ᛏᚱᚨᚾᛉᛚᚨᛏᛖ
Translated Language Learning

Siddhartha

Indicum Carmen
An Indian Poem

Hermann Hesse

Latin / English

Copyright © 2024 Tranzlaty
All rights reserved
Published by Tranzlaty
Siddhartha – Eine Indische Dichtung
ISBN: 978-1-83566-690-6
Original text by Hermann Hesse
First published in German in 1922
www.tranzlaty.com

Filius Brahman
The Son of the Brahman

In umbra domus
In the shade of the house
in sole fluminis
in the sunshine of the riverbank
prope scaphas
near the boats
sub Sal silvae
in the shade of the Sal-wood forest
in umbra ficulnea
in the shade of the fig tree
hoc est ubi Siddhartha creverant
this is where Siddhartha grew up
fuit filius pulcher Brahman, iuvenis falconis
he was the handsome son of a Brahman, the young falcon
crevit amicus Govinda
he grew up with his friend Govinda
Govinda Brahman filius erat
Govinda was also the son of a Brahman
ad ripas fluminis sol perusta scapulis suis
by the banks of the river the sun tanned his light shoulders
lavacrum, ablutiones sacras facere, oblationes sacras facere
bathing, performing the sacred ablutions, making sacred offerings
In mango horto, umbra in oculos nigros infunditur
In the mango garden, shade poured into his black eyes
quando puer, cum matre canebat
when playing as a boy, when his mother sang
quando sacra facta sunt
when the sacred offerings were made
cum pater eius grammaticus eum docuisset
when his father, the scholar, taught him
quando sapientes loquebatur
when the wise men talked

Diu Siddhartha sapientum disputationibus communicaverat
For a long time, Siddhartha had been partaking in the discussions of the wise men
utebatur disputando cum Govinda
he practiced debating with Govinda
artem reflexionis cum Govinda exercuit
he practiced the art of reflection with Govinda
et meditatus est
and he practiced meditation
Iam sciebat loqui Om tacite
He already knew how to speak the Om silently
sciebat verbum verborum
he knew the word of words
tacite locutus est in se trahens
he spoke it silently into himself while inhaling
ex se exhalans tacite locutus est
he spoke it silently out of himself while exhaling
hoc fecit cum omni intentione animae suae
he did this with all the concentration of his soul
frontem eius cingebat ardore spiritus lucidi
his forehead was surrounded by the glow of the clear-thinking spirit
Iam sciebat quomodo Atman sentiret in ima sui esse
He already knew how to feel Atman in the depths of his being
posset sentire incorruptibiles
he could feel the indestructible
sciebat quid esset unum cum universo
he knew what it was to be at one with the universe
Laetitia exsiluit in corde patris
Joy leapt in his father's heart
quia filius eius velox ad discendum erat
because his son was quick to learn
sitivit scientia
he was thirsty for knowledge
Pater eius eum videre potuit ut magnus vir sapiens cresceret

his father could see him growing up to become a great wise man
videre eum fieri sacerdos
he could see him becoming a priest
viderit eum fieri principem inter Brachmanas
he could see him becoming a prince among the Brahmans
Beatitudo in pectore matris exsiluit, cum vidit eum ambulantem
Bliss leapt in his mother's breast when she saw him walking
Beatitudo exsiluit in corde suo, cum vidit eum discumbere et surgere
Bliss leapt in her heart when she saw him sit down and get up
Siddhartha fortis et pulcher
Siddhartha was strong and handsome
ille qui graciles pedes ambulabat
he, who was walking on slender legs
salutavit eam cum honore
he greeted her with perfect respect
Amor Brahmanorum corda iuvenum filiarum tetigit
Love touched the hearts of the Brahmans' young daughters
capti cum Siddhartha per vicos oppidi
they were charmed when Siddhartha walked through the lanes of the town
luminosa frons, oculi regis, coxis gracili
his luminous forehead, his eyes of a king, his slim hips
Maxime autem amabatur Govinda
But most of all he was loved by Govinda
Govinda, amicus eius, filius Brahman
Govinda, his friend, the son of a Brahman
Amavit Siddhartha oculus et vox dulcis
He loved Siddhartha's eye and sweet voice
amavit viam ambulavit
he loved the way he walked
et perfectam pudorem motuum suorum amavit
and he loved the perfect decency of his movements
dilexit omnia Siddhartha fecit et dixit

he loved everything Siddhartha did and said
sed quod maxime amabat, spiritus ejus erat
but what he loved most was his spirit
amavit transcendentem, igneam cogitationem
he loved his transcendent, fiery thoughts
amavit suam ardentem voluntatem et altam vocationem
he loved his ardent will and high calling
Govinda scivit se Brahman non commune fieri
Govinda knew he would not become a common Brahman
non, ne piger fieret
no, he would not become a lazy official
non, non avarus fieret mercator
no, he would not become a greedy merchant
non vanus et vanus orator
not a vain, vacuous speaker
neque sordidus sacerdos dolosus
nor a mean, deceitful priest
et non fieret honestus et stultus ovis
and he also would not become a decent, stupid sheep
ovis in grege multorum
a sheep in the herd of the many
et nolebat fieri unum ex his
and he did not want to become one of those things
unus ex illis decem milia Brahmanorum esse nolebat
he did not want to be one of those tens of thousands of Brahmans
Siddhartha sequi voluit; carus, splendidus
He wanted to follow Siddhartha; the beloved, the splendid
in diebus venturis, cum Siddhartha fieret deus, ipse ibi esset
in days to come, when Siddhartha would become a god, he would be there
cum gloriosus se ibi fore
when he would join the glorious, he would be there
Govinda eum sequi voluit amicum suum
Govinda wanted to follow him as his friend
ille socius et famulus

he was his companion and his servant
Hic est hasta eius et umbra eius
he was his spear-carrier and his shadow
Siddhartha amabatur ab omnibus
Siddhartha was loved by everyone
Gaudium erat omnibus
He was a source of joy for everybody
jucundum fuit omnibus
he was a delight for them all
At ille Siddhartha sibi non gaudebat
But he, Siddhartha, was not a source of joy for himself
non delectatur in se
he found no delight in himself
ambulavit in viis roseis ficulneae hortus
he walked the rosy paths of the fig tree garden
sedit in umbra caerulea in horto contemplationis
he sat in the bluish shade in the garden of contemplation
membra sua cotidie in poenitentiae balneo lavit
he washed his limbs daily in the bath of repentance
immolavit in umbra mango silva
he made sacrifices in the dim shade of the mango forest
gestus perfecti pudoris
his gestures were of perfect decency
erat omnium amor et gaudium
he was everyone's love and joy
sed tamen omni carebat gaudio in corde suo
but he still lacked all joy in his heart
Somnia et inquietae cogitationes in mentem venit
Dreams and restless thoughts came into his mind
ex aqua fluvii somnia
his dreams flowed from the water of the river
somnia excussum sidera noctis
his dreams sparked from the stars of the night
de radiis solis liquefacta suo
his dreams melted from the beams of the sun

somniorum accesserunt ad eum, et facta est ei inquietudo animae
dreams came to him, and a restlessness of the soul came to him
anima eius ex sacrificiis ardebat
his soul was fuming from the sacrifices
e versibus Rig-Vedæ efflavit
he breathed forth from the verses of the Rig-Veda
versus infusi guttatim
the verses were infused into him, drop by drop
versus ex veterum Brahmanorum dogmatibus
the verses from the teachings of the old Brahmans
Siddhartha inceperat nutrire fastidium in se
Siddhartha had started to nurse discontent in himself
dubitare coeperat de amore patris
he had started to feel doubt about the love of his father
dubitabat amorem matris
he doubted the love of his mother
et dubitavit de amore amici sui, Govinda .
and he doubted the love of his friend, Govinda
dubitabat an amor illi gaudium in saecula saeculorum
he doubted if their love could bring him joy forever and ever
amor non lactaverunt eum
their love could not nurse him
amor sui non pascere eum
their love could not feed him
amor satisfacere non potuit
their love could not satisfy him
coepi suspicari doctrina patris sui
he had started to suspect his father's teachings
forte ostenderat ei omnia, quae sciebat
perhaps he had shown him everything he knew
Erant alii magistri, sapientes Brahmanae
there were his other teachers, the wise Brahmans
fortassis iam ipsi quantum sapientiae suae revelarunt

perhaps they had already revealed to him the best of their wisdom
timebat enim iam se exspectantem
he feared that they had already filled his expecting vessel
non obstante ubertate doctrinae suae, vas non erat plenum
despite the richness of their teachings, the vessel was not full
spiritus non erat contentus
the spirit was not content
anima non cessabit
the soul was not calm
cor non impletur
the heart was not satisfied
ablutiones erant bonae, sed aquae erant
the ablutions were good, but they were water
ablutiones non ablue peccatum
the ablutions did not wash off the sin
non sanaverunt sitim spiritus
they did not heal the spirit's thirst
timor cordis non levabunt
they did not relieve the fear in his heart
Sacrificia et invocatio deorum optima erant
The sacrifices and the invocation of the gods were excellent
sed itane fuit?
but was that all there was?
num felicia sacrificia dabant?
did the sacrifices give a happy fortune?
quid de diis?
and what about the gods?
Itane Prajapati qui mundum creaverat?
Was it really Prajapati who had created the world?
Nonne Atman creaverat mundum?
Was it not the Atman who had created the world?
Atman, solus, singularis
Atman, the only one, the singular one
Nonne creationes erant?
Were the gods not creations?

nonne sicut me et tu creati sunt?
were they not created like me and you?
an di non erant tempori obnoxii?
were the Gods not subject to time?
di mortales erant? Bonum erat?
were the Gods mortal? Was it good?
ius erat? significativum erat?
was it right? was it meaningful?
maximumne opus erat diis sacrificare?
was it the highest occupation to make offerings to the gods?
Cui enim alii offerebantur?
For whom else were offerings to be made?
quis alius colendus?
who else was to be worshipped?
quis alius, nisi ille?
who else was there, but Him?
Solus unus, Atman
The only one, the Atman
Atman et ubi inveniendus est?
And where was Atman to be found?
ubi mansit?
where did He reside?
ubi cor aeternum verberavit?
where did His eternal heart beat?
ubi aliud nisi in semet ipso?
where else but in one's own self?
in intima parte incorruptibilis
in its innermost indestructible part
an id quod quisque in se habuit?
could he be that which everyone had in himself?
Sed ubi erat iste homo?
But where was this self?
ubi haec intima?
where was this innermost part?
ubi haec fuit ultima pars?
where was this ultimate part?

Non erat caro et os
It was not flesh and bone
neque cogitatio neque conscientia
it was neither thought nor consciousness
hoc est quod sapientes docuit
this is what the wisest ones taught
Ubi ergo erat?
So where was it?
ipse, ipse, Atman
the self, myself, the Atman
Ad hunc locum perveniendum ;
To reach this place, there was another way
fuitne hic alius modus quaerendus?
was this other way worth looking for?
Heu, nemo sic ei ostendit
Alas, nobody showed him this way
nemo sciens aliter
nobody knew this other way
patre nesciebat
his father did not know it
et doctores ac sapientes nescierunt
and the teachers and wise men did not know it
Noverunt omnia, Brahmanae
They knew everything, the Brahmans
et libri sancti eorum omnia sciebant
and their holy books knew everything
curaverunt omnia
they had taken care of everything
ipsi curaverunt de mundi creatione
they took care of the creation of the world
originem sermonis, cibum, attrahens, exhalans
they described origin of speech, food, inhaling, exhaling
describunt sensuum dispositionem
they described the arrangement of the senses
acta deorum narrabant
they described the acts of the gods

quorum libri sciebant infinite multa
their books knew infinitely much
sed satisne erat haec omnia nosse?
but was it valuable to know all of this?
Eratne non unum esse quod sciatur?
was there not only one thing to be known?
adhucne non id quod maxime interest scire?
was there still not the most important thing to know?
multi versus sanctorum librorum de hac re intima et ultima locuti sunt
many verses of the holy books spoke of this innermost, ultimate thing
nominatim in Upanishades Samaveda
it was spoken of particularly in the Upanishades of Samaveda
sunt mirabilia versibus
they were wonderful verses
"Anima tua totus est mundus", hoc ibi scriptum est
"Your soul is the whole world", this was written there
et scriptum est quod homo in sopore occurrit intima sua
and it was written that man in deep sleep would meet with his innermost part
et ipse resideret in Atman
and he would reside in the Atman
Mira sapientia his versibus
Marvellous wisdom was in these verses
omnis scientia sapientissimorum hic in magicis verbis collecta fuerat
all knowledge of the wisest ones had been collected here in magic words
sicut mel ab apibus
it was as pure as honey collected by bees
Imo versus non sunt despiciendi
No, the verses were not to be looked down upon
quae continebant magnas illuminationes
they contained tremendous amounts of enlightenment
sapientiam continebant, quae collegit et conservavit;

they contained wisdom which lay collected and preserved
sapientia collecta ab innumeris sapientum generationibus Brahmanae
wisdom collected by innumerable generations of wise Brahmans
Sed ubi erant Brachmani?
But where were the Brahmans?
ubi erant sacerdotes?
where were the priests?
ubi sapientes vel poenitentes?
where the wise men or penitents?
ubi erant qui successerant?
where were those that had succeeded?
ubi erant qui plus sciebant quam omnis scientia?
where were those who knew more than deepest of all knowledge?
ubi erant qui etiam sapientiam illustratam vixerunt?
where were those that also lived out the enlightened wisdom?
Vbi erat gnarus qui Atman e somno eduxerat?
Where was the knowledgeable one who brought Atman out of his sleep?
qui hanc scientiam in diem adduxit?
who had brought this knowledge into the day?
qui hanc scientiam in vita susceperunt?
who had taken this knowledge into their life?
qui hanc scientiam omni gradu ceperunt?
who carried this knowledge with every step they took?
qui dictis factis sua duxerat?
who had married their words with their deeds?
Siddhartha cognovit multos venerabiles Brahmanae
Siddhartha knew many venerable Brahmans
patre puro
his father, the pure one
scolasticus, venerabilis
the scholar, the most venerable one
Pater admiratione dignus erat

His father was worthy of admiration
quieti et nobiles mores erant
quiet and noble were his manners
pura vita erat, sapiens verba erant
pure was his life, wise were his words
post frontem tenerae ac bonae cogitationes vixit
delicate and noble thoughts lived behind his brow
sed, cum hoc sciret, in beatitudine vivebat?
but even though he knew so much, did he live in blissfulness?
numquid pacem habuit, non tamen omnibus scientibus?
despite all his knowledge, did he have peace?
nonne et homo iustus erat perscrutator ?
was he not also just a searching man?
adhuc non sitiens?
was he still not a thirsty man?
Nonne e sacris fontibus identidem haurire debebat?
Did he not have to drink from holy sources again and again?
annon de oblationibus bibit?
did he not drink from the offerings?
nonne ex libris bibit?
did he not drink from the books?
lites Brachmanarum non bibit?
did he not drink from the disputes of the Brahmans?
Cur cottidie debet abluere peccata?
Why did he have to wash off sins every day?
an cotidie ad purgationem contendat?
must he strive for a cleansing every day?
atque etiam cotidie
over and over again, every day
Nonne in eo erat Atman?
Was Atman not in him?
nonne pri- stus fons est ex animo ?
did not the pristine source spring from his heart?
pristinum principium inveniendum est in se ipso
the pristine source had to be found in one's own self
pristinum principium possidendum!

the pristine source had to be possessed!
facere aliud quaerebat
doing anything else else was searching
quodlibet aliud transitum est circumitu
taking any other pass is a detour
iens aliter ducit ad amissam
going any other way leads to getting lost
Haec erant cogitationes Siddhartha
These were Siddhartha's thoughts
haec erat sitis, haec dolori
this was his thirst, and this was his suffering
Saepe sibi ex Chandogya-Upanishad locutus est:
Often he spoke to himself from a Chandogya-Upanishad:
"Vere nomen Brahman Satyam" est.
"Truly, the name of the Brahman is Satyam"
"Qui scit tale, cottidie celestem intrabit".
"he who knows such a thing, will enter the heavenly world every day"
Saepe coelestis mundus prope visus est
Often the heavenly world seemed near
sed nunquam omnino ad caelestem mundum
but he had never reached the heavenly world completely
ultimum sitim numquam exstinguitur
he had never quenched the ultimate thirst
Et inter omnes sapientissimos et sapientissimos viros nemo pervenerat
And among all the wise and wisest men, none had reached it
ab eis mandatum accepit
he received instructions from them
sed non perfecte ad caelestia mundi
but they hadn't completely reached the heavenly world
non penitus sitim
they hadn't completely quenched their thirst
quia haec sitis aeterna sitis est
because this thirst is an eternal thirst

"Govinda" Siddhartha locutus est ad amicum suum
"Govinda" Siddhartha spoke to his friend
"Carissima Govinda, veni mecum sub arbore Banyan".
"Govinda, my dear, come with me under the Banyan tree"
"Exeamus meditationem"
"let's practise meditation"
Et ad Banyan arbore
They went to the Banyan tree
sub arbore Banyan sederunt
under the Banyan tree they sat down
Siddhartha erat hic
Siddhartha was right here
Govinda viginti passus est
Govinda was twenty paces away
Siddhartha sedet se et iterum murmurans versum
Siddhartha seated himself and he repeated murmuring the verse
Om arcus, sagitta anima
Om is the bow, the arrow is the soul
Brahman est sagittae scopum
The Brahman is the arrow's target
scopum ut incessanter hit
the target that one should incessantly hit
consueto tempore exercitationis in meditatione praeterierat
the usual time of the exercise in meditation had passed
Govinda surrexit, vespere venerat
Govinda got up, the evening had come
erat tempus praestare vesperum ablutionem
it was time to perform the evening's ablution
nomen Siddhartha appellavit, sed Siddhartha non respondit
He called Siddhartha's name, but Siddhartha did not answer
Siddhartha sedebat ibi in cogitatione amissa
Siddhartha sat there, lost in thought
Oculi eius rigide feruntur ad longius scopum
his eyes were rigidly focused towards a very distant target
extremum linguae paulum inter dentes eminet

the tip of his tongue was protruding a little between the teeth
non respirare videbatur
he seemed not to breathe
Sic resedit contemplatione involutus
Thus sat he, wrapped up in contemplation
in cogitatione Om
he was deep in thought of the Om
anima mittitur Brahman sicut sagitta
his soul sent after the Brahman like an arrow
Olim Samanas iter per oppidum Siddhartha
Once, Samanas had travelled through Siddhartha's town
erant reruni in peregrinatione
they were ascetics on a pilgrimage
tres invalidi viri aridorum non senes neque iuvenes
three skinny, withered men, neither old nor young
pulverulenta cruentus umeris
dusty and bloody were their shoulders
fere nudus, sole ambustus, solitudini circumdatus
almost naked, scorched by the sun, surrounded by loneliness
peregrini et inimici in mundum
strangers and enemies to the world
advenae et dracones in the realm of homines
strangers and jackals in the realm of humans
Post eos insufflavit calidum odorem quietis passionis
Behind them blew a hot scent of quiet passion
odor perniciosius servitium
a scent of destructive service
odorem crudelis abnegationis
a scent of merciless self-denial
factum est vespere
the evening had come
post contemplationis horam, Siddhartha Govinda locutus est
after the hour of contemplation, Siddhartha spoke to Govinda
"Mane cras mane, mi amice, Siddhartha ad Samanas ibit".
"Early tomorrow morning, my friend, Siddhartha will go to the Samanas"

"Fiet Samana";
"He will become a Samana"
Govinda palluit cum haec verba audivit
Govinda turned pale when he heard these words
et legit in immobile vultum amici sui
and he read the decision in the motionless face of his friend
determinatio unstoppable erat, sicut sagitta emissa ab arcu
the determination was unstoppable, like the arrow shot from the bow
Govinda primo intuitu intellexit; nunc incipit
Govinda realized at first glance; now it is beginning
Nunc Siddhartha accipit viam suam
now Siddhartha is taking his own way
nunc incipit pullulare fatum suum
now his fate is beginning to sprout
et propter Siddhartha, fatum Govindae pullulat
and because of Siddhartha, Govinda's fate is sprouting too
et palluit sicut arida fixa pellis
he turned pale like a dry banana-skin
"O Siddhartha", exclamavit
"Oh Siddhartha," he exclaimed
"Pater tuus hoc facere permittit?"
"will your father permit you to do that?"
Siddhartha vidi tamquam mox evigilantes
Siddhartha looked over as if he was just waking up
sicut sagitta est anima Govinda legit
like an Arrow he read Govinda's soul
legere metum et obsequium in eo
he could read the fear and the submission in him
"O Govinda" tacite dixit, "ne verba perdam".
"Oh Govinda," he spoke quietly, "let's not waste words"
"Cras prima luce vitam Samanas incipiam".
"Tomorrow at daybreak I will begin the life of the Samanas"
"nihil dicamus de eo".
"let us speak no more of it"

Siddhartha ingressa est cubiculum ubi pater eius sedebat
Siddhartha entered the chamber where his father was sitting
Pater autem erat in mat bast
his father was was on a mat of bast
Siddhartha egressus post patrem suum
Siddhartha stepped behind his father
et stans post eum
and he remained standing behind him
stetit donec pater sensit aliquem stantem post se
he stood until his father felt that someone was standing behind him
Dixit Brahman: "Estne tu, Siddhartha?"
Spoke the Brahman: "Is that you, Siddhartha?"
"Tum dic quid venerit dicere"
"Then say what you came to say"
Locutus est Siddhartha: "Permissu tuo, mi pater".
Spoke Siddhartha: "With your permission, my father"
"Veni nuntiare tibi quod cupiam domum tuam cras relinquere".
"I came to tell you that it is my longing to leave your house tomorrow"
"Ire ad reruni volo";
"I wish to go to the ascetics"
"Samana fieri cupio"
"My desire is to become a Samana"
"Ne pater meus huic resistat".
"May my father not oppose this"
Brahman tacuit, et tam diu mansit
The Brahman fell silent, and he remained so for long
stellae in parva fenestra erraverunt
the stars in the small window wandered
et mutaverunt positiones
and they changed their relative positions
Silens et immobilis stabat filius brachiis
Silent and motionless stood the son with his arms folded
tace et immobilis sedit pater in mat

silent and motionless sat the father on the mat
et stellae tramites in caelo
and the stars traced their paths in the sky
Tum pater
Then spoke the father
"Brachmane non decet verba dura et irata loqui"
"it is not proper for a Brahman to speak harsh and angry words"
Sed indignatio in corde meo.
"But indignation is in my heart"
"Nolo iterum hanc petitionem audire".
"I wish not to hear this request for a second time"
Tarde, Brahman rosa
Slowly, the Brahman rose
Siddhartha tacitus stetit, bracchia complicata
Siddhartha stood silently, his arms folded
"Quid moraris?" interrogavit patrem
"What are you waiting for?" asked the father
Siddhartha locutus est, "Tu scis quid expecto"
Spoke Siddhartha, "You know what I'm waiting for"
pater indignatus thalamum reliquit
Indignant, the father left the chamber
indigne ferens, se ad lectum suum accubuit;
indignant, he went to his bed and lay down
hora praeterierat, sed somnus super oculos non venit
an hour passed, but no sleep had come over his eyes
Brahman surgens deambulavit
the Brahman stood up and he paced to and fro
et exivit domum suam in nocte
and he left the house in the night
Per fenestram parvam cubiculi intus respexit
Through the small window of the chamber he looked back inside
et ibi vidit Siddhartha stantem
and there he saw Siddhartha standing
bracchia plicata sunt neque se loco movisse

his arms were folded and he had not moved from his spot
Pallida micabat stola clara
Pale shimmered his bright robe
Sollicito corde, pater ad lectum rediit
With anxiety in his heart, the father returned to his bed
alterum insomnis hora transierunt
another sleepless hour passed
cum nullus somnus super oculos venisset, Brahman iterum surrexit
since no sleep had come over his eyes, the Brahman stood up again
deambulavit et ambulavit extra domum
he paced to and fro, and he walked out of the house
et vidit lunam surrexisse
and he saw that the moon had risen
Per fenestram cubiculi intus respexit
Through the window of the chamber he looked back inside
stabat Siddhartha, loco immobilis
there stood Siddhartha, unmoved from his spot
bracchia plicabantur, ut erat
his arms were folded, as they had been
lunam cogitabat ex nudo tibiarum
moonlight was reflecting from his bare shins
Sollicitus in corde pater cubitum ivit
With worry in his heart, the father went back to bed
rediit post horam
he came back after an hour
et iterum post duas horas rediit
and he came back again after two hours
per fenestram respexit
he looked through the small window
Vidit Siddhartha stantem lunae lumen
he saw Siddhartha standing in the moon light
stetit ad lucem stellarum in tenebris
he stood by the light of the stars in the darkness
Et reversus est post horam

And he came back hour after hour
tacitus in thalamum inspexit
silently, he looked into the chamber
vidit eum in eodem loco stantem
he saw him standing in the same place
implevit cor suum in ira
it filled his heart with anger
repletur inquietudine
it filled his heart with unrest
implevit cor suum
it filled his heart with anguish
implevit cor eius tristitia
it filled his heart with sadness
noctis hora venerat
the night's last hour had come
pater rediit et deinc in cubiculum
his father returned and stepped into the room
vidit iuvenem stantem
he saw the young man standing there
longus et quasi extraneus ei videbatur
he seemed tall and like a stranger to him
"Siddhartha" dixit "quid moraris?"
"Siddhartha," he spoke, "what are you waiting for?"
"Tu scis quid expecto"
"You know what I'm waiting for"
"Visne semper stare et exspectes?
"Will you always stand that way and wait?
"Semper stare et expectare".
"I will always stand and wait"
"expectabis donec mane, meridies et vespere fiat?"
"will you wait until it becomes morning, noon, and evening?"
"Exspectabo donec fiat mane, meridies et vespere";
"I will wait until it become morning, noon, and evening"
"Tu fessus fies, Siddhartha"
"You will become tired, Siddhartha"
"Ego fessus sum"

"I will become tired"
"Obdormis, Siddhartha"
"You will fall asleep, Siddhartha"
"Non dormiam"
"I will not fall asleep"
"Morieris, Siddhartha".
"You will die, Siddhartha"
"Moriar", respondit Siddhartha
"I will die," answered Siddhartha
"Et vis potius mori, quam patri parere?"
"And would you rather die, than obey your father?"
"Siddhartha patri suo semper obtemperavit".
"Siddhartha has always obeyed his father"
"Sic consilium tuum deseres?"
"So will you abandon your plan?"
"Siddhartha faciet quod locutus est ei pater suus ut faceret".
"Siddhartha will do what his father will tell him to do"
Prima luce in cubiculum effulsit
The first light of day shone into the room
Brahman vidit Siddhartha genua trementia molliter
The Brahman saw that Siddhartha knees were softly trembling
In Siddhartha non vidit faciem trepidantis
In Siddhartha's face he saw no trembling
oculi fixi procul
his eyes were fixed on a distant spot
Hoc erat cum pater intellexit
This was when his father realized
nunc Siddhartha non diutius habitavit cum eo in domo sua
even now Siddhartha no longer dwelt with him in his home
Vidit iam eum
he saw that he had already left him
Pater tetigit Siddhartha in humero
The Father touched Siddhartha's shoulder
"Vis" inquit "ire in silvam et eris Samana";
"You will," he spoke, "go into the forest and be a Samana"
"Cum beatitudinem invenis in silva, revertere";

"When you find blissfulness in the forest, come back"
"Veni et doce me beatum esse"
"come back and teach me to be blissful"
"Si dolorem invenis, tunc revertere";
"If you find disappointment, then return"
"Reddeamusque simul deosque libemus iterum".
"return and let us make offerings to the gods together, again"
"Ite nunc et matrem osculare"
"Go now and kiss your mother"
"Dic ei quo vadis"
"tell her where you are going"
"At mihi tempus est ire ad flumen".
"But for me it is time to go to the river"
"tempus meum est ad primam ablutionem faciendam".
"it is my time to perform the first ablution"
Accepitque manum de humero filii sui et exivit foras
He took his hand from the shoulder of his son, and went outside
Siddhartha vacillabat latus conabatur ambulare
Siddhartha wavered to the side as he tried to walk
Et reposuit membra sub potestate et adoravit patrem
He put his limbs back under control and bowed to his father
ivit ad matrem suam, ut faceret sicut dixerat pater ejus
he went to his mother to do as his father had said
dum lente cruribus rigidis relinquatur umbra proxima casae proximae resurrexit
As he slowly left on stiff legs a shadow rose near the last hut
quis illic accubans, et cum peregrino conjunctus?
who had crouched there, and joined the pilgrim?
"Govinda, venisti" Siddhartha dixit et risit
"Govinda, you have come" said Siddhartha and smiled
"Veni," dixit Govinda
"I have come," said Govinda

Apud Samanas
With the Samanas

In vespera huius diei reruni prehenduntur
In the evening of this day they caught up with the ascetics
reruni; invalidi Samanas
the ascetics; the skinny Samanas
societatem et obedientiam sibi offerebant
they offered them their companionship and obedience
Eorum societas et obedientia accepta sunt
Their companionship and obedience were accepted
Siddhartha Brahman pauperi vestimenta sua in platea dedit
Siddhartha gave his garments to a poor Brahman in the street
nihil aliud quam linteum et terrenum, non fucatum
He wore nothing more than a loincloth and earth-coloured, unsown cloak
semel in die comedit et nunquam cocta
He ate only once a day, and never anything cooked
XV diebus ieiunavit, viginti octo diebus ieiunavit
He fasted for fifteen days, he fasted for twenty-eight days
Caro femur et genis
The flesh waned from his thighs and cheeks
De somniis febricitantibus in oculis dilatatis teriit
Feverish dreams flickered from his enlarged eyes
ungues longos lente creverunt in digitos arentes
long nails grew slowly on his parched fingers
et in mento sicci villosi barba creverunt
and a dry, shaggy beard grew on his chin
Aspectus eius in glaciem conversus est cum mulieribus offendit
His glance turned to ice when he encountered women
ambulavit per civitatem pulchre indutus populo
he walked through a city of nicely dressed people
os suum twitched contemnentes eos
his mouth twitched with contempt for them
vidit negotiatores mercatores et principes venationis

He saw merchants trading and princes hunting
vidit lugentes plangentes pro mortuis
he saw mourners wailing for their dead
et vidit meretrices offerentes semetipsos
and he saw whores offering themselves
medicis quaerit infirmos
physicians trying to help the sick
sacerdotes aptissimum diem determinant ad seminis
priests determining the most suitable day for seeding
amantes filios et matres nutrientes
lovers loving and mothers nursing their children
atque haec non uno aspectu digna fuit
and all of this was not worthy of one look from his eyes
totum mentitur, totum putuit, totum putuit mendacium
it all lied, it all stank, it all stank of lies
omnia simulabat significantia et laeta et pulchra
it all pretended to be meaningful and joyful and beautiful
et totum solum putrefactio occultatur
and it all was just concealed putrefaction
mundus amarum gustavit; vita erat cruciatu
the world tasted bitter; life was torture

Una meta stetit ante Siddhartha
A single goal stood before Siddhartha
eius propositum erat inanis
his goal was to become empty
propositum erat vacuum siti
his goal was to be empty of thirst
inane velle et inanis somniorum
empty of wishing and empty of dreams
inanis gaudii et tristitiae
empty of joy and sorrow
suum propositum erat sibi mortuum esse
his goal was to be dead to himself
suum propositum non esse se amplius
his goal was not to be a self any more

eius propositum fuit ut quieti sitis exinanito corde
his goal was to find tranquillity with an emptied heart
propositum fuit ut miraculis per se cogitationibus pateat
his goal was to be open to miracles in unselfish thoughts
Ad hoc assequendum propositum suum
to achieve this was his goal
cum omnes sui superati et mortui essent
when all of his self was overcome and had died
cum omne desiderium et omne desiderium silet in corde
when every desire and every urge was silent in the heart
ultima pars eius evigilare
then the ultimate part of him had to awake
intima sui, quae non est sui ipsius;
the innermost of his being, which is no longer his self
hoc magnum secretum
this was the great secret

Tacite, Siddhartha se radiis solis ardentibus exposuit
Silently, Siddhartha exposed himself to the burning rays of the sun
dolore ardebat et siti ardebat
he was glowing with pain and he was glowing with thirst
et ibi stetit donec nec dolorem nec sitim percepit
and he stood there until he neither felt pain nor thirst
Tacite ibi stetit tempore pluvioso
Silently, he stood there in the rainy season
e crinibus umeris rigens aqua rorabat
from his hair the water was dripping over freezing shoulders
aqua rorante torpore coxis cruribusque
the water was dripping over his freezing hips and legs
et poenitens stabat ibi
and the penitent stood there
ibi stetit donec frigus amplius sentire non potuit
he stood there until he could not feel the cold any more
ibi stetit donec corpus eius tacuit
he stood there until his body was silent

ibi stetit donec corpus eius quievit
he stood there until his body was quiet
Tacite, in frutectis spinis constitit
Silently, he cowered in the thorny bushes
sanguis destillavit in cute ardenti
blood dripped from the burning skin
cruor stillavit exulcerationes
blood dripped from festering wounds
et Siddhartha mansit rigida et immobilis
and Siddhartha stayed rigid and motionless
stetit, donec nullus cruor
he stood until no blood flowed any more
stetit donec nihil amplius
he stood until nothing stung any more
stetit donec nihil amplius ardebat
he stood until nothing burned any more
Siddhartha rectus sedit et didicit parce spirare
Siddhartha sat upright and learned to breathe sparingly
didicit ut cum paucis flatibus
he learned to get along with few breaths
didicit prohibere spirandi
he learned to stop breathing
Incipiens a spiritu didicit cordis pulsus sedare
He learned, beginning with the breath, to calm the beating of his heart
didicit ad redigendum pulsus cordis sui
he learned to reduce the beats of his heart
meditatus dum ordiantur pauci
he meditated until his heartbeats were only a few
et ordiantur prope
and then his heartbeats were almost none
Vetustissima Samanas instructus, Siddhartha abnegationem sui exercuit
Instructed by the oldest of the Samanas, Siddhartha practised self-denial
meditationem exercuit, secundum nova praecepta Samana

he practised meditation, according to the new Samana rules
Ardea quis fermentum volitans super silvam
A heron flew over the bamboo forest
Siddhartha heron accepit in animam suam
Siddhartha accepted the heron into his soul
volavit in saltibus et montibus
he flew over forest and mountains
Heron erat, pisces comedit
he was a heron, he ate fish
sensit famem stimulis herodis
he felt the pangs of a heron's hunger
dixit herodii coaxare
he spoke the heron's croak
et mortuus est herodis mortem
he died a heron's death
Mortuus draco iacebat in ripa arenosa
A dead jackal was lying on the sandy bank
Siddhartha anima elapsa intra corpus draconum mortui
Siddhartha's soul slipped inside the body of the dead jackal
mortuus erat draconis imposito ripis et tumidus
he was the dead jackal laying on the banks and bloated
putuit et concidit et per hyenas discubuit
he stank and decayed and was dismembered by hyenas
a vulturibus detraxerat et in sceletum convertit
he was skinned by vultures and turned into a skeleton
conversus in pulverem et campestria
he was turned to dust and blown across the fields
Et anima Siddhartha rediit
And Siddhartha's soul returned
perierat, tabescebat, et sicut pulvis di- sebatur
it had died, decayed, and was scattered as dust
quod tristis ebrietas cycli gustaverat
it had tasted the gloomy intoxication of the cycle
nova siti exspectatur, quasi in hiatu venator
it awaited with a new thirst, like a hunter in the gap
in hiatu quo e cyclo effugere potuit

in the gap where he could escape from the cycle
in gap ubi aeternitas sine dolore coepit
in the gap where an eternity without suffering began
sensus et memoria occidit
he killed his senses and his memory
in mille alias formas ex se elapsa est
he slipped out of his self into thousands of other forms
animal, cadaver, lapis
he was an animal, a carrion, a stone
erat lignum et aqua
he was wood and water
et evigilavit omni tempore ut iterum se veterem suum
and he awoke every time to find his old self again
sive sol sive luna, iterum se ipse fuit
whether sun or moon, he was his self again
et conversus in exolvuntur
he turned round in the cycle
sensit sitim, sitim devicit, novam sensit sitim
he felt thirst, overcame the thirst, felt new thirst

Siddhartha multum didicit cum esset apud Samanas
Siddhartha learned a lot when he was with the Samanas
didicit multis ducens ab ipso
he learned many ways leading away from the self
didicit dimittere
he learned how to let go
ivit via abnegationis mediante dolore
He went the way of self-denial by means of pain
didicit se abnegationis per voluntariam passionem et dolorem superans
he learned self-denial through voluntarily suffering and overcoming pain
famem, sitim et languorem superavit
he overcame hunger, thirst, and tiredness
Viam abnegationis ivit per meditationem
He went the way of self-denial by means of meditation

abnegationis viam ivit, per imaginando mentem ab omnibus conceptionibus vacuam esse
he went the way of self-denial through imagining the mind to be void of all conceptions
his et aliis modis dimittere didicit
with these and other ways he learned to let go
millies a se
a thousand times he left his self
per horas et dies mansit in se non-
for hours and days he remained in the non-self
Omnes hi ducti ab ipso
all these ways led away from the self
sed eorum semita semper reducta est ad seipsum
but their path always led back to the self
Siddhartha millies fugit a se
Siddhartha fled from the self a thousand times
sed reditus ad seipsum inevitabilis fuit
but the return to the self was inevitable
quamvis in nulla re moratus, revertens inevitabilis fuit
although he stayed in nothingness, coming back was inevitable
quamvis in pecoribus et lapidibus remaneret, revertens inevitabilis fuit
although he stayed in animals and stones, coming back was inevitable
invenit se in sole vel in luce lunae iterum
he found himself in the sunshine or in the moonlight again
in umbra vel in pluvia iterum invenit
he found himself in the shade or in the rain again
atque iterum se ipsum; Siddhartha
and he was once again his self; Siddhartha
iterumque cruciatus cycli, qui ei coactus fuerat, sensit
and again he felt the agony of the cycle which had been forced upon him

iuxta suam vixit Govinda umbra eius

by his side lived Govinda, his shadow
Govinda eadem via ambulavit et eosdem conatus sumit
Govinda walked the same path and undertook the same efforts
loquebantur ad invicem non plus quam exercitia
they spoke to one another no more than the exercises required
interdum per castella duo
occasionally the two of them went through the villages
iverunt petere cibum sibi et suis magistris
they went to beg for food for themselves and their teachers
"Quomodo nos putas profecturos, Govinda" interrogavit?
"How do you think we have progressed, Govinda" he asked
"Nonne aliqua proposita pervenimus?" Govinda respondit
"Did we reach any goals?" Govinda answered
"Dicimus, et discimus".
"We have learned, and we'll continue learning"
"Magnus eris Samana, Siddhartha"
"You'll be a great Samana, Siddhartha"
"Cito, omnem exercitationem didicisti".
"Quickly, you've learned every exercise"
"Saepe veteres Samanas mirati sunt"
"often, the old Samanas have admired you"
"Unus dies eris vir sanctus, o Siddhartha".
"One day, you'll be a holy man, oh Siddhartha"
Locutus est Siddhartha, "Non possum non sentire quod sic non est, mi amice"
Spoke Siddhartha, "I can't help but feel that it is not like this, my friend"
"Quae didici esse apud Samanas, potuit citius didicere".
"What I've learned being among the Samanas could have been learned more quickly"
"Potuit simplicius per"
"it could have been learned by simpler means"
"in qualibet taberna disci potuit"
"it could have been learned in any tavern"
didi potuit ubi sunt meretrices.

"it could have been learned where the whorehouses are"
"Discere potui inter carrucarios et aleatores"
"I could have learned it among carters and gamblers"
Loquebatur Govinda, "Siddhartha iocatur mecum".
Spoke Govinda, "Siddhartha is joking with me"
"Quomodo inter miseros meditatio didicisti?"
"How could you have learned meditation among wretched people?"
"Quomodo meretrices tibi docuerunt anhelitum tenentem?"
"how could whores have taught you about holding your breath?"
"Quomodo aleatores docuerunt improbitatem contra dolorem?"
"how could gamblers have taught you insensitivity against pain?"
Siddhartha tacite locutus est, quasi secum ipse loqueretur
Siddhartha spoke quietly, as if he was talking to himself
"Quid est meditatio?"
"What is meditation?"
"Quid relinquet corpus?"
"What is leaving one's body?"
"Quid est jejunium?"
"What is fasting?"
"Quid tenens anhelitum?"
"What is holding one's breath?"
"Fugat a se;"
"It is fleeing from the self"
"Brevis cruciatus effugium est sui ipsius"
"it is a short escape of the agony of being a self"
" Brevis est torpens sensuum contra dolorem " ;
"it is a short numbing of the senses against the pain"
"devitat vanitatem vitae"
"it is avoiding the pointlessness of life"
"Idem torpens est quod agitator plaustri bovis in diversorio invenit".

"The same numbing is what the driver of an ox-cart finds in the inn"
"bibens pauca phialas de rice-vinum vel fermentatum Cocoes lactis"
"drinking a few bowls of rice-wine or fermented coconut-milk"
"Tunc non sentiet se amplius"
"Then he won't feel his self anymore"
"Deinde non sentiet dolores vitae amplius"
"then he won't feel the pains of life anymore"
"Invenit ergo brevem sensuum torpens";
"then he finds a short numbing of the senses"
"Cum dormierit super phialam oryzae vini, idem inveniet quod invenimus".
"When he falls asleep over his bowl of rice-wine, he'll find the same what we find"
invenit quod invenimus cum corpora nostra per longa exercitia evadimus.
"he finds what we find when we escape our bodies through long exercises"
"Omnes nos manemus in non-se"
"all of us are staying in the non-self"
« Ita est, o Govinda ».
"This is how it is, oh Govinda"
Locutus est Govinda, "Ais, o amice".
Spoke Govinda, "You say so, oh friend"
"et tamen scis Siddhartha non esse agitator plaustri bovis".
"and yet you know that Siddhartha is no driver of an ox-cart"
"et scis Samana ebriosus non esse".
"and you know a Samana is no drunkard"
"Verum est quod potator sensus suos torpet"
"it's true that a drinker numbs his senses"
verum est quod breviter fugit et quiescit.
"it's true that he briefly escapes and rests"
"sed a errore redibit et omnia immutata invenit".
"but he'll return from the delusion and finds everything to be unchanged"

"non sapientior factus est"
"he has not become wiser"
Collegit omnem illuminationem.
"he has gathered any enlightenment"
"Non resurrexit pluribus gradibus"
"he has not risen several steps"
Et locutus est Siddhartha risu
And Siddhartha spoke with a smile
"Nescio, numquam ebriosus fui".
"I do not know, I've never been a drunkard"
"Scio me brevem sensuum torpens".
"I know that I find only a short numbing of the senses"
"In exercitiis et meditationibus invenio"
"I find it in my exercises and meditations"
" et invenio, quantum distet a sapientia, sicut parvulus in utero matris ".
"and I find I am just as far removed from wisdom as a child in the mother's womb"
"Hoc scio, o Govinda".
"this I know, oh Govinda"

Et iterum, alio tempore, coepit Siddhartha loqui
And once again, another time, Siddhartha began to speak
Siddhartha silva reliquerat una cum Govinda
Siddhartha had left the forest, together with Govinda
petere cibum in villa reliquerunt
they left to beg for some food in the village
"Quid nunc, inquit, o Govinda?"
he said, "What now, oh Govinda?"
"Nos sumus in viam rectam?"
"are we on the right path?"
"veniemus propius ad illuminationem?"
"are we getting closer to enlightenment?"
"Venimus propius ad salutem?"
"are we getting closer to salvation?"
"An forte in circulo vivimus?"

"Or do we perhaps live in a circle?"
"nos, qui nos cyclum effugere arbitrati sumus".
"we, who have thought we were escaping the cycle"
Locutus est Govinda, "multum didicimus"
Spoke Govinda, "We have learned a lot"
"Siddhartha, adhuc multum discendum est"
"Siddhartha, there is still much to learn"
"Non imus in circulis"
"We are not going around in circles"
"Nos movere sursum, circulus spiralis"
"we are moving up; the circle is a spiral"
"Iam multa gradus ascendimus"
"we have already ascended many levels"
Respondit Siddhartha, "Quot annos nata putas Samana nostra vetustissima esse?"
Siddhartha answered, "How old would you think our oldest Samana is?"
"Quot annos, venerabilis magister noster?"
"how old is our venerable teacher?"
Locutus est Govinda, "antiquior noster unus esset circiter sexaginta annos natus".
Spoke Govinda, "Our oldest one might be about sixty years of age"
Locutus est Siddhartha, "vixit annos sexaginta".
Spoke Siddhartha, "He has lived for sixty years"
"et tamen ad nirvana non pervenit".
"and yet he has not reached the nirvana"
" Septuaginta et octoginta convertet "
"He'll turn seventy and eighty"
"te et me, sicut illi senescimus".
"you and me, we will grow just as old as him"
"et exercitia nostra faciemus"
"and we will do our exercises"
"et ieiunemus, et meditabimur".
"and we will fast, and we will meditate"
"Sed non ad nirvana"

"But we will not reach the nirvana"
"Non perveniant nirvana et non"
"he won't reach nirvana and we won't"
"Est autem Samanas Ipsius ibi sunt"
"there are uncountable Samanas out there"
"fortasse ne unus quidem nirvana"
"perhaps not a single one will reach the nirvana"
"Invenimus consolationem, invenimus torpor, discimus facta".
"We find comfort, we find numbness, we learn feats"
"Haec discimus alios fallere".
"we learn these things to deceive others"
"Sed quod maximi momenti est, semita semitarum non inveniemus"
"But the most important thing, the path of paths, we will not find"
Govinda locutus est "Si non diceres tantum verba terribilis, Siddhartha!"
Spoke Govinda "If you only wouldn't speak such terrible words, Siddhartha!"
"tot docti homines".
"there are so many learned men"
"quomodo nemo eorum non inuenit semitam?"
"how could not one of them not find the path of paths?"
"Quomodo tot Brahmans non reperit?"
"how can so many Brahmans not find it?"
"Quomodo tot severi ac venerabiles Samanas non inveniunt?"
"how can so many austere and venerable Samanas not find it?"
"Quomodo omnes, qui quaerunt, non inveniunt?"
"how can all those who are searching not find it?"
quomodo sancti viri non inveniunt eam?
"how can the holy men not find it?"
Sed Siddhartha locutus est tam tristitia quam ludibrium
But Siddhartha spoke with as much sadness as mockery
cum silentio, leviter tristis, voce leviter irridens

he spoke with a quiet, a slightly sad, a slightly mocking voice
"Mox, Govinda, amicus tuus iter Samanas relinquet".
"Soon, Govinda, your friend will leave the path of the Samanas"
"Per te ambulavit tam diu latus"
"he has walked along your side for so long"
" siti patior " ;
"I'm suffering of thirst"
"In hac longissima Samana via, sitis mea quam fortis permansit semper".
"on this long path of a Samana, my thirst has remained as strong as ever"
"Semper sitivi scientiam"
"I always thirsted for knowledge"
"Ego semper plenus quaestionum"
"I have always been full of questions"
"Brachmanas petii quotannis".
"I have asked the Brahmans, year after year"
Sancte Vedas rogaui jugiter.
"and I have asked the holy Vedas, year after year"
" et piam Samanas rogavi jugiter " ;
"and I have asked the devoted Samanas, year after year"
"Fortasse potui discere ab ave hornbill".
"perhaps I could have learned it from the hornbill bird"
"Fortasse rogavi sphingas"
"perhaps I should have asked the chimpanzee"
"Non me diu".
"It took me a long time"
"et nondum discere complevi"
"and I am not finished learning this yet"
"O Govinda, didici nihil discendum esse!"
"oh Govinda, I have learned that there is nothing to be learned!"
"Nulla quidem talis res est quam doctrina".
"There is indeed no such thing as learning"
"Est una scientia"

"There is just one knowledge"
"Vbique haec scientia est, hoc est Atman".
"this knowledge is everywhere, this is Atman"
"Cognitio haec in me est, et in te";
"this knowledge is within me and within you"
Et haec scientia est in omni creatura.
"and this knowledge is within every creature"
"Nihil peius inimicum habet cognitio quam cupiditas sciendi".
"this knowledge has no worse enemy than the desire to know it"
"Hoc est quod credo"
"that is what I believe"
Ad hoc, Govinda in via substitit
At this, Govinda stopped on the path
Surrexit manus, et locutus est
he rose his hands, and spoke
"Si modo non molestas amico tuo hoc genere sermonis"
"If only you would not bother your friend with this kind of talk"
" Vere, verba tua excita cor meum ".
"Truly, your words stir up fear in my heart"
"Vide quid sanctitati orationis accideret?"
"consider, what would become of the sanctity of prayer?"
"quid futurum erat venerabili ordini Bramanorum?"
"what would become of the venerability of the Brahmans' caste?"
quid sanctitati Samanis accideret?
"what would happen to the holiness of the Samanas?"
" Quid tunc de illo sancto ".
"What would then become of all of that is holy"
"quid adhuc esset pretiosum?"
"what would still be precious?"
Et Govinda mussavit versum ex Upanishad sibi
And Govinda mumbled a verse from an Upanishad to himself

"Qui considerans purificatus spiritus se amittit in meditatione Atmani".
"He who ponderingly, of a purified spirit, loses himself in the meditation of Atman"
"Ineffabilis verbis est beatitudo cordis ejus";
"inexpressible by words is the blissfulness of his heart"
Sed Siddhartha tacuit
But Siddhartha remained silent
Cogitabat de verbis quae sibi Govinda dixerat
He thought about the words which Govinda had said to him
et cogitabat verba eorum usque ad finem
and he thought the words through to their end
de omnibus, quod sanctum videbatur, reliquum fore
he thought about what would remain of all that which seemed holy
Quid restat? Quid potest experiri?
What remains? What can stand the test?
Et quassavit caput
And he shook his head

duo iuvenes vixerunt in Samana per annos circiter tres
the two young men had lived among the Samanas for about three years
quidam nuntius, rumor, fabula ad eos pervenit
some news, a rumour, a myth reached them
pluries fama fuerat
the rumour had been retold many times
Apparuerat homo quidam nomine Gotama
A man had appeared, Gotama by name
excelsus, Buddha
the exalted one, the Buddha
passionem mundi in se superaverat
he had overcome the suffering of the world in himself
renascentiae cursus constiterat
and he had halted the cycle of rebirths
Dictus pererrare terram, docens

He was said to wander through the land, teaching
Dictus discipulorum circumdari
he was said to be surrounded by disciples
dicebatur absque possessione, domo, vel uxore
he was said to be without possession, home, or wife
dicebatur in modo pallii ascetici
he was said to be in just the yellow cloak of an ascetic
sed erat hilari fronte
but he was with a cheerful brow
Dictus est vir beatus
and he was said to be a man of bliss
Brachmanes et principes coram eo adoraverunt
Brahmans and princes bowed down before him
et facti sunt discipuli eius
and they became his students
Haec fabula, haec fama, haec fabula sonuit
This myth, this rumour, this legend resounded
surrexit odor ejus, passim in oppidis
its fragrance rose up, here and there, in the towns
Brachmanae de hac legenda locutus est
the Brahmans spoke of this legend
et saltu, Samanas locutus est
and in the forest, the Samanas spoke of it
identidem nomen Gotama Buddha ad aures puerorum pervenit
again and again, the name of Gotama the Buddha reached the ears of the young men
fuit bona et mala disputatio Gotamae
there was good and bad talk of Gotama
quidam eum laudaverunt Gotamam, alii eum
some praised Gotama, others defamed him
Quasi plaga in terra
It was as if the plague had broken out in a country
rumore circumfuso quod in uno vel alio loco erat homo
news had been spreading around that in one or another place there was a man

vir prudens, sapiens
a wise man, a knowledgeable one
vir cuius sermo et spiritus satis erat ad sanandum omnes
a man whose word and breath was enough to heal everyone
eius praesentia quemvis pestilentia infectum sanare potuit
his presence could heal anyone who had been infected with the pestilence
Talis nuntius ibat per terram, et omnes loquebantur de illo
such news went through the land, and everyone would talk about it
multi rumores crediderunt, multi dubitaverunt
many believed the rumours, many doubted them
multi autem in itinere quam primum
but many got on their way as soon as possible
iverunt ad quaerendum sapientem adiutorem
they went to seek the wise man, the helper
sapiens familiae Sakya
the wise man of the family of Sakya
Possedit, ut credentes, summam illuminationem
He possessed, so the believers said, the highest enlightenment
pristinae vitae meminerat; pervenerat nirvana
he remembered his previous lives; he had reached the nirvana
et numquam in cyclum rediit
and he never returned into the cycle
numquam iterum mersa atris flumine formarum corporearum
he was never again submerged in the murky river of physical forms
Multa de eo mira et incredibilia delata sunt
Many wonderful and unbelievable things were reported of him
fecerat miracula
he had performed miracles
vicisset diabolum
he had overcome the devil
Dixerat

he had spoken to the gods
Sed inimici et increduli dicti Gotama fuit vanus seductor
But his enemies and disbelievers said Gotama was a vain seducer
aiebant se in deliciis dierum egisse
they said he spent his days in luxury
dicebant oblationes contempsit
they said he scorned the offerings
dicebant se nescire
they said he was without learning
se neque meditata neque castimonia se scire
they said he knew neither meditative exercises nor self-castigation
Fabula Buddha cecinit dulce
The myth of Buddha sounded sweet
Odor magicae ex his opinionibus manavit
The scent of magic flowed from these reports
Nam mundus infirmus erat et vita durior erat
After all, the world was sick, and life was hard to bear
et ecce hic subsidio prodire videbatur
and behold, here a source of relief seemed to spring forth
hic nuntius vocare videbatur
here a messenger seemed to call out
consolatus, mitis, plenus promissionum nobilium
comforting, mild, full of noble promises
Ubique rumor Buddha audiebatur, iuvenes audiebantur
Everywhere where the rumour of Buddha was heard, the young men listened up
ubique in Indiae terris cupiditatem senserunt
everywhere in the lands of India they felt a longing
Ubique, ubi scrutati sunt, spem sentiebant
everywhere where the people searched, they felt hope
omnis peregrinus et advena gratus fuit cum de eo nuntiaret
every pilgrim and stranger was welcome when he brought news of him
excelsus, Sakyamuni

the exalted one, the Sakyamuni
Fabula etiam Samanas in saltu pervenerat
The myth had also reached the Samanas in the forest
et Siddhartha et Govinda fabulae quoque audiverunt
and Siddhartha and Govinda heard the myth too
tardius, guttatim audiverunt fabula
slowly, drop by drop, they heard the myth
omnis gutta erat cum spe
every drop was laden with hope
omnis gutta erat in dubio
every drop was laden with doubt
Non raro loquebatur de illo
They rarely talked about it
quia senior Samanas non sic fabula
because the oldest one of the Samanas did not like this myth
audiverat hanc allegatam esse asceticam Buddha
he had heard that this alleged Buddha used to be an ascetic
audivit eum in silva fuisse
he heard he had lived in the forest
sed ad luxuriam et ad mundanas voluptates converterat
but he had turned back to luxury and worldly pleasures
et de hoc Gotama non habebat existimationem
and he had no high opinion of this Gotama

"**O Siddhartha," Govinda locutus est olim amico suo**
"Oh Siddhartha," Govinda spoke one day to his friend
"**Hodie in villa fui**";
"Today, I was in the village"
"**et Brahman me invitavit in domum suam**".
"and a Brahman invited me into his house"
"**et in domo sua erat filius Brahman de Magadha**";
"and in his house, there was the son of a Brahman from Magadha"
"**Buddha oculis suis vidit**"
"he has seen the Buddha with his own eyes"
et exaudivit eum docebit.

"and he has heard him teach"
"Immo hoc dolorem meum pectus fecerat cum respirabam".
"Verily, this made my chest ache when I breathed"
et hoc cogitabam apud me;
"and I thought this to myself:"
"si modo ex ore perfecti viri istius doctrinas audivimus."
"if only we heard the teachings from the mouth of this perfected man!"
"Loquere, amice, nolumus illuc quoque ire"
"Speak, friend, wouldn't we want to go there too"
"Nonne bonum sit audire doctrinam ab ore Buddha?"
"wouldn't it be good to listen to the teachings from the Buddha's mouth?"
Locutus est Siddhartha, "putavi te apud Samanas manere".
Spoke Siddhartha, "I had thought you would stay with the Samanas"
"Semper credideram propositum tuum victurum esse septuaginta";
"I always had believed your goal was to live to be seventy"
"Cogitavi te illa facinora et exercitia servare".
"I thought you would keep practising those feats and exercises"
"et cogitavi te Samana fieres"
"and I thought you would become a Samana"
"Sed ecce, satis bene Govindam nesciebam".
"But behold, I had not known Govinda well enough"
" Parum scivi de corde suo " ;
"I knew little of his heart"
"Nunc igitur novam viam velis accipere"
"So now you want to take a new path"
"et vis illuc ire ubi Buddha dogma diffundit".
"and you want to go there where the Buddha spreads his teachings"
Dixit Govinda, "Irrisis me".
Spoke Govinda, "You're mocking me"
"Ille me, si placet, Siddhartha!"

"Mock me if you like, Siddhartha!"
"Sed non etiam desiderium haec doctrina elaborasti?"
"But have you not also developed a desire to hear these teachings?"
"non dixisti" inquit "non multo longiorem viam Samanas ambulare?"
"have you not said you would not walk the path of the Samanas for much longer?"
Ad hoc, Siddhartha suo more risit
At this, Siddhartha laughed in his very own manner
quomodo vocem sumpsit tactum tristitiae
the manner in which his voice assumed a touch of sadness
sed adhuc habuit tactum illud ludibrii
but it still had that touch of mockery
Siddhartha locutus est, "Govinda, bene locutus es".
Spoke Siddhartha, "Govinda, you've spoken well"
"Recte meministi quae dixi"
"you've remembered correctly what I said"
"Si modo alterius rei meministi ex me audisti".
"If only you remembered the other thing you've heard from me"
"Diffidens sum defessus contra doctrinas et doctrinas"
"I have grown distrustful and tired against teachings and learning"
"fides mea verbis, quae nobis a magistris afferuntur, parva est";
"my faith in words, which are brought to us by teachers, is small"
"Sed faciamus, mi"
"But let's do it, my dear"
"Libenter audire istas doctrinas".
"I am willing to listen to these teachings"
" Etsi in corde meo spem non habeo "
"though in my heart I do not have hope"
"Credo nos iam optimum fructum harum doctrinarum gustasse"

"I believe that we've already tasted the best fruit of these teachings"
Dixit Govinda: Voluntas tua cor meum delectat.
Spoke Govinda, "Your willingness delights my heart"
"Sed dic, quomodo id fieri potest?"
"But tell me, how should this be possible?"
"Quomodo igitur Gotamae doctrinas optimum fructum nobis iam patefecit?"
"How can the Gotama's teachings have already revealed their best fruit to us?"
sed verba eius non audivimus.
"we have not heard his words yet"
Dixit Siddhartha, "Hunc fructum comedamus".
Spoke Siddhartha, "Let us eat this fruit"
"et reliquas opperiamur, o Govinda!"
"and let us wait for the rest, oh Govinda!"
Sed hic fructus consistit in eo quod nos a Samana vocamus.
"But this fruit consists in him calling us away from the Samanas"
"et nos iam Gotamae gratiam recepimus!"
"and we have already received it thanks to the Gotama!"
"Utrum plus habet, placidis exspectemus cordibus".
"Whether he has more, let us await with calm hearts"

Hoc ipso die Siddhartha seniori Samana locutus est
On this very same day Siddhartha spoke to the oldest Samana
dixit ei de consilio suo ut Samanas egrederetur
he told him of his decision to leaves the Samanas
seniorem cum comitate et modestia docuit
he informed the oldest one with courtesy and modesty
sed Samana iratus est quod duo iuvenes vellent eum exire
but the Samana became angry that the two young men wanted to leave him
et loquebatur magna et usus est rudibus verbis
and he talked loudly and used crude words
Govinda obstupuit et erubuit

Govinda was startled and became embarrassed
Sed Siddhartha os suum admovet auriculam Govindae
But Siddhartha put his mouth close to Govinda's ear
"Iam, senem volo ostendere quid ab eo didicerim".
"Now, I want to show the old man what I've learned from him"
Siddhartha in conspectu Samana
Siddhartha positioned himself closely in front of the Samana
intenta anima, senis aspectu cepit
with a concentrated soul, he captured the old man's glance
potestate privavit et mutum fecit
he deprived him of his power and made him mute
tulit liberum arbitrium suum
he took away his free will
et subiecit eum in propria voluntate et praecepit ei
he subdued him under his own will, and commanded him
oculi eius immobiles facti sunt, et voluntas eius resoluta est
his eyes became motionless, and his will was paralysed
brachiis dependentibus sine viribus
his arms were hanging down without power
cecidisset victimam ad Siddhartha scriptor incantatores
he had fallen victim to Siddhartha's spell
Siddhartha cogitationes Samana in suam potestatem redegit
Siddhartha's thoughts brought the Samana under their control
exsequi quod jussa habebat
he had to carry out what they commanded
Sicque senex varios arcus fecit
And thus, the old man made several bows
gestus benedi- centiae fecit
he performed gestures of blessing
pie optare bonum iter dixit
he spoke stammeringly a godly wish for a good journey
juvenes bona vota cum gratiarum actione redierunt
the young men returned the good wishes with thanks
irent cum salutationibus
they went on their way with salutations

In via, Govinda iterum locutus est
On the way, Govinda spoke again
"O Siddhartha, plus a Samana didicisti quam scivi".
"Oh Siddhartha, you have learned more from the Samanas than I knew"
"Difficile est Samana vetus alligent".
"It is very hard to cast a spell on an old Samana"
"Vere, si ibi manseris, mox per aquam ambulare didiceris".
"Truly, if you had stayed there, you would soon have learned to walk on water"
"Non quaero ambulare super aquam" dixit Siddhartha
"I do not seek to walk on water" said Siddhartha
"Sit veteres Samanas talibus facinoribus contenti!"
"Let old Samanas be content with such feats!"

Gotama

In Savathi omnis puer noverat nomen sublimium Buddha
In Savathi, every child knew the name of the exalted Buddha
omnis domus ad adventum suum parata est
every house was prepared for his coming
unaquaeque domus implebat eleemosynas ex discipulis Gotamae
each house filled the alms-dishes of Gotama's disciples
Gotamae discipuli taciti petentes
Gotama's disciples were the silently begging ones
Prope oppidum Gotama est ventus locus ad manendum
Near the town was Gotama's favourite place to stay
mansit in horto Jetavana
he stayed in the garden of Jetavana
mercator dives Anathapindika hortum Gotamae dederat
the rich merchant Anathapindika had given the garden to Gotama
ei dono dederat
he had given it to him as a gift
erat obediens cultor elatus
he was an obedient worshipper of the exalted one
duos pullos reruni accepisset fabulas et responsa
the two young ascetics had received tales and answers
omnibus hisce fabulis et responsionibus ostendit eos in domo Gotamae
all these tales and answers pointed them to Gotama's abode
venerunt in oppidum Savathi
they arrived in the town of Savathi
iverunt ad primam portam oppidi
they went to the very first door of the town
et cibum oraverunt ad januam
and they begged for food at the door
Mulier cibum
a woman offered them food
et acceperunt cibum

and they accepted the food
Siddhartha interrogavit mulier
Siddhartha asked the woman
"O caritas, ubi Buddha habitat?"
"oh charitable one, where does the Buddha dwell?"
"Nos sumus duo Samanas de silva"
"we are two Samanas from the forest"
"Venimus ad uidendum perfectum".
"we have come to see the perfected one"
"Venimus audire de ore eius doctrinas".
"we have come to hear the teachings from his mouth"
Dixit mulier, "Samana tu de silva".
Spoke the woman, "you Samanas from the forest"
"Tu vere ad dextram locum"
"you have truly come to the right place"
"nosces, in Jetavana, hortus Anathapindikae";
"you should know, in Jetavana, there is the garden of Anathapindika"
id est, ubi habitat excelsus.
"that is where the exalted one dwells"
"ibi peregrini pernoctabunt".
"there you pilgrims shall spend the night"
"sat spatium innumerabilibus, qui huc confluunt".
"there is enough space for the innumerable, who flock here"
"Et ipsi veniunt audire de ore Ipsius".
"they too come to hear the teachings from his mouth"
Hoc fecit beatus Govinda, et plenus gaudio
This made Govinda happy, and full of joy
inquit, "pervenimus";
he exclaimed, "we have reached our destination"
"Defectum est iter nostrum!"
"our path has come to an end!"
"Sed dic, o mater peregrinorum".
"But tell us, oh mother of the pilgrims"
"scisne eum Buddha?"
"do you know him, the Buddha?"

"Numquid vidisti eum oculis tuis?"
"have you seen him with your own eyes?"
Dixit mulier: "Saepe vidi eum exaltatum".
Spoke the woman, "Many times I have seen him, the exalted one"
" Multis diebus vidi eum ";
"On many days I have seen him"
" per angiportum tacitus vidi eum ambulantem ";
"I have seen him walking through the alleys in silence"
"Vidi pallio pallio";
"I have seen him wearing his yellow cloak"
"Vidi eleemosynam suam in silentio".
"I have seen him presenting his alms-dish in silence"
" foribus domorum eum vidi ";
"I have seen him at the doors of the houses"
" et vidi eum saturitate repletum relinquentem ";
"and I have seen him leaving with a filled dish"
Govinda foemina jucunde auscultavit
Delightedly, Govinda listened to the woman
et multo magis petere et audire cupiebat
and he wanted to ask and hear much more
Sed Siddhartha hortatus est ut ambularet
But Siddhartha urged him to walk on
Mulieri gratias egerunt et ad sinistram
They thanked the woman and left
vix ad partes petere
they hardly had to ask for directions
multi peregrini et monachi ibant in Jetavana .
many pilgrims and monks were on their way to the Jetavana
perventum est ad eam noctem;
they reached it at night, so there were constant arrivals
et qui petierant recepit
and those who sought shelter got it
Duo Samanas vitam in silva esse consuerunt
The two Samanas were accustomed to life in the forest
ita sine ullo tumultu celeriter locum morandi invenerunt

so without making any noise they quickly found a place to stay
et quievit ibi usque mane
and they rested there until the morning

Orto sole mirantur magnitudinem multitudinis
At sunrise, they saw with astonishment the size of the crowd
multorum credentium venerant
a great many number of believers had come
et hic magnus numerus curiosorum hominum pernoctaverat
and a great number of curious people had spent the night here
In omnibus viis horti mirifici monachi cum stolis flavis ambulaverunt
On all paths of the marvellous garden, monks walked in yellow robes
sub arboribus passim sederunt in alta contemplatione
under the trees they sat here and there, in deep contemplation
vel erant in colloquio de rebus spiritualibus
or they were in a conversation about spiritual matters
nemorosos hortos quasi civitatem
the shady gardens looked like a city
civitas plena populo, sicut apes indu
a city full of people, bustling like bees
Maior pars monachorum exivit cum lancibus suis eleemosynam
The majority of the monks went out with their alms-dish
Exierunt colligere cibum pro prandio
they went out to collect food for their lunch
hoc esset unum cibum diei
this would be their only meal of the day
Buddha ipse, illuminatus, orabat etiam in matutinis
The Buddha himself, the enlightened one, also begged in the mornings
Siddhartha vidit eum et statim agnovit eum
Siddhartha saw him, and he instantly recognised him
Agnovit eum tamquam Deum demonstrasse

he recognised him as if a God had pointed him out
Vir simplex vidit in stola crocea
He saw him, a simple man in a yellow robe
ferculum eleemosynae portabat in manu, tacite ambulans
he was bearing the alms-dish in his hand, walking silently
"Ecce hic!" Siddhartha dixit quiete ad Govinda
"Look here!" Siddhartha said quietly to Govinda
"Haec Buddha"
"This one is the Buddha"
Attente Govinda aspexit monachum flavum
Attentively, Govinda looked at the monk in the yellow robe
hic monachus nullo modo ab aliquo diversus esse videbatur
this monk seemed to be in no way different from any of the others
sed mox, Govinda etiam intellexit hoc unum esse
but soon, Govinda also realized that this is the one
Et secuti sunt eum
And they followed him and observed him
Buddha ibat, modeste et profunde in cogitationibus
The Buddha went on his way, modestly and deep in his thoughts
vultu placido nec laetus nec tristis erat
his calm face was neither happy nor sad
vultu placide ac intus ridere videbatur
his face seemed to smile quietly and inwardly
eius risu latebat, quies et tranquillitas
his smile was hidden, quiet and calm
via Buddha ambulavit simillimus sanus puer
the way the Buddha walked somewhat resembled a healthy child
ambulavit sicut omnes monachos suos
he walked just as all of his monks did
pedes secundum certa regula posuit
he placed his feet according to a precise rule
os et gressum, vultumque silenter deposuit
his face and his walk, his quietly lowered glance

manu pensilis tacite quilibet digitus eius
his quietly dangling hand, every finger of it
haec omnia pacem
all these things expressed peace
Omnia haec perfectio
all these things expressed perfection
non quaesivit nec imitatus est
he did not search, nor did he imitate
ille leniter inspiravit intus inexhausta tranquillitas
he softly breathed inwardly an unwhithering calm
extus est sine lumine
he shone outwardly an unwhithering light
inviolabilem pacem habuit
he had about him an untouchable peace
agnoverunt eum duo Samanas sola animi sui perfectione
the two Samanas recognised him solely by the perfection of his calm
agnoverunt eum per quietem vultus sui
they recognized him by the quietness of his appearance
tranquillitatem in vultu, in qua nulla quaerebatur
the quietness in his appearance in which there was no searching
nulla cupiditas, neque imitatio
there was no desire, nor imitation
nulla cura videri
there was no effort to be seen
sola lux et pax in aspectu eius
only light and peace was to be seen in his appearance
"Hodie doctrinas audiemus ex ore eius" dixit Govinda .
"Today, we'll hear the teachings from his mouth" said Govinda
Siddhartha non respondit mihi
Siddhartha did not answer
Sensit parum curiositatem doctrinae
He felt little curiosity for the teachings
non credebat se aliquid novi docturos

he did not believe that they would teach him anything new
haec Buddha dogmata iterum atque iterum audiverat
he had heard the contents of this Buddha's teachings again and again
sed hae relationes tantum repraesentabant secunda manu informationes
but these reports only represented second hand information
At Gotamae caput attente intuens
But attentively he looked at Gotama's head
umeros, pedes, manus pendere tacite
his shoulders, his feet, his quietly dangling hand
sicut si omnis digitus manus huius de doctrina ista
it was as if every finger of this hand was of these teachings
digitos vero
his fingers spoke of truth
digiti eius spirabant et exhalabantur odorem veritatis
his fingers breathed and exhaled the fragrance of truth
digitis renidebant vero
his fingers glistened with truth
Haec Buddha verax erat ad gestum ultimi digiti
this Buddha was truthful down to the gesture of his last finger
Siddhartha potuit videre hunc virum sanctum fuisse
Siddhartha could see that this man was holy
Numquam ante, Siddhartha hominem tantum veneratus est
Never before, Siddhartha had venerated a person so much
nunquam prius amaverat quantum iste
he had never before loved a person as much as this one
Ambo Buddha usque ad oppidum pervenerunt
They both followed the Buddha until they reached the town
et tunc reversi sunt ad silentium
and then they returned to their silence
ipsi hac die abstinere voluerunt
they themselves intended to abstain on this day
Viderunt Gotamam redeuntes cibum sibi datum
They saw Gotama returning the food that had been given to him

quod edebat, ne gulae quidem satiasse potuit
what he ate could not even have satisfied a bird's appetite
et viderunt eum cedentem in umbra mango
and they saw him retiring into the shade of the mango-trees

ad vesperam calor defervuerat
in the evening the heat had cooled down
omnes in castris inceperunt tumultuari et convenerunt
everyone in the camp started to bustle about and gathered around
audiverunt Buddha doctrinam et vocem eius
they heard the Buddha teaching, and his voice
et vox quoque perfecta
and his voice was also perfected
vox eius summae tranquillitatis
his voice was of perfect calmness
vox eius plena pacis
his voice was full of peace
Gotama docuit doctrinam doloris
Gotama taught the teachings of suffering
docuit originem doloris
he taught of the origin of suffering
docebat de via ad dolorem
he taught of the way to relieve suffering
Placide et plane quietis eius oratio fluxit
Calmly and clearly his quiet speech flowed on
Passio erat vita et plenus tribulationibus mundus
Suffering was life, and full of suffering was the world
sed salus a labore inventa est
but salvation from suffering had been found
salus consecuta est ab eo, qui iter Buddhae incederet
salvation was obtained by him who would walk the path of the Buddha
Molli et firma voce locuta est praecelsa
With a soft, yet firm voice the exalted one spoke
Quattuor praecipua doctrina

he taught the four main doctrines
ipse octuplum iter docuit
he taught the eight-fold path
solitam viam doctrinis patienter ivit
patiently he went the usual path of the teachings
eius doctrina exempla continebat
his teachings contained the examples
suam doctrinam usurparunt repetitiones
his teaching made use of the repetitions
splendide et quiete ferebatur super audientium vocem
brightly and quietly his voice hovered over the listeners
vox eius quasi lux
his voice was like a light
vox eius quasi caelum sidereum
his voice was like a starry sky
Cum Buddha orationem finivit, multi peregrini extiterunt
When the Buddha ended his speech, many pilgrims stepped forward
rogaverunt ut in civitatem recipiatur
they asked to be accepted into the community
confugerunt in doctrina
they sought refuge in the teachings
Et accepit eos Gotama loquendo
And Gotama accepted them by speaking
"Audivisti bene dogmata"
"You have heard the teachings well"
"junge nos et ambulemus in sanctitate";
"join us and walk in holiness"
"Omni dolori finem imposuit"
"put an end to all suffering"
Ecce Govinda, verecunda, etiam exstitit et locutus est
Behold, then Govinda, the shy one, also stepped forward and spoke
« Et ad exaltatum et ad doctrinam eius confugio ».
"I also take my refuge in the exalted one and his teachings"

et petiit ut in communitatem suorum discipulorum recipiatur
and he asked to be accepted into the community of his disciples
et receptus est in communitatem discipulorum Gotamae
and he was accepted into the community of Gotama's disciples

Buddha receperat noctis
the Buddha had retired for the night
Govinda conversus ad Siddhartha et avide locutus est
Govinda turned to Siddhartha and spoke eagerly
"Siddhartha, non est meum obiurgandi locum"
"Siddhartha, it is not my place to scold you"
« Audivimus et exaltatum ».
"We have both heard the exalted one"
" ambo dogmata percepimus " ;
"we have both perceived the teachings"
" Audivit Govinda dogma "
"Govinda has heard the teachings"
"confugit in doctrina"
"he has taken refuge in the teachings"
"At, amice honorande, a te petendus est".
"But, my honoured friend, I must ask you"
"non vis etiam viam salutis ambulare?"
"don't you also want to walk the path of salvation?"
"Vis dubitare?"
"Would you want to hesitate?"
"Visne diutius exspectare?"
"do you want to wait any longer?"
Siddhartha excitavit quasi dormiret
Siddhartha awakened as if he had been asleep
Diu in faciem Govindae inspexit
For a long time, he looked into Govinda's face
Tum tacite, voce sine irrisione
Then he spoke quietly, in a voice without mockery
"Amice Govinda, nunc hunc gradum tulisti".

"Govinda, my friend, now you have taken this step"
"Nunc viam hanc elegisti"
"now you have chosen this path"
"Semper, o Govinda, amicus meus fuisti".
"Always, oh Govinda, you've been my friend"
"Tu semper ambulavit gradum post me"
"you've always walked one step behind me"
"Saepe cogitavi de vobis"
"Often I have thought about you"
"Nonne Govinda semel etiam per se gradum".
"'Won't Govinda for once also take a step by himself'"
"Nonne Govinda gradum sine me accipies?"
"'won't Govinda take a step without me?'"
"Nonne anima sua gradum accipit?"
"'won't he take a step driven by his own soul?'"
"Ecce iam conversus in hominem".
"Behold, now you've turned into a man"
"Viam tuam eliges tibi"
"you are choosing your path for yourself"
« **Volo ut eamus ad finem** ».
"I wish that you would go it up to its end"
"O mi amice, spero quod salutem inveneris!"
"oh my friend, I hope that you shall find salvation!"
Govinda nondum eam penitus intellexit
Govinda, did not completely understand it yet
iteravit quaestionem impatiens sono
he repeated his question in an impatient tone
"Loquere, quaeso, mi mi!"
"Speak up, I beg you, my dear!"
"Dic mihi, quandoquidem aliter fieri non potuit".
"Tell me, since it could not be any other way"
"Nonne tu etiam cum excelso Buddha confugies?"
"won't you also take your refuge with the exalted Buddha?"
Siddhartha imposuit manum in humero Govinda
Siddhartha placed his hand on Govinda's shoulder
"Tu non audisti bonam voluntatem meam pro te"

"You failed to hear my good wish for you"
"Repetitio mea ad vos volo"
"I'm repeating my wish for you"
" Opto ut hanc viam velis ire " .
"I wish that you would go this path"
" Opto ut ad huius viae finem ascendas "
"I wish that you would go up to this path's end"
Utinam salutem invenias.
"I wish that you shall find salvation!"
Hoc momento, Govinda intellexit amicum suum ab eo discessisse
In this moment, Govinda realized that his friend had left him
Quod cum animadvertisset, coepit flere
when he realized this he started to weep
"Siddhartha!" inquit lamentabiliter
"Siddhartha!" he exclaimed lamentingly
Siddhartha benigne locutus est ei
Siddhartha kindly spoke to him
"Noli oblivisci, Govinda, quae tu es".
"don't forget, Govinda, who you are"
"Tu nunc unus ex Samanas Buddha"
"you are now one of the Samanas of the Buddha"
" Domum tuam ac parentes renuntiasti " ;
"You have renounced your home and your parents"
"abrenuntiasti natalibus et possessionibus tuis".
"you have renounced your birth and possessions"
"Abrenuntiasti liberum arbitrium"
"you have renounced your free will"
" abrenuntiasti omnem amicitiam "
"you have renounced all friendship"
"Hoc est quod doctrina requirat".
"This is what the teachings require"
"Hoc est quod vult exaltatus".
"this is what the exalted one wants"
"Hoc est quod volebas pro te".
"This is what you wanted for yourself"

"Cras, o Govinda, te relinquo".
"Tomorrow, oh Govinda, I will leave you"
Diu in horto ambulabant amici
For a long time, the friends continued walking in the garden
Diu ibi iacuerunt nec somnum invenerunt
for a long time, they lay there and found no sleep
Govinda etiam atque etiam hortatus est
And over and over again, Govinda urged his friend
"cur ad Gotamae dogmata confugere non vis?"
"why would you not want to seek refuge in Gotama's teachings?"
"Quam culpam invenis in his dogmatibus?"
"what fault could you find in these teachings?"
Sed Siddhartha recessit ab amico suo
But Siddhartha turned away from his friend
quotienscumque dixit, "Contende, Govinda!"
every time he said, "Be content, Govinda!"
"Bona doctrina sublimis".
"Very good are the teachings of the exalted one"
"Quomodo ego in dogmatibus eius culpam invenio?"
"how could I find a fault in his teachings?"

valde mane in mane
it was very early in the morning
unus de senioribus monachis per hortum
one of the oldest monks went through the garden
ad eos qui confugerant vocabat
he called to those who had taken their refuge in the teachings
vocavit eos ut operaretur in pallio flavo
he called them to dress them up in the yellow robe
et eos in primis doctrinis et officiis suae dignitatis instruat
and he instruct them in the first teachings and duties of their position
Govinda semel iterumque amplexus est adulescentia sua
Govinda once again embraced his childhood friend
et cum novitiis

and then he left with the novices
Sed Siddhartha ambulavit per hortum, cogitatione perdita
But Siddhartha walked through the garden, lost in thought
Tunc forte Gotama obviam venit elatus
Then he happened to meet Gotama, the exalted one
salutavit eum
he greeted him with respect
Buddha aspectu erat plena benignitate et tranquillitate
the Buddha's glance was full of kindness and calm
adulescens animum vocat
the young man summoned his courage
rogavit venerabilis pro licentia loqui ei
he asked the venerable one for the permission to talk to him
Tacite, adnuit elatus assensum
Silently, the exalted one nodded his approval
Siddhartha locutus est, "Heri, o exaltata";
Spoke Siddhartha, "Yesterday, oh exalted one"
"Me dignatus sum audire mirabilia tua dogmata"
"I had been privileged to hear your wondrous teachings"
"Cum amico meo e longinquo ad audiendum doctrinas tuas".
"Together with my friend, I had come from afar, to hear your teachings"
"Et nunc amicus meus cum populo tuo manebit".
"And now my friend is going to stay with your people"
"Confugit ad te".
"he has taken his refuge with you"
"Sed iterum incipiam peregrinationem meam".
"But I will again start on my pilgrimage"
"Ut placet" venerabilis vir blande locutus est
"As you please," the venerable one spoke politely
"Nimis audax est oratio mea", Siddhartha continued
"Too bold is my speech," Siddhartha continued
"sed Nolo in hac nota deserere elevatum".
"but I do not want to leave the exalted on this note"
« Honestas cogitationes meas cum sanctissima communicare volo ».

"I want to share with the most venerable one my honest thoughts"
" Placetne venerabili uno momento auscultare diutius?"
"Does it please the venerable one to listen for one moment longer?"
Tacite, Buddha assensum suum adnuit
Silently, the Buddha nodded his approval
Siddhartha locutus est, "o sanctissime".
Spoke Siddhartha, "oh most venerable one"
"Unum est quod in tuis dogmatibus maxime admiratus sum"
"there is one thing I have admired in your teachings most of all"
"Omnia in tuis dogmatibus clarissime"
"Everything in your teachings is perfectly clear"
"probatur quod loqueris".
"what you speak of is proven"
"Tu exhibes mundum ut catenam perfectam"
"you are presenting the world as a perfect chain"
" catena quae numquam et nusquam rumpitur "
"a chain which is never and nowhere broken"
"Eterna catena nexus quorum causarum et effectuum sunt".
"an eternal chain the links of which are causes and effects"
"Numquam hoc tam clare visum est".
"Never before, has this been seen so clearly"
"Nunquam antea hoc tam irrefragabiliter oblatum est".
"never before, has this been presented so irrefutably"
"Verum, cor cuiuslibet Brahmanis habet fortiora amore verberare".
"truly, the heart of every Brahman has to beat stronger with love"
" vidit mundum per doctrinas tuas perfecte connexas " ;
"he has seen the world through your perfectly connected teachings"
"sine hiatus, clarum ut crystallum"
"without gaps, clear as a crystal"
non casu fretus, non deorum fretus.

"not depending on chance, not depending on Gods"
"habet eam accipere sive sit bonum sive malum".
"he has to accept it whether it may be good or bad"
"vivendum est ex eo sive dolore sive gaudio".
"he has to live by it whether it would be suffering or joy"
"sed de uniformitate mundi nolo disputare".
"but I do not wish to discuss the uniformity of the world"
"Potest hoc esse essentiale".
"it is possible that this is not essential"
" omnia quae fiunt iuncta sunt "
"everything which happens is connected"
" magna et parva circumdantur omnia " .
"the great and the small things are all encompassed"
"connexa sunt eisdem viribus temporis".
"they are connected by the same forces of time"
eadem causarum lege connexa sunt.
"they are connected by the same law of causes"
"causas existendi et moriendi".
"the causes of coming into being and of dying"
"Hoc est quod de sublimibus tuis doctrinis clare elucet".
"this is what shines brightly out of your exalted teachings"
"At, secundum tuam ipsius doctrinam, exiguus hiatus est".
"But, according to your very own teachings, there is a small gap"
« haec unitas et necessaria series omnium in uno loco contrita est ».
"this unity and necessary sequence of all things is broken in one place"
« Mundus unitatis hic ab alio invaditur ».
"this world of unity is invaded by something alien"
"est aliquid novum quod prius non fuerat".
"there is something new, which had not been there before"
"est aliquid quod demonstrari non potest".
"there is something which cannot be demonstrated"
"est aliquid quod probari non potest"
"there is something which cannot be proven"

"Haec sunt vestra dogmata vincendi mundum".
"these are your teachings of overcoming the world"
"Haec sunt tua doctrina salutis".
"these are your teachings of salvation"
"At cum hoc parvo hiatu aeternum rursus frangit".
"But with this small gap, the eternal breaks apart again"
"Cum hac parva contritione, lex mundi irrita fit";
"with this small breach, the law of the world becomes void"
"Ignosce quaeso hanc obiectionem exprimendam"
"Please forgive me for expressing this objection"
Gotama quiete eum audiverat immotus
Quietly, Gotama had listened to him, unmoved
Nunc fatus, genere perfecto, voce et ingenua voce
Now he spoke, the perfected one, with his kind and polite clear voice
"Audisti doctrinam, o fili Brahman".
"You've heard the teachings, oh son of a Brahman"
"et bene tibi hoc penitus cogitasti"
"and good for you that you've thought about it this deeply"
"Invenisti lacunam in doctrinis meis, errorem".
"You've found a gap in my teachings, an error"
"De hoc ulterius cogitare debes"
"You should think about this further"
Sed admone, o inquisitor scientiae, perplexitatem sententiarum.
"But be warned, oh seeker of knowledge, of the thicket of opinions"
"monendum est de verbis disputandi"
"be warned of arguing about words"
"Nihil ad opiniones";
"There is nothing to opinions"
"Ut sint pulchra vel deformis"
"they may be beautiful or ugly"
"Sententias dolor sit vel stultum"
"opinions may be smart or foolish"
"quisque sententias potest sustinere vel eas abiicias".

"everyone can support opinions, or discard them"
"At doctrinas, quas a me audisti, nullae sunt sententiae".
"But the teachings, you've heard from me, are no opinion"
"Propositum eorum est mundum quaerentibus scientiam explicare"
"their goal is not to explain the world to those who seek knowledge"
"Habent alium finem";
"They have a different goal"
"eorum finis est salus a dolore";
"their goal is salvation from suffering"
"Hoc est quod Gotama docet, nihil aliud".
"This is what Gotama teaches, nothing else"
"Vtinam tibi, o princeps, non mihi succenseas" inquit adulescens
"I wish that you, oh exalted one, would not be angry with me" said the young man
"Non locutus sum vobis, ut disputarem cum vobis;
"I have not spoken to you like this to argue with you"
"Nolo de verbis disputare".
"I do not wish to argue about words"
"Recte dicis; parum est opinionibus"
"You are truly right, there is little to opinions"
"At ego unum plura".
"But let me say one more thing"
"Non dubitavi in te uno momento"
"I have not doubted in you for a single moment"
"Non dubitavi unum momentum quod tu Buddha"
"I have not doubted for a single moment that you are Buddha"
"Non dubitavi quin ad summum pervenisse propositum";
"I have not doubted that you have reached the highest goal"
"supremus finis ad quem tot Bragmanorum viis sunt".
"the highest goal towards which so many Brahmans are on their way"
"Salutem a morte invenisti";
"You have found salvation from death"

"**Venit ad te in curriculo inquisitionis tuae**"
"It has come to you in the course of your own search"
"**Venit ad te in via tua**"
"it has come to you on your own path"
"**Venit ad te per cogitationem et meditationem**"
"it has come to you through thoughts and meditation"
"**pervenit ad vos per effectum et per illustrationem**".
"it has come to you through realizations and enlightenment"
"**sed non venit ad vos per doctrinam.**"
"but it has not come to you by means of teachings!"
" **Et haec est cogitatio mea** ";
"And this is my thought"
"**per doctrinas nemo obtinebit salutem.**"
"nobody will obtain salvation by means of teachings!"
"**Non poteris horam illuminationis tuae deferre**".
"You will not be able to convey your hour of enlightenment"
"**Verba eorum quae tibi evenerunt non momentum efferre**".
"words of what has happened to you won't convey the moment!"
"**doctrina Buddha illustratorum multa continent**".
"The teachings of the enlightened Buddha contain much"
" **docet multos iuste vivere** ".
"it teaches many to live righteously"
" **docet multos malos vitare** ";
"it teaches many to avoid evil"
"**Sed unum est quod haec doctrina non continet**".
"But there is one thing which these teachings do not contain"
"**sunt clara ac veneranda, sed dogmata fallunt**".
"they are clear and venerable, but the teachings miss something"
"**sacramentum doctrinarum non continet**"
"the teachings do not contain the mystery"
"**mysterium eorum quae exaltatus in se expertus est**".
"the mystery of what the exalted one has experienced for himself"
"**in centenis milibus solus expertus est**".

"among hundreds of thousands, only he experienced it"
"Hoc est, quod cogitavi et intellexi, cum audivi doctrinas".
"This is what I have thought and realized, when I heard the teachings"
"Haec est causa peregrinationis meae continuans"
"This is why I am continuing my travels"
"Quare non alia, meliora dogmata peto".
"this is why I do not to seek other, better teachings"
"Scio nihil esse melius doctrina"
"I know there are no better teachings"
" Discedere ab omnibus doctrinis et omnibus doctoribus relinquo " ;
"I leave to depart from all teachings and all teachers"
"Me aut mori aut finire relinquo";
"I leave to reach my goal by myself, or to die"
"Saepe hodie cogitabo, o exaltate";
"But often, I'll think of this day, oh exalted one"
" et hanc horam cum uirum sanctum uiderunt oculi mei."
"and I'll think of this hour, when my eyes beheld a holy man"
Oculi Buddha quiete respexit ad terram
The Buddha's eyes quietly looked to the ground
quiete, in aequo animo, vultus ejus inscrutabilis ridebat
quietly, in perfect equanimity, his inscrutable face was smiling
venerabilis aliquis tardius locutus est
the venerable one spoke slowly
« Utinam cogitationes vestras non erretis ».
"I wish that your thoughts shall not be in error"
"Utinam ad propositum perveniatis!"
"I wish that you shall reach the goal!"
"Sed est aliquid, quod te rogo, ut dicas mihi";
"But there is something I ask you to tell me"
Vidisti multitudinem Samanas meae?
"Have you seen the multitude of my Samanas?"
"confugerunt ad doctrinam;"
"they have taken refuge in the teachings"
"Credis satius esse eos dogmata deserere?"

"do you believe it would be better for them to abandon the teachings?"
"an redibunt in mundum cupiditatum?"
"should they to return into the world of desires?"
"Absit talis cogitatio ab animo meo", exclamavit Siddhartha
"Far is such a thought from my mind" exclaimed Siddhartha
« Volo ut omnes maneant in doctrina ».
"I wish that they shall all stay with the teachings"
"Vtinam ad propositum perveniant!"
"I wish that they shall reach their goal!"
"Non est meum locum iudicare vitam alterius".
"It is not my place to judge another person's life"
" Non possum solus vitam meam judicare " .
"I can only judge my own life "
"Decernere oportet, delegandum est, recusandum est";
"I must decide, I must chose, I must refuse"
"Salus ab ipso est quod nos Samanas quaerimus";
"Salvation from the self is what we Samanas search for"
"O exaltate, si unus ex discipulis tuis essem".
"oh exalted one, if only I were one of your disciples"
"Ego metuo ne mihi contingat".
"I'd fear that it might happen to me"
"stare videtur, tranquillus essem et redimendus".
"only seemingly, would my self be calm and be redeemed"
"sed vere viveret ac cresceret".
"but in truth it would live on and grow"
"Quia tunc ego me dogmata reponerem".
"because then I would replace my self with the teachings"
"Meum esse officium meum, ut te sequar"
"my self would be my duty to follow you"
"Mea se fore amica mea pro vobis"
"my self would be my love for you"
"et ipse esset communitas monachorum."
"and my self would be the community of the monks!"
Cum dimidium risu Gotama respexit in oculis alieni
With half of a smile Gotama looked into the stranger's eyes

oculi eius indubitanter aperti et benigni erant
his eyes were unwaveringly open and kind
iubet ut vix notabilis gestus exiret
he bid him to leave with a hardly noticeable gesture
"Sapis, o Samana" venerabilis locutus
"You are wise, oh Samana" the venerable one spoke
"Tu scis sapienter loqui, amice";
"You know how to talk wisely, my friend"
"Scire nimium sapientiam!"
"Be aware of too much wisdom!"
Buddha declinaverunt
The Buddha turned away
Siddhartha nunquam obliviscar eius aspectu
Siddhartha would never forget his glance
dimidium risus semper signatum in memoria Siddhartha
his half smile remained forever etched in Siddhartha's memory
Siddhartha sibi putavit
Siddhartha thought to himself
"Nunquam antea hominem aspectum vidi et hoc modo ridere"
"I have never before seen a person glance and smile this way"
"Nihil aliud sedet et ambulat sicut facit"
"no one else sits and walks like he does"
" Vtinam hoc modo possit intueri et ridere ".
"truly, I wish to be able to glance and smile this way"
" Opto ut hoc etiam modo sedere et ambulare possit " ;
"I wish to be able to sit and walk this way, too"
"liberati, venerabiles, absconditi, aperti, pueriles et arcani";
"liberated, venerable, concealed, open, childlike and mysterious"
« in intima sui parte pervenire debet ».
"he must have succeeded in reaching the innermost part of his self"
"Tantum ergo potest aliquem intuitum et hoc modo ambulare"

"only then can someone glance and walk this way"
"Ego quoque ut ad intima sui parte pervenirem".
"I will also seek to reach the innermost part of my self"
"Vidi hominem" Siddhartha thought
"I saw a man" Siddhartha thought
"unus homo, ante quem oculos demittere volo".
"a single man, before whom I would have to lower my glance"
"nolo ante oculos quemquam demittere meum";
"I do not want to lower my glance before anyone else"
"Nulla doctrina me amplius alliciet"
"No teachings will entice me more anymore"
"Quia doctrina huius hominis me non decepit".
"because this man's teachings have not enticed me"
"Buddha sum privatus" putavit Siddhartha
"I am deprived by the Buddha" thought Siddhartha
" privatus sum, licet ille dederit tantum";
"I am deprived, although he has given so much"
"Me privavit amici mei"
"he has deprived me of my friend"
"Amicus meus qui credidit in me"
"my friend who had believed in me"
"Amicus meus qui nunc credit in eum"
"my friend who now believes in him"
"Amicus meus qui fuerat umbra mea"
"my friend who had been my shadow"
"et nunc est umbra Gotamae".
"and now he is Gotama's shadow"
"sed me Siddhartha dedit".
"but he has given me Siddhartha"
"Ille me ipse dedit"
"he has given me myself"

Excitatio
Awakening

Siddhartha relicto mango nemus post eum
Siddhartha left the mango grove behind him
sed anteactam vitam sensit etiam remansisse
but he felt his past life also stayed behind
Buddha, perfectus, remanebat
the Buddha, the perfected one, stayed behind
et Govinda post etiam mansit
and Govinda stayed behind too
et anteacta vita ab eo recessit
and his past life had parted from him
cogitabat ambulantem lente
he pondered as he was walking slowly
de hoc sensu cogitabat, quod eum compleverat
he pondered about this sensation, which filled him completely
Cogitabat alte, quasi mergens in profundam aquam
He pondered deeply, like diving into a deep water
submisit se ad humum sensui
he let himself sink down to the ground of the sensation
se subsidere ad locum ubi sunt causae
he let himself sink down to the place where the causes lie
cognoscere causas est ipsa ratio cogitandi
to identify the causes is the very essence of thinking
ita sibi videbatur
this was how it seemed to him
eoque solo sensus in realizations convertitur
and by this alone, sensations turn into realizations
et hi sensus non pereunt
and these sensations are not lost
sed sensus fiunt
but the sensations become entities
et sensus incipiunt emittere quod intus est
and the sensations start to emit what is inside of them
ostendunt vera sua sicut lucis radiis

they show their truths like rays of light
Tarde ambulans, Siddhartha cogitabat
Slowly walking along, Siddhartha pondered
Adolescens se amplius non esse intellexit
He realized that he was no youth any more
intellexit se in hominem convertisse
he realized that he had turned into a man
Intellexit se aliquid reliquisse eum
He realized that something had left him
similiter et anguis cutis vetustate relinquitur
the same way a snake is left by its old skin
quod fuerat in adulescentia, nihil iam in eo fuisse
what he had throughout his youth no longer existed in him
pars eius esse solebat; volunt habere doctores
it used to be a part of him; the wish to have teachers
velle audire doctrinam
the wish to listen to teachings
Ultimum etiam magistrum qui in eius itinere apparuerat reliquerat
He had also left the last teacher who had appeared on his path
summum etiam ac sapientissimum magistrum reliquerat
he had even left the highest and wisest teacher
sanctissimus Buddha reliquerat
he had left the most holy one, Buddha
partem cum eo habebat, eius doctrinam acceptare non poterat
he had to part with him, unable to accept his teachings
Tardius ambulavit in cogitationibus suis
Slower, he walked along in his thoughts
"Sed quid hoc?"
and he asked himself, "But what is this?"
"quid a doctrinis et a magistris discere voluisti?"
"what have you sought to learn from teachings and from teachers?"
et quid erant qui te tantum docuerunt?
"and what were they, who have taught you so much?"

"**quid sunt, si te docere potuerunt?**"
"what are they if they have been unable to teach you?"
Et invenit: Ipse erat.
And he found, "It was the self"
Finis et essentia fuit de quo discere volui.
"it was the purpose and essence of which I sought to learn"
"Ipse ego me liberare volui"
"It was the self I wanted to free myself from"
" ipse quem vincere volebam " ;
"the self which I sought to overcome"
"At ego eam vincere non potui".
"But I was not able to overcome it"
"Nisi falli possem"
"I could only deceive it"
"Nisi hoc potui fugere";
"I could only flee from it"
"Nisi celare potui"
"I could only hide from it"
"Verum, nulla res in hoc mundo tam occupatas cogitationes meas servavit".
"Truly, no thing in this world has kept my thoughts so busy"
"In mysterio vitae meae occupatus sum".
"I have been kept busy by the mystery of me being alive"
"me unum sacramentum"
"the mystery of me being one"
"sacramentum, si ab omnibus separatur et ab omnibus separatur".
"the mystery if being separated and isolated from all others"
"Siddhartha mei mysterium est!"
"the mystery of me being Siddhartha!"
" Et nihil est in hoc mundo minus de me scio."
"And there is no thing in this world I know less about"
se cogitans lente incedentem
he had been pondering while slowly walking along
hae cogitationes substitit adprehendit illum
he stopped as these thoughts caught hold of him

et statim alia cogitatio ex his cogitationibus orta est
and right away another thought sprang forth from these thoughts
"Una causa est cur nihil de me scio"
"there's one reason why I know nothing about myself"
"Una causa est cur Siddhartha aliena a me remansit"
"there's one reason why Siddhartha has remained alien to me"
"Hoc totum ex una causa".
"all of this stems from one cause"
Me timui, et fugiebam.
"I was afraid of myself, and I was fleeing"
"Quaesivi utrumque Atman et Brahman"
"I have searched for both Atman and Brahman"
"in hoc volebam me ipsum dissecare".
"for this I was willing to dissect my self"
"Et volens omnia eius stratis decoriabit".
"and I was willing to peel off all of its layers"
"Medium omnium caeperum invenire volui in interioribus ignotis".
"I wanted to find the core of all peels in its unknown interior"
"Atman, vita, pars divina, pars ultima"
"the Atman, life, the divine part, the ultimate part"
"Sed in processu meipsum amisi";
"But I have lost myself in the process"
Siddhartha aperuit oculos suos et circumspiciebat
Siddhartha opened his eyes and looked around
circumspiciens, risu vultum implevit
looking around, a smile filled his face
sensus excitandi diu somniorum per illum
a feeling of awakening from long dreams flowed through him
sensus a capite usque ad digitos
the feeling flowed from his head down to his toes
non ita multo ante quam iterum ambulavit
And it was not long before he walked again
cito ambulavit sicut homo qui scit quid habet

he walked quickly, like a man who knows what he has got to do

"nunc Siddhartha iterum me non dimittam!"
"now I will not let Siddhartha escape from me again!"
"Ego non iam volo cogitationes meas et vitam cum Atman incipere"
"I no longer want to begin my thoughts and my life with Atman"
"nec volo cogitationes meas a mundi passione incipere".
"nor do I want to begin my thoughts with the suffering of the world"
"nolo me occidere et dissecare diutius".
"I do not want to kill and dissect myself any longer"
"Yoga-Veda me amplius non docebit".
"Yoga-Veda shall not teach me anymore"
nec Atharva-Veda, nec reruni.
"nor Atharva-Veda, nor the ascetics"
" non erit ulla doctrina " ;
"there will not be any kind of teachings"
"Volo discere a me et esse discipulus meus"
"I want to learn from myself and be my student"
"Ego nosse cupio, secretum Siddhartha"
"I want to get to know myself; the secret of Siddhartha"

Circumspexit, ut si mundum primum videret
He looked around, as if he was seeing the world for the first time
Pulchra et varia erat mundus
Beautiful and colourful was the world
novis et arcanum erat mundus
strange and mysterious was the world
Hic cæruleus, hic flavus erat, hic viridis erat
Here was blue, there was yellow, here was green
caelum et flumen
the sky and the river flowed
silva et montes rigidi

the forest and the mountains were rigid
totus mundus esset pulchra
all of the world was beautiful
omnia arcana magica
all of it was mysterious and magical
et in medio eius, Siddhartha, excitatio
and in its midst was he, Siddhartha, the awakening one
et erat in via ad se
and he was on the path to himself
haec omnia flavus & cæruleus & rivus & silva Siddhartha . intrarunt
all this yellow and blue and river and forest entered Siddhartha
primum per oculos intravit
for the first time it entered through the eyes
Mara non erat carmen
it was no longer a spell of Mara
non erat velum Maianae
it was no longer the veil of Maya
non erat inanis et coincidentalis
it was no longer a pointless and coincidental
res non diversitas mera apparentia
things were not just a diversity of mere appearances
apparentiae despiciendi penitus ratus Brahman
appearances despicable to the deeply thinking Brahman
Brahman cogitatio diversitatem contemnit et unitatem quaerit
the thinking Brahman scorns diversity, and seeks unity
Hyacinthum erat flumen et hyacinthum erat
Blue was blue and river was river
singulare divinumque latuit in Siddhartha
the singular and divine lived hidden in Siddhartha
modo divinitatis et consilii erat hic esse croceus et illic blue
divinity's way and purpose was to be yellow here, and blue there
ibi caelum, illic silva, hic Siddhartha

there sky, there forest, and here Siddhartha
Propositum et essentialia proprietates non alicubi post sunt
The purpose and essential properties was not somewhere behind the things
ad et essentialia erat intus in omnibus
the purpose and essential properties was inside of everything
"Quam surdus et stultus fui!" cogitavit
"How deaf and stupid have I been!" he thought
et ambulavit velociter per
and he walked swiftly along
"Cum quis textum legit, symbola et litteras non spernet".
"When someone reads a text he will not scorn the symbols and letters"
non vocabit symbola deceptiones vel coincidentia.
"he will not call the symbols deceptions or coincidences"
sed leget ea ut scripta sunt.
"but he will read them as they were written"
"distendabit et diliget eos litteras per litteras".
"he will study and love them, letter by letter"
"Librum mundi legere volui et litteras contempsisti".
"I wanted to read the book of the world and scorned the letters"
"Librum mihi legere volui et symbola sprevi".
"I wanted to read the book of myself and scorned the symbols"
"Oculos vocavi et lingua coincidentalis".
"I called my eyes and my tongue coincidental"
"Nunquam dixi formas sine substantia";
"I said they were worthless forms without substance"
"Minime, hoc peracto, evigilavi".
"No, this is over, I have awakened"
"Ego quidem evigilavi".
"I have indeed awakened"
"Non ante hunc ipsum diem natus sum"
"I had not been born before this very day"
Has cogitationes cogitans, Siddhartha semel iterum substitit

In thinking these thoughts, Siddhartha suddenly stopped once again
constitit quasi serpens iacens coram eo
he stopped as if there was a snake lying in front of him
subito etiam aliud sensit
suddenly, he had also become aware of something else
Fuit quidem sicut aliquis qui nuper excitatus est
He was indeed like someone who had just woken up
et erat quasi novus natus infantem incipiens de novo vitam
he was like a new-born baby starting life anew
et debebat iterum in principio
and he had to start again at the very beginning
Mane longe aliter
in the morning he had had very different intentions
ad patrem suum redire putaverat
he had thought to return to his home and his father
Nunc autem restitit sicut serpens iacebat in uia sua
But now he stopped as if a snake was lying on his path
et fecit effectum ubi erat
he made a realization of where he was
"Ego non sum ille fui"
"I am no longer the one I was"
" Ascetica non sum amplius "
"I am no ascetic anymore"
"Ego non sum sacerdos amplius"
"I am not a priest anymore"
"Brahman non sum amplius"
"I am no Brahman anymore"
"Quid faciam apud patrem meum?"
"Whatever should I do at my father's place?"
"Studium fac oblationes? Meditatio Practice?"
"Study? Make offerings? Practise meditation?"
"Sed haec omnia supra me sunt"
"But all this is over for me"
"Hoc totum non est in semita mea"
"all of this is no longer on my path"

Immobilis, Siddhartha ibi stabat
Motionless, Siddhartha remained standing there
et, ut uno momento temporis et respirationis tempore, refrixit cor eius
and for the time of one moment and breath, his heart felt cold
sensit frigus in pectore
he felt a coldness in his chest
idem sentit animal parvum, cum videt, quam solum sit
the same feeling a small animal feels when it sees how alone it is
Multos annos sine domicilio nihil senserat
For many years, he had been without home and had felt nothing
Iam sensit sine domo
Now, he felt he had been without a home
Etiamsi in summa meditatione fuerat filius patris
Still, even in the deepest meditation, he had been his father's son
fuerat Brahman, magni ordinis
he had been a Brahman, of a high caste
fuerat clericus
he had been a cleric
Iam nihil erat nisi Siddhartha, evigilans
Now, he was nothing but Siddhartha, the awoken one
aliud superfuit
nothing else was left of him
Vehementer, frigus attraxit et sensit
Deeply, he inhaled and felt cold
cucurrit per corpus
a shiver ran through his body
Nemo tam solus ut erat
Nobody was as alone as he was
Nullus erat nobilis qui non pertinebat ad nobiles
There was no nobleman who did not belong to the noblemen
non fuit operarius qui non pertinent ad operarios
there was no worker that did not belong to the workers

inter se omnes confugerant
they had all found refuge among themselves
sumebant vitam eorum et linguas suas
they shared their lives and spoke their languages
non sunt Brahman, qui nec Brahmanae censendi sunt
there are no Brahman who would not be regarded as Brahmans
et non sunt Brachmanae qui non vivunt ut Brahmans
and there are no Brahmans that didn't live as Brahmans
non sunt ascetici qui cum Samanate refugere non possent
there are no ascetic who could not find refuge with the Samanas
et etiam desertissimus heremita in silva non erat solus
and even the most forlorn hermit in the forest was not alone
et ipse locus cingitur
he was also surrounded by a place he belonged to
etiam ad castellanum in quo domi erat
he also belonged to a caste in which he was at home
Govinda eum reliquerat et monachus factus est
Govinda had left him and became a monk
et mille monachi fratres eius
and a thousand monks were his brothers
utebantur autem eodem pallio
they wore the same robe as him
credebant in fide eius et lingua eius
they believed in his faith and spoke his language
At ille, Siddhartha, ubi est?
But he, Siddhartha, where did he belong to?
Cum quo vitam communicat?
With whom would he share his life?
Cuius lingua loquatur?
Whose language would he speak?
mundus liquefactum in circuitu eius
the world melted away all around him
stabat solus sicut stella in caelo
he stood alone like a star in the sky

frigore et desperatione circumdederunt eum
cold and despair surrounded him
sed Siddhartha ex hoc momento emersit
but Siddhartha emerged out of this moment
Siddhartha emersit plus sui veri quam prius
Siddhartha emerged more his true self than before
et constantius quam umquam fuit
he was more firmly concentrated than he had ever been
Sensit; "Hic fuerat ultimus tremor excitationis".
He felt; "this had been the last tremor of the awakening"
"Extremum certamen huius nativitatis";
"the last struggle of this birth"
Et non multum fuit usque dum iterum ambularet
And it was not long until he walked again in long strides
coepit ire celeriter et impatiens
he started to proceed swiftly and impatiently
iam non domum
he was no longer going home
iam non ad patrem
he was no longer going to his father

Pars Duo
Part Two

***

Kamala

Siddhartha didicit aliquid novi per omnes gradus suae semitae
Siddhartha learned something new on every step of his path
quia mundus mutatus est et cor eius consecratum
because the world was transformed and his heart was enchanted
solem orientem vidit super montes
He saw the sun rising over the mountains
et vidit solem in litore maris occidentem
and he saw the sun setting over the distant beach
Noctu stellas in caelo fixis locis vidit
At night, he saw the stars in the sky in their fixed positions
et vidit lunam quasi scapham in caerula natantem
and he saw the crescent of the moon floating like a boat in the blue
Vidit arbores, stellas, animalia et nubes
He saw trees, stars, animals, and clouds
irides, saxa, herbae, flores, rivi et flumina
rainbows, rocks, herbs, flowers, streams and rivers
vidit ros in dumis mane
he saw the glistening dew in the bushes in the morning
vidit procul montes excelsos, qui erant caerulei;
he saw distant high mountains which were blue
flavit ventus per rice-agri
wind blew through the rice-field
quae omnia millena et varia semper ibi fuerunt
all of this, a thousand-fold and colourful, had always been there
Sol et luna semper refulserunt

the sun and the moon had always shone
flumina semper insonuerunt, semper apes pulsavere
rivers had always roared and bees had always buzzed
sed haec omnia olim Velo fallax
but in former times all of this had been a deceptive veil
illi nihil aliud fuerat quam fugax
to him it had been nothing more than fleeting
existimabatur aspici diffidentia
it was supposed to be looked upon in distrust
destinatum erat cogitatione penetrari et destrui
it was destined to be penetrated and destroyed by thought
quia non erat essentia existendi
since it was not the essence of existence
cum haec essentia sit ultra, altera parte visibilis
since this essence lay beyond, on the other side of, the visible
Nunc autem liberati oculi cis steterunt
But now, his liberated eyes stayed on this side
vidit et sensit visibilem
he saw and became aware of the visible
quaesivit esse domi in hoc mundo
he sought to be at home in this world
verum essentiam non quaerere
he did not search for the true essence
non intendit mundum ultra
he did not aim at a world beyond
hoc mundo satis pulchrum erat
this world was beautiful enough for him
sic spectans omnia puerilia fecit
looking at it like this made everything childlike
Pulchra erant luna et stellae
Beautiful were the moon and the stars
pulchra amnis ripasque
beautiful was the stream and the banks
silva et petrae, hircus et bruchus
the forest and the rocks, the goat and the gold-beetle
flos et papilio; pulchra et pulchra erat

the flower and the butterfly; beautiful and lovely it was
iterum ambulare per mundum erat parvulis
to walk through the world was childlike again
hoc modo evigilatus est
this way he was awoken
sic patuit prope
this way he was open to what is near
hoc modo sine diffidentia erat
this way he was without distrust
aliter sol caput
differently the sun burnt the head
aliter silvae umbra tepuit illum
differently the shade of the forest cooled him down
aliter cucurbita et Musa gustavit
differently the pumpkin and the banana tasted
Breves dies erant, breves erant noctes
Short were the days, short were the nights
omni hora celeriter quasi velo in mare currunt
every hour sped swiftly away like a sail on the sea
et sub velo erat navis thesauris plena gaudio
and under the sail was a ship full of treasures, full of joy
Siddhartha vidit coetus simiarum movens per altum conopeum
Siddhartha saw a group of apes moving through the high canopy
erant in ramis arborum
they were high in the branches of the trees
et audiit efferum cantu avarum
and he heard their savage, greedy song
Siddhartha vidit ovem masculum sequentem feminam unam et coitum cum ea
Siddhartha saw a male sheep following a female one and mating with her
In stagno arundineto vidit milum avide venatum ad cenam suam

In a lake of reeds, he saw the pike hungrily hunting for its dinner
piscibus propellentibus se a pilo
young fish were propelling themselves away from the pike
sunt terrebis, wiggling et scintillans
they were scared, wiggling and sparkling
pulli piscibus insilierunt catervatim ex aqua
the young fish jumped in droves out of the water
odor fortitudinis et passionis exivit fortiter de aqua
the scent of strength and passion came forcefully out of the water
et miluus odorem excitauit
and the pike stirred up the scent
Quae omnia semper fuerunt
All of this had always existed
et ille non viderat nec cum illo fuisset
and he had not seen it, nor had he been with it
Erat autem cum eo, et erat de eo
Now he was with it and he was part of it
Lux et umbra per oculos currunt
Light and shadow ran through his eyes
sidera et lunam percurrentes cor suum
stars and moon ran through his heart

Siddhartha recordatus est omnium quae in paradiso Jetavana erant
Siddhartha remembered everything he had experienced in the Garden Jetavana
recordatus est doctrinae quam ibi audivit de divina Buddha.
he remembered the teaching he had heard there from the divine Buddha
vale recordatus a Govinda
he remembered the farewell from Govinda
Recordatus est conversationis cum excelso
he remembered the conversation with the exalted one

Iterum recordatus est verborum suorum, quae dixit ad exaltatum
Again he remembered his own words that he had spoken to the exalted one
et recordatus est omne verbum
he remembered every word
se ea quae non sciverat dixerat
he realized he had said things which he had not really known
obstupuit ipse quod Gotamas dixerat
he astonished himself with what he had said to Gotama
Buddha thesaurus et secretus doctrinarum non erat
the Buddha's treasure and secret was not the teachings
arcanum autem inenarrabile et non docibile
but the secret was the inexpressible and not teachable
arcanum quod in hora illuminationis suae expertus fuerat
the secret which he had experienced in the hour of his enlightenment
arcanum nihil nisi hoc ipsum quod iam expertum erat
the secret was nothing but this very thing which he had now gone to experience
arcanum erat quod nunc experiri coepit
the secret was what he now began to experience
Nunc experiri debuit
Now he had to experience his self
iam diu se ipsum esse Atman
he had already known for a long time that his self was Atman
Sciebat Atman eadem naturas sempiternas ac Brahman
he knew Atman bore the same eternal characteristics as Brahman
Sed nunquam vere hunc sui
But he had never really found this self
quia in laqueo cogitationis seipsum capere voluisset
because he had wanted to capture the self in the net of thought
corpus autem non erat pars sui
but the body was not part of the self
non erat sensuum spectaculum

it was not the spectacle of the senses
ita nec cogitatio nec mens rationalis
so it also was not the thought, nor the rational mind
non fuit sapientia doctus , non erat doctis ingenio
it was not the learned wisdom, nor the learned ability
ex his nihil concludi potuit
from these things no conclusions could be drawn
Immo, mundus cogitationis etiam in hac parte erat
No, the world of thought was also still on this side
Utraeque cogitationes, tum sensus, pulchrae erant
Both, the thoughts as well as the senses, were pretty things
sed latuit ultima significatio post utrumque
but the ultimate meaning was hidden behind both of them
uterque audiendus et ludunt
both had to be listened to and played with
neque contemni neque plus aequo
neither had to be scorned nor overestimated
occultae voces veritatis intimae erant
there were secret voices of the innermost truth
has voces attente percipi
these voices had to be attentively perceived
Nihil aliud appetere voluit
He wanted to strive for nothing else
facturum quod vox ei mandasset
he would do what the voice commanded him to do
habitet ubi voces eum monuerunt
he would dwell where the voices advised him to
Cur sedit Gotama sub arbore Bodhi?
Why had Gotama sat down under the Bodhi tree?
Vocem in corde suo audivit
He had heard a voice in his own heart
vox quae jusserat ut sub hac arbore requiem quaereret
a voice which had commanded him to seek rest under this tree
posset ad sacrificandum
he could have gone on to make offerings
lavationes facere potuit

he could have performed his ablutions
potuit id temporis exegisse orationem
he could have spent that moment in prayer
manducare neque bibere voluisset
he had chosen not to eat or drink
non dormire aut somniare voluisset
he had chosen not to sleep or dream
sed voci paret
instead, he had obeyed the voice
Sic obedire bono fuit
To obey like this was good
Bonum est non obedire exteriori mandato
it was good not to obey to an external command
bonum fuit voci solum obedire
it was good to obey only the voice
paratos esse sicut hoc erat bonum et necessarium
to be ready like this was good and necessary
nihil aliud necesse fuit
there was nothing else that was necessary

nocte Siddhartha pervenit ad fluvium
in the night Siddhartha got to a river
dormivit in casa portitor
he slept in the straw hut of a ferryman
hac nocte Siddhartha somnium
this night Siddhartha had a dream
Govinda stabat in conspectu eius
Govinda was standing in front of him
erat indutus stolam luteam ascetic
he was dressed in the yellow robe of an ascetic
Tristis erat quam Govinda respexit
Sad was how Govinda looked
maestus, "cur me dereliquisti?"
sadly he asked, "Why have you forsaken me?"
Siddhartha Govindam amplexa est et brachia eius circumdedit

Siddhartha embraced Govinda, and wrapped his arms around him
traxitque eum iuxta pectus et osculatus est eum
he pulled him close to his chest and kissed him
at Govinda iam non erat, sed femina
but it was not Govinda anymore, but a woman
plenum pectus papaver ex habitu mulieris
a full breast popped out of the woman's dress
Siddhartha iacebat et bibit de pectore
Siddhartha lay and drank from the breast
dulciter et fortiter lac ex hoc pectore gustavit
sweetly and strongly tasted the milk from this breast
Is cum muliere et viro
It tasted of woman and man
gustavit solem silvasque
it tasted of sun and forest
quod gustavit animalis et flos
it tasted of animal and flower
ex omni fructu et omni desiderio
it tasted of every fruit and every joyful desire
Inebriabat eum et inscium ei reddidit
It intoxicated him and rendered him unconscious
Siddhartha experrectus e somno
Siddhartha woke up from the dream
pallidus amnis per ostium casae coruscis
the pale river shimmered through the door of the hut
obscurum vocationem noctuae penitus silvae
a dark call of an owl resounded deeply through the forest
Siddhartha interrogavit portitor trans flumen
Siddhartha asked the ferryman to get him across the river
Portitor eum trans flumen obtinuit in bamboo-ratis
The ferryman got him across the river on his bamboo-raft
rutilabat aqua luce diluculi
the water shimmered reddish in the light of the morning
"Hoc flumen pulchrum est", dixit socio suo
"This is a beautiful river," he said to his companion

"Ita," inquit portitor, "flumen pulcherrimum"
"Yes," said the ferryman, "a very beautiful river"
"Ille plus quam aliquid amo"
"I love it more than anything"
"Saepe ego eum audivi".
"Often I have listened to it"
"Saepe vidi in oculis"
"often I have looked into its eyes"
et semper ab eo didici.
"and I have always learned from it"
"Multa disci possunt a rivo".
"Much can be learned from a river"
"Gratias tibi ago, benefactor meus" Siddhartha . locutus est
"I thank you, my benefactor" spoke Siddhartha
trans flumen evectus
he disembarked on the other side of the river
"Nullum habeo donum quod tibi pro hospitio tuo dare potui, mi carissimi"
"I have no gift I could give you for your hospitality, my dear"
"et ego quoque nullam mercedem pro labore tuo"
"and I also have no payment for your work"
" Homo sum sine domo ;"
"I am a man without a home"
"Filius sum Brahman et Samana";
"I am the son of a Brahman and a Samana"
"Vidi" dixit portitor
"I did see it," spoke the ferryman
"Non expecto aliquam mercedem a te"
"I did not expect any payment from you"
"Mos est hospitum dona ferre".
"it is custom for guests to bear a gift"
"sed aut hoc a te non exspectavi".
"but I did not expect this from you either"
" Dabis mihi donum alio tempore " .
"You will give me the gift another time"
"Putasne?" interrogavit Siddhartha, bemusedly

"Do you think so?" asked Siddhartha, bemusedly
"Certus sum" respondit portitor
"I am sure of it," replied the ferryman
"Hoc quoque a flumine didici".
"This too, I have learned from the river"
"Omne quod redit!"
"everything that goes comes back!"
"Tu quoque, Samana, redibis".
"You too, Samana, will come back"
" Nunc valete ! Sit mihi merces amicitia ".
"Now farewell! Let your friendship be my reward"
"Commemorate me, cum diis offeretis".
"Commemorate me, when you make offerings to the gods"
Olli subridens inter se diviserunt
Smiling, they parted from each other
Smiling, Siddhartha gauisus est de amicitia
Smiling, Siddhartha was happy about the friendship
et gavisus est de beneficio portitor
and he was happy about the kindness of the ferryman
"Est Govinda similis", cum risu cogitavit
"He is like Govinda," he thought with a smile
"Omnes qui occurro in uia mea sunt sicut Govinda"
"all I meet on my path are like Govinda"
"Omnes grati sunt quod habent";
"All are thankful for what they have"
"sed ii sunt qui ius habent ad gratias agendas".
"but they are the ones who would have a right to receive thanks"
"Omnes submissi et amici esse vellem"
"all are submissive and would like to be friends"
"Omnes libet parere et parum cogitare"
"all like to obey and think little"
"Omnes homines tamquam pueri"
"all people are like children"

Circa meridiem per villam venit

At about noon, he came through a village
Ante casalia caeni pueri in platea volutabant
In front of the mud cottages, children were rolling about in the street
ludebant cucurbita semina et conchylia
they were playing with pumpkin-seeds and sea-shells
clamaverunt et luctaretur inter se
they screamed and wrestled with each other
sed timide omnes ignoto fugerunt Samana
but they all timidly fled from the unknown Samana
In fine pagi, via per rivum ducitur
In the end of the village, the path led through a stream
iuxta rivum puella genuflexus
by the side of the stream, a young woman was kneeling
lavabat vestimenta sua in stream
she was washing clothes in the stream
Cum Siddhartha eam salutasset, caput levavit
When Siddhartha greeted her, she lifted her head
et subridens suspexit
and she looked up to him with a smile
album videre non poterat in oculis candida
he could see the white in her eyes glistening
Et benedixit ei
He called out a blessing to her
Haec consuetudo erat inter peregrinos
this was the custom among travellers
et quaesivit quantum esset ad magnam civitatem
and he asked how far it was to the large city
Tunc surgens venit ad eum
Then she got up and came to him
os illi madefactum pulchre coruscis in facie iuvenum
beautifully her wet mouth was shimmering in her young face
Faceta ioculare cum eo
She exchanged humorous banter with him
Quaesivit utrum iam comedisset
she asked whether he had eaten already

et quaesivit curiosa
and she asked curious questions
"Verum est Samanas nocte sola dormivisse?"
"is it true that the Samanas slept alone in the forest at night?"
"verum Samanas mulieres cum illis habere non licet".
"is it true Samanas are not allowed to have women with them"
Cum loqueretur, posuit pedem suum sinistrum in dextro suo
While talking, she put her left foot on his right one
motus mulieris quae vellet inchoare voluptatem sexualem
the movement of a woman who would want to initiate sexual pleasure
quod vocant "arborem ascendere"
the textbooks call this "climbing a tree"
Siddhartha sensit sanguinem calefacere sursum
Siddhartha felt his blood heating up
iterum de somnio cogitare
he had to think of his dream again
leviter flectere ad mulierem
he bend slightly down to the woman
et osculatus est labris brunneis papillae pectoris
and he kissed with his lips the brown nipple of her breast
Suspiciens, vultum vidit subridens
Looking up, he saw her face smiling
et oculi eius repleti sunt libidinis;
and her eyes were full of lust
Siddhartha etiam sensit desiderium eius
Siddhartha also felt desire for her
Sensit fontem sexualitatis movens
he felt the source of his sexuality moving
sed nunquam ante mulierem attigit
but he had never touched a woman before
haesitavit paulisper
so he hesitated for a moment
manus iam paratas porrigere
his hands were already prepared to reach out for her
sed tunc vocem intimae sui audivit

but then he heard the voice of his innermost self
expavescit voce
he shuddered with awe at his voice
et haec vox non dixit ei
and this voice told him no
omnibus carminibus evanuit puella blanditur
all charms disappeared from the young woman's smiling face
non vidit aliud nisi humido aspectu
he no longer saw anything else but a damp glance
omne animal videre poterat esse in calidum feminam
all he could see was female animal in heat
Comis, fovi maxillam
Politely, he petted her cheek
et avertit se ab ea et non comparuit
he turned away from her and disappeared away
Mulier confusa reliquit a gradibus
he left from the disappointed woman with light steps
et disparuit in Bamboo
and he disappeared into the bamboo-wood

ad urbem magnam ante vesperum
he reached the large city before the evening
et gavisus est pervenisse ad urbem
and he was happy to have reached the city
quia sensit necessitatem esse apud homines
because he felt the need to be among people
aut diutius in silvis vixerat
or a long time, he had lived in the forests
primum diu sub tecto dormivit
for first time in a long time he slept under a roof
Ante urbem erat hortus pulcherrimus munita
Before the city was a beautifully fenced garden
viator venit per parva coetus servorum
the traveller came across a small group of servants
servi cophinos pomorum portabant
the servants were carrying baskets of fruit

quattuor servi sellam decentem portabant
four servants were carrying an ornamental sedan-chair
in hac sella mulier sedit, domina
on this chair sat a woman, the mistress
erat in cervicalia rubra sub varia tegmine
she was on red pillows under a colourful canopy
Siddhartha substitit ad ostium horti viridarii
Siddhartha stopped at the entrance to the pleasure-garden
et spectavit pompam ire per
and he watched the parade go by
vidit servos et ancillas
he saw saw the servants and the maids
canistra vidit et sellam lecticam
he saw the baskets and the sedan-chair
et vidit dominam super sellam
and he saw the lady on the chair
Sub capillo nigro vidit faciem subtilissimam
Under her black hair he saw a very delicate face
purpureo ore rubeo quasi recenter fici findatur
a bright red mouth, like a freshly cracked fig
supercilia, quae bene pascebantur et in arcus altitudinis depicta erant
eyebrows which were well tended and painted in a high arch
erant dolor et vigilans oculis tenebris
they were smart and watchful dark eyes
clara et alta collo rosa viridis et aurei vestis
a clear, tall neck rose from a green and golden garment
manus quiescebant, longae et tenues
her hands were resting, long and thin
habebat aureas armillas in manibus
she had wide golden bracelets over her wrists
Siddhartha vidit quam pulchra esset et laetatum est cor eius
Siddhartha saw how beautiful she was, and his heart rejoiced
Inclinavit se, cum appropinquavit sella
He bowed deeply, when the sedan-chair came closer
iterumque revoluto aspexit pulchram, venustam faciem

straightening up again, he looked at the fair, charming face
legit dolor oculos cum arcubus altis
he read her smart eyes with the high arcs
in odore aliquid nesciebat
he breathed in a fragrance of something he did not know
Cum risu, pulchra mulier in momento annuit
With a smile, the beautiful woman nodded for a moment
tum in horto disparuit
then she disappeared into the garden
et tunc servi non conparuit
and then the servants disappeared as well
"Hanc urbem ingredior omine lepido" Siddhartha cogitatio
"I am entering this city with a charming omen" Siddhartha thought
Statim se in hortum extractum sensit
He instantly felt drawn into the garden
sed de situ suo
but he thought about his situation
sciret quomodo eum servi et ancillae inspexissent
he became aware of how the servants and maids had looked at him
despicabilem, diffidentem, eiecerunt
they thought him despicable, distrustful, and rejected him
"Ego adhuc sum Samana" putabat
"I am still a Samana" he thought
"Ego adhuc sum asceticus et mendicus";
"I am still an ascetic and beggar"
"Non oportet me sic manere".
"I must not remain like this"
"hortum hoc modo intrare non potero", risit
"I will not be able to enter the garden like this," he laughed
quaesivit proximum qui per viam horti
he asked the next person who came along the path about the garden
et petiit nomen mulieris
and he asked for the name of the woman

nuntiaverunt hunc hortum esse Kamala, nobilem meretricem
he was told that this was the garden of Kamala, the famous courtesan
dixitque eam etiam in urbe possedisse
and he was told that she also owned a house in the city
Deinde cum meta in urbem ingressus est
Then, he entered the city with a goal
Quod cum peteret, permisit civitatem, ut eum sugeret
Pursuing his goal, he allowed the city to suck him in
ibat per fluxus viarum
he drifted through the flow of the streets
et stetit in platea civitatis
he stood still on the squares in the city
requievit in gradibus lapideis iuxta flumen
he rested on the stairs of stone by the river
Vespere autem facto, amicos tonsoris fecit
When the evening came, he made friends with a barber's assistant
eum in umbra arcus laborantem viderat
he had seen him working in the shade of an arch
et invenit eum iterum orantem in templo Vishnu .
and he found him again praying in a temple of Vishnu
narravit de fabulis Vishnu et Lakshmi
he told about stories of Vishnu and the Lakshmi
Inter scaphas fluvii hac nocte dormivit
Among the boats by the river, he slept this night
Siddhartha ad eum venit antequam clientes primi in tabernam suam venerunt
Siddhartha came to him before the first customers came into his shop
tonsoris adiutorem tondet barbam et tondebat
he had the barber's assistant shave his beard and cut his hair
comam pectit et unguento perfudit
he combed his hair and anointed it with fine oil
Deinde ivit ad lavandum in flumine

Then he went to take his bath in the river

post meridiem, pulchra Kamala hortum eius appropinquavit
late in the afternoon, beautiful Kamala approached her garden
Siddhartha stabat ad ostium iterum
Siddhartha was standing at the entrance again
arcum fecit et accepit salutationem meretricis
he made a bow and received the courtesan's greeting
ille attentio cuiusdam servi
he got the attention of one of the servant
rogat ut certiorem faciat dominam suam
he asked him to inform his mistress
"Adolescens Brahman voluerit loqui ad eam"
"a young Brahman wishes to talk to her"
Interposito tempore servus rediit
After a while, the servant returned
servus interrogavit Siddhartha sequi eum
the servant asked Siddhartha to follow him
Siddhartha secutus est servum in pellem
Siddhartha followed the servant into a pavilion
Kamala iacebat hic in lecto
here Kamala was lying on a couch
et dimisit eum servus solus cum ea
and the servant left him alone with her
"Nonne tu etiam heri stas, me salutans?" interrogavit Kamala
"Weren't you also standing out there yesterday, greeting me?" asked Kamala
"Verum est me iam vidi et te heri salutavi".
"It's true that I've already seen and greeted you yesterday"
"At non heri barbam et comam longam geris?"
"But didn't you yesterday wear a beard, and long hair?"
et non erat pulvis in crinibus tuis?
"and was there not dust in your hair?"
"Bene observasti, omnia vidisti"
"You have observed well, you have seen everything"
"Siddhartha vidisti filium Brahman".

"You have seen Siddhartha, the son of a Brahman"
"Brahman qui domum suam reliquit ut Samana fieret"
"the Brahman who has left his home to become a Samana"
"Brahman qui fuit Samana per tres annos".
"the Brahman who has been a Samana for three years"
"Sed nunc dimisi illam viam et veni in hanc civitatem".
"But now, I have left that path and came into this city"
"et primum conveni, antequam urbem intrarem, tu eras".
"and the first one I met, even before I had entered the city, was you"
"Hoc dicere, Veni ad te, o Kamala!"
"To say this, I have come to you, oh Kamala!"
"Antequam, Siddhartha omnem mulierem oculis in terram allocutus est"
"before, Siddhartha addressed all woman with his eyes to the ground"
"Tu prima femina quam aliter alloquor".
"You are the first woman whom I address otherwise"
"Numquam adhuc oculos meos in terram volo".
"Never again do I want to turn my eyes to the ground"
"Non convertam cum venio per pulchra mulier"
"I won't turn when I'm coming across a beautiful woman"
Kamala risit et lusit cum ea pavonum plumis ventilabrum
Kamala smiled and played with her fan of peacocks' feathers
"Et hoc solum ut dicas, Siddhartha ad me venit?"
"And only to tell me this, Siddhartha has come to me?"
"Ad hoc et tibi gratias ago quod tam pulcher sit"
"To tell you this and to thank you for being so beautiful"
"Velim te rogare ut sis amicus et magister"
"I would like to ask you to be my friend and teacher"
"Nihil enim scio de ea arte quam tu cepi".
"for I know nothing yet of that art which you have mastered"
Hoc Kamala risit
At this, Kamala laughed aloud
"Numquam ante hoc mihi accidit, mi amice";
"Never before this has happened to me, my friend"

"**Samana e silva ad me venit et discere a me voluit!**"
"a Samana from the forest came to me and wanted to learn from me!"
"**Numquam ante hoc mihi accidit**".
"Never before this has happened to me"
"**Samana venit ad me capillis longis et vetus, lodicula discerpta!**"
"a Samana came to me with long hair and an old, torn loincloth!"
"**Multi iuvenes veniunt ad me**".
"Many young men come to me"
"**et sunt etiam filii Brahmanorum inter eos**".
"and there are also sons of Brahmans among them"
"**sed veniunt in pulchro veste**"
"but they come in beautiful clothes"
"**Veniunt in calceis**"
"they come in fine shoes"
"**Habent unguentum in capillum**
"they have perfume in their hair"
"**et habent pecuniam in manticis suis**"
"and they have money in their pouches"
"**Sic similes sunt iuvenes qui ad me veniunt**".
"This is how the young men are like, who come to me"
Locutus est Siddhartha, "Iam incipio discere a te".
Spoke Siddhartha, "Already I am starting to learn from you"
"**Etiam heri iam discebam**";
"Even yesterday, I was already learning"
"**Ego barbam meam iam exui**"
"I have already taken off my beard"
" **comas pexi** " ;
"I have combed the hair"
"**et oleum habeo in coma**"
"and I have oil in my hair"
" **Parum est quod adhuc in me deest** " ;
"There is little which is still missing in me"

"O optima, vestes splendidas, calceos, pecuniam in pera mea".
"oh excellent one, fine clothes, fine shoes, money in my pouch"
"Cognosces Siddhartha duriora sibi proposita".
"You shall know Siddhartha has set harder goals for himself"
"et pervenit ad has metas".
"and he has reached these goals"
"Quomodo non perveniam ad metam?"
"How shouldn't I reach that goal?"
"Finis quem hesterno die pro me posui"
"the goal which I have set for myself yesterday"
"ut sis amicus tuus et amoris gaudia discas a te".
"to be your friend and to learn the joys of love from you"
"Videbis quod cito scies, Kamala".
"You'll see that I'll learn quickly, Kamala"
"Iam didici duriora quam ea quae tu me docere existimaris".
"I have already learned harder things than what you're supposed to teach me"
"Et nunc ad eam"
"And now let's get to it"
"Non contentus es cum Siddhartha sicut ille?"
"You aren't satisfied with Siddhartha as he is?"
"oleo in crinibus sed sine vestibus".
"with oil in his hair, but without clothes"
"Siddhartha sine calceis, sine pecunia"
"Siddhartha without shoes, without money"
Kamala ridens exclamavit, "Minime mi".
Laughing, Kamala exclaimed, "No, my dear"
"Non mihi satisfacit, sed"
"he doesn't satisfy me, yet"
"Vestimenta sunt quae habere debet".
"Clothes are what he must have"
"Vestimenta pulchra et calceamentis opus est".
"pretty clothes, and shoes is what he needs"
"Pulchellus calceos et multas pecunias in pera"
"pretty shoes, and lots of money in his pouch"

"et debet habere dona pro Kamala".
"and he must have gifts for Kamala"
"Scisne nunc, Samana de silva?"
"Do you know it now, Samana from the forest?"
"Nonne verba mea notas?"
"Did you mark my words?"
"Ita, verba tua notavi", Siddhartha exclamavit
"Yes, I have marked your words," Siddhartha exclaimed
"Quomodo notanda sunt verba ex tali ore?"
"How should I not mark words which are coming from such a mouth!"
"Os tuum sicut ficus recenter finditur, Kamala"
"Your mouth is like a freshly cracked fig, Kamala"
"Os meum rubet et etiam recens"
"My mouth is red and fresh as well"
"Idoneus erit tibi compositus, aspicies".
"it will be a suitable match for yours, you'll see"
"Sed dic mihi, pulchra Kamala"
"But tell me, beautiful Kamala"
"Nonne tu omnino Samana de silva timeas"
"aren't you at all afraid of the Samana from the forest""
"Samana qui venit discere quomodo amare"
"the Samana who has come to learn how to make love"
"Quidquid enim timeam a Samana?"
"Whatever for should I be afraid of a Samana?"
"Samana stultus a silva"
"a stupid Samana from the forest"
"Samana qui venit ex draconibus".
"a Samana who is coming from the jackals"
"Samana, quae ne adhuc quidem novit quae feminae sunt?"
"a Samana who doesn't even know yet what women are?"
"O fortis est, Samana".
"Oh, he's strong, the Samana"
"Et nihil timet"
"and he isn't afraid of anything"
"Poterat te opprimere, formosa puella";

"He could force you, beautiful girl"
"Potuit te rapere et te laedere".
"He could kidnap you and hurt you"
"Minime, Samana, hoc non timeo".
"No, Samana, I am not afraid of this"
"Numquid unquam Samana aut Brahman aliquis pertimuit, ut veniret et eum caperet?"
"Did any Samana or Brahman ever fear someone might come and grab him?"
Num timet aliquis suam eruditionem surripere?
"could he fear someone steals his learning?
"Poterat quisquam suam religiosam devotionem";
"could anyone take his religious devotion"
"Potestne eius altitudinem cogitationis accipere?
"is it possible to take his depth of thought?
"Non, quia haec sua ipsius sunt".
"No, because these things are his very own"
"solum dare scientiam quam dare voluerit".
"he would only give away the knowledge he is willing to give"
" se tantum dare quae vult dare ";
"he would only give to those he is willing to give to"
"similiter hoc est etiam cum Kamala".
"precisely like this it is also with Kamala"
"et idem est cum jucunditatibus amoris;"
"and it is the same way with the pleasures of love"
"Pulchrum et rubrum os Kamala est", respondit Siddhartha
"Beautiful and red is Kamala's mouth," answered Siddhartha
"sed noli eam contra voluntatem Kamala osculari"
"but don't try to kiss it against Kamala's will"
"quia non habebis ex eo unam guttam suavitatis".
"because you will not obtain a single drop of sweetness from it"
"facile discis, Siddhartha".
"You are learning easily, Siddhartha"
"hoc quoque scire debes".
"you should also learn this"

"Amor obtinetur mendicando, emendo";
"love can be obtained by begging, buying"
"Potes id donum accipere"
"you can receive it as a gift"
"Vel invenire potes in platea"
"or you can find it in the street"
"Sed amor non furtum"
"but love cannot be stolen"
"In hoc, cum perversa via ascendisti".
"In this, you have come up with the wrong path"
"misericordia esset, si amore tali prave vis occupari".
"it would be a pity if you would want to tackle love in such a wrong manner"
Siddhartha adoravit risus
Siddhartha bowed with a smile
"Esset pietatis, Kamala, tam ius"
"It would be a pity, Kamala, you are so right"
" Esset tam magnae pietatis " ;
"It would be such a great pity"
"Nemo, ne unam guttam suavitatis ex ore tuo perdam".
"No, I shall not lose a single drop of sweetness from your mouth"
nec perdes suavitatem ex ore meo.
"nor shall you lose sweetness from my mouth"
"Ita constat. Siddhartha redibit"
"So it is agreed. Siddhartha will return"
"Siddhartha redibit semel quod habet quod adhuc caret".
"Siddhartha will return once he has what he still lacks"
"Veniet cum vestibus, calceis et pecunia".
"he will come back with clothes, shoes, and money"
"Sed loquere, amabilia Kamala, non potuisti mihi unum munusculum dare adhuc consilium?"
"But speak, lovely Kamala, couldn't you still give me one small advice?"
"Date consilium? Quidni?"
"Give you an advice? Why not?"

"Quis non placet consilium dare pauperi, nescienti Samana?"
"Who wouldn't like to give advice to a poor, ignorant Samana?"
"Carissime Kamala, quo eundum est ut haec tria celerrime inveniam?"
"Dear Kamala, where I should go to find these three things most quickly?"
"Amice, multi hoc scire volunt"
"Friend, many would like to know this"
"Fac quod didiceris et pecuniam petas".
"You must do what you've learned and ask for money"
"Nulla alia via est homini pauperi pecuniam acquirere".
"There is no other way for a poor man to obtain money"
"Quid facere potuisti?"
"What might you be able to do?"
"Possum cogitare. Possum exspectare. Possum jejunare" dixit Siddhartha
"I can think. I can wait. I can fast" said Siddhartha
"Nihil aliud?" interrogavit Kamala
"Nothing else?" asked Kamala
"Immo etiam carmina scribere possum"
"yes, I can also write poetry"
"Visne mihi osculum dare pro carmine?"
"Would you like to give me a kiss for a poem?"
"Velim, si tibi carmen placet"
"I would like to, if I like your poem"
"Quidnam esset titulus ejus?"
"What would be its title?"
Siddhartha locutus est, postquam de illo momento cogitavit
Siddhartha spoke, after he had thought about it for a moment
"In hortum suum umbrosum exivit Kamala pulchra"
"Into her shady garden stepped the pretty Kamala"
"In horti foribus stabat Samana fusca";
"At the garden's entrance stood the brown Samana"
Vidensque penitus florem loti, adoravit hominem illum.
"Deeply, seeing the lotus's blossom, Bowed that man"

Et subridens Kamala gratias egit.
"and smiling, Kamala thanked him"
"Amabilius, juvenem, quam vota pro diis."
"More lovely, thought the young man, than offerings for gods"
Kamala manus ita plaudit ut armillae aureae clangant
Kamala clapped her hands so loud that the golden bracelets clanged
"Pulcheri sunt versiculi tui, o fusca Samana";
"Beautiful are your verses, oh brown Samana"
"et vero, nihil perdo cum tibi osculum pro illis".
"and truly, I'm losing nothing when I'm giving you a kiss for them"
Annuens oculis
She beckoned him with her eyes
caput iugo eius ut faciem eius tetigerit
he tilted his head so that his face touched hers
et posuit os suum super os suum
and he placed his mouth on her mouth
os quod erat quasi recenter finditur ficus
the mouth which was like a freshly cracked fig
Diu Kamala eum osculatus est
For a long time, Kamala kissed him
et cum Siddhartha nimio stupore persensit quomodo eum docebat
and with a deep astonishment Siddhartha felt how she taught him
sensit quam sapiens fuit
he felt how wise she was
sensit quomodo se continuit
he felt how she controlled him
sensit quomodo abjecerit
he felt how she rejected him
sensit quomodo decepit eum
he felt how she lured him
et sentiebat quomodo oscula plura essent
and he felt how there were to be more kisses

omne osculum ab aliis
every kiss was different from the others
adhuc erat, cum oscula
he was still, when he received the kisses
Penitus spirans, stans ubi erat
Breathing deeply, he remained standing where he was
obstupuit sicut puer de rebus cognitis
he was astonished like a child about the things worth learning
Cognitio ante oculos eius
the knowledge revealed itself before his eyes
"Pulchrimi versus sunt" inquit Kamala
"Very beautiful are your verses" exclaimed Kamala
"si dives essem, aureos tibi darem pro illis".
"if I were rich, I would give you pieces of gold for them"
"At difficile erit tibi cum versibus pecuniam mereri".
"But it will be difficult for you to earn enough money with verses"
"quia multam pecuniam debes, si amicus Kamala esse vis"
"because you need a lot of money, if you want to be Kamala's friend"
"Viam osculari potes, Kamala!" titubantia Siddhartha
"The way you're able to kiss, Kamala!" stammered Siddhartha
"Ita hoc possum facere".
"Yes, this I am able to do"
Non careo ergo vestibus, calceis, armillis.
"therefore I do not lack clothes, shoes, bracelets"
"Habeo omnia bella"
"I have all the beautiful things"
"Sed quid de te fiet?"
"But what will become of you?"
"Non potes aliud facere?"
"Aren't you able to do anything else?"
"Potesne plus quam cogitare, jejunare, et facere carmina?"
"can you do more than think, fast, and make poetry?"
"Ego quoque carmina sacrificalia" dixit Siddhartha .
"I also know the sacrificial songs" said Siddhartha

"sed illa carmina iam cantare nolo"
"but I do not want to sing those songs anymore"
"Ego quoque scio quomodo carmina magica facere"
"I also know how to make magic spells"
"sed nolo amplius loqui"
"but I do not want to speak them anymore"
" Legi scripturas " ;
"I have read the scriptures"
"Desine!" Kamala interpellavit eum
"Stop!" Kamala interrupted him
"Tu legere et scribere potes?"
"You're able to read and write?"
"Profecto hoc facere possum multi homines"
"Certainly, I can do this, many people can"
"Plerique non possunt," Kamala respondit
"Most people can't," Kamala replied
"Ego quoque unus sum ex iis qui id facere non possunt".
"I am also one of those who can't do it"
"Optime bonum est quod legere et scribere potes"
"It is very good that you're able to read and write"
"etiam in magicis carminibus uti"
"you will also find use for the magic spells"
Hoc momento ancilla accurrit
In this moment, a maid came running in
susurrabat nuntium in aurem dominae suae
she whispered a message into her mistress's ear
"Non est mihi peregrinus", exclamavit Kamala
"There's a visitor for me" exclaimed Kamala
"Festina et abice te, Siddhartha".
"Hurry and get yourself away, Siddhartha"
"nullus huc te videat, hoc memento!"
"nobody may see you in here, remember this!"
"Cras, iterum te videbo"
"Tomorrow, I'll see you again"
Kamala ancillae suae iussit Siddhartha vestimenta alba dare
Kamala ordered her maid to give Siddhartha white garments

et Siddhartha invenit se ab ancilla trahi
and then Siddhartha found himself being dragged away by the maid
e conspectu omnium semitarum in hortum perlatus est
he was brought into a garden-house out of sight of any paths
tum in hortos ductus
then he was led into the bushes of the garden
hortatus est ut se quam primum ex horto surgeret
he was urged to get himself out of the garden as soon as possible
et dixit se non videri
and he was told he must not be seen
fecit ut sibi fuerat imperatum
he did as he had been told
solitus erat saltus
he was accustomed to the forest
ita ut sine sono
so he managed to get out without making a sound

involutis vestibus sub bracchio ad urbem rediit
he returned to the city carrying the rolled up garments under his arm
In diversorio, ubi degunt viatores, per ostium se collocavit
At the inn, where travellers stay, he positioned himself by the door
sine verbis poposcit cibum
without words he asked for food
sine verbo accepit fragmen rice-placentae
without a word he accepted a piece of rice-cake
cogitabat quomodo semper orabat
he thought about how he had always begged
"Fortasse quamprimum cras rogabo neminem pro cibo amplius".
"Perhaps as soon as tomorrow I will ask no one for food anymore"
Repente in eo superbia exarsit

Suddenly, pride flared up in him
Non erat Samana amplius
He was no Samana any more
non erat ei conveniens ut cibum peteret
it was no longer appropriate for him to beg for food
rice-libum dedit cani
he gave the rice-cake to a dog
et nocte illa sine cibo mansit
and that night he remained without food
Siddhartha cogitabat sibi de civitate
Siddhartha thought to himself about the city
« Simplex vita est quam homines in hoc mundo agunt ».
"Simple is the life which people lead in this world"
"Haec vita nullas difficultates praebet"
"this life presents no difficulties"
"Omnia difficilia et laboriosa cum Samana essem";
"Everything was difficult and toilsome when I was a Samana"
"sicut Samana omnia desperata"
"as a Samana everything was hopeless"
" nunc omnia facilia sunt "
"but now everything is easy"
"facilis est sicut lectio in osculando Kamala".
"it is easy like the lesson in kissing from Kamala"
"Vestibus opus est et pecunia, nihil aliud"
"I need clothes and money, nothing else"
"Haec proposita parva sunt et deduceretur"
"these goals are small and achievable"
"Quae proposita non faciunt hominem aliquem somnum perdere"
"such goals won't make a person lose any sleep"

postridie ad domum Kamala rediit
the next day he returned to Kamala's house
"Res bene operantur" clamabat ad eum
"Things are working out well" she called out to him
"Expectant te Kamaswami scriptor"

"They are expecting you at Kamaswami's"
"Est mercator civitatis ditissimus";
"he is the richest merchant of the city"
"Si volet, te recipiet in suum servitium".
"If he likes you, he'll accept you into his service"
"sed te sapias, fusca Samana"
"but you must be smart, brown Samana"
"Et alii dixero ei de te"
"I had others tell him about you"
"Esto officiosus in eum, potens est"
"Be polite towards him, he is very powerful"
"At moneo, ne nimis modestus sis!"
"But I warn you, don't be too modest!"
"Nolo te servum eius fieri".
"I do not want you to become his servant"
fies eius aequalis.
"you shall become his equal"
"Aut ego vobiscum sum contentus erit"
"or else I won't be satisfied with you"
"Kamaswami est incipiens ad vetus et piger"
"Kamaswami is starting to get old and lazy"
"Si tibi placuerit, multum te committet".
"If he likes you, he'll entrust you with a lot"
Siddhartha gratias egit et derisit
Siddhartha thanked her and laughed
Invenit quod non comedi
she found out that he had not eaten
et misit ei panem et fructus suos
so she sent him bread and fruits
"Fuistine felix" dixit cum discesserunt
"You've been lucky" she said when they parted
"Ego ostium unum post alium tibi"
"I'm opening one door after another for you"
"Quam veniam? Habesne carmina?"
"How come? Do you have a spell?"
"Dixi tibi scivi cogitare, exspectare et jejunare".

"I told you I knew how to think, to wait, and to fast"
"sed nullius usus hoc putares".
"but you thought this was of no use"
"At multis rebus utile est"
"But it is useful for many things"
"Kamala, videbis stultos Samanas discendo bonos esse".
"Kamala, you'll see that the stupid Samanas are good at learning"
"Aspicies se posse facere multa bella in silva"
"you'll see they are able to do many pretty things in the forest"
"Quae similia vobis non possunt"
"things which the likes of you aren't capable of"
"Pridie heri adhuc villosus eram mendicus".
"The day before yesterday, I was still a shaggy beggar"
"Nuper quam heri osculatus sum Kamala"
"as recently as yesterday I have kissed Kamala"
"et mox mercator ero et pecuniam habebo".
"and soon I'll be a merchant and have money"
" atque ego omnia ista quae tu insistis ".
"and I'll have all those things you insist upon"
"Estne," fatebatur, "sed ubi esses sine me?"
"Well yes," she admitted, "but where would you be without me?"
"Quid vis esse, si Kamala te non adiuvat?"
"What would you be, if Kamala wasn't helping you?"
"Carus Kamala" dixit Siddhartha
"Dear Kamala" said Siddhartha
et erectus est in altitudine sua
and he straightened up to his full height
"Cum venissem ad te in hortum tuum, primum gradum feci".
"when I came to you into your garden, I did the first step"
"Meum fuit consilium discere amorem ex hac pulcherrima muliere".
"It was my resolution to learn love from this most beautiful woman"
"Illo momento hoc senatus consultum fecissem"

"that moment I had made this resolution"
"et sciebam me id facere".
"and I knew I would carry it out"
"Sciebam te adiuvaturum me".
"I knew that you would help me"
"primo aspectu tuo hortus in ostio iam scivi".
"at your first glance at the entrance of the garden I already knew it"
"Sed quid, si noluissem?" interrogavit Kamala
"But what if I hadn't been willing?" asked Kamala
"Velles" respondit Siddhartha
"You were willing" replied Siddhartha
"Cum ieceris saxum in aquam, velocissimo cursu ad imum accipit".
"When you throw a rock into water, it takes the fastest course to the bottom"
"Hoc sic est, cum Siddhartha habet metam";
"This is how it is when Siddhartha has a goal"
"Siddhartha nihil facit; exspectat, cogitat, ieiunat".
"Siddhartha does nothing; he waits, he thinks, he fasts"
sed ea quae mundi sunt pertransit sicut petra per aquam
"but he passes through the things of the world like a rock through water"
"Transivit per aquam nihil facere"
"he passed through the water without doing anything"
"ad fundum aquarum trahitur";
"he is drawn to the bottom of the water"
"sese se ad imum aquae"
"he lets himself fall to the bottom of the water"
"Eum propositum allicit ad eam";
"His goal attracts him towards it"
"non admittit quicquam animae suae intromittere quod fini possit obsistere".
"he doesn't let anything enter his soul which might oppose the goal"
"Hoc est quod didicit Siddhartha apud Samanas".

"This is what Siddhartha has learned among the Samanas"
"Hoc est quod stulti magicam vocant"
"This is what fools call magic"
"A daemonibus fieri putant"
"they think it is done by daemons"
"sed nihil fit a daemonibus".
"but nothing is done by daemons"
"non sunt daemones in hoc mundo".
"there are no daemons in this world"
"Omnes magicas facere possunt, si velint".
"Everyone can perform magic, should they choose to"
" Quisque potest sua proposita attingere si cogitare possit "
"everyone can reach his goals if he is able to think"
"Quisque potest sua proposita pervenire, si expectare potest".
"everyone can reach his goals if he is able to wait"
"Quisque potest sua proposita pervenire, si potest ieiunare".
"everyone can reach his goals if he is able to fast"
Audivit eum Kamala; dilexit eam vocem suam
Kamala listened to him; she loved his voice
et vultus ex oculis eius dilexit
she loved the look from his eyes
"Fortasse ita est ut dicis, amice";
"Perhaps it is as you say, friend"
Sed fortasse alia explicatio est.
"But perhaps there is another explanation"
"Siddhartha est pulcher homo"
"Siddhartha is a handsome man"
"mulieres aspectu delectat".
"his glance pleases the women"
" ad eum fortuna venit propter hoc "
"good fortune comes towards him because of this"
Uno osculo Siddhartha renuntiat
With one kiss, Siddhartha bid his farewell
"Utinam ita sit, mi magister".
"I wish that it should be this way, my teacher"

" Utinam oculi mei tibi placeant "
"I wish that my glance shall please you"
" Opto ut mihi fortunam semper afferas "
"I wish that that you always bring me good fortune"

Cum puerilis populus
With the Childlike People

Siddhartha ad Kamaswami mercator
Siddhartha went to Kamaswami the merchant
ductus est in domum opulentam
he was directed into a rich house
servi eum inter stragula pretiosa in cubiculum duxerunt
servants led him between precious carpets into a chamber
in thalamo erat, ubi patremfamilias exspectabat
in the chamber was where he awaited the master of the house
Kamaswami celeriter intravit in cubiculum
Kamaswami entered swiftly into the room
erat leniter movere hominem
he was a smoothly moving man
habebat canos valde et ingeniosissimos, oculos cautos
he had very gray hair and very intelligent, cautious eyes
et habebat os avarum
and he had a greedy mouth
Hospes et hospes comiter salutaverunt
Politely, the host and the guest greeted one another
"Dixi te esse Brahman" mercatorem incepit
"I have been told that you were a Brahman" the merchant began
"Dixi te virum doctum".
"I have been told that you are a learned man"
"et etiam aliud mihi dictum est".
"and I have also been told something else"
"in servitio mercatoris esse petis".
"you seek to be in the service of a merchant"
"Numquid egestatis, Brahman, ut servire petis?"
"Might you have become destitute, Brahman, so that you seek to serve?"
"Non," inquit Siddhartha, "non egens factus sum".
"No," said Siddhartha, "I have not become destitute"
"neque vnquam destitutus sum" addidit Siddhartha

"nor have I ever been destitute" added Siddhartha
« **Sciatis quia a Samanas venio** ».
"You should know that I'm coming from the Samanas"
"cum illis diu vixi".
"I have lived with them for a long time"
"Venis a Samana"
"you are coming from the Samanas"
"quomodo potes esse nisi destitutus?"
"how could you be anything but destitute?"
"nonne Samanas omnino caret possessionibus?"
"Aren't the Samanas entirely without possessions?"
"Sine possessione sum, si id est quod dicis", inquit Siddhartha .
"I am without possessions, if that is what you mean" said Siddhartha
"At ego sine sponte pos- sum".
"But I am without possessions voluntarily"
et ideo non sum destitutus.
"and therefore I am not destitute"
"Sed quid paras vivere sine possessione?"
"But what are you planning to live from, being without possessions?"
"Hoc nondum cogitavi, domine"
"I haven't thought of this yet, sir"
" Plusquam triennium sine possessionibus fui " ;
"For more than three years, I have been without possessions"
"et numquam cogitavi de iis quae vivam".
"and I have never thought about of what I should live"
"De rebus alienis sic vixisti".
"So you've lived of the possessions of others"
"Verum est, hoc quomodo est?"
"Presumable, this is how it is?"
"Mercatores bene vivunt etiam ex aliis quae possident".
"Well, merchants also live of what other people own"
"Bene dixit mercator"
"Well said," granted the merchant

"sed nihil pro nihilo acciperet ab alio".
"But he wouldn't take anything from another person for nothing"
"se mercaturam suam in reditu" daturum dixit Kamaswami .
"he would give his merchandise in return" said Kamaswami
" Sic quidem esse videtur " ;
"So it seems to be indeed"
" Quisque accipit, quisque dat, talis est vita".
"Everyone takes, everyone gives, such is life"
"At si me interrogantem non sapiunt, habeo quaestionem"
"But if you don't mind me asking, I have a question"
"Sine possessione, quid vis dare?"
"being without possessions, what would you like to give?"
"Omnis dat quod habet".
"Everyone gives what he has"
" Belliger dat vires ;"
"The warrior gives strength"
"mercator mercaturam" dat.
"the merchant gives merchandise"
"Magister dat doctrinam"
"the teacher gives teachings"
"Ryzam agricola dat"
"the farmer gives rice"
"piscator dat piscem"
"the fisher gives fish"
"Ita vero. Et quid est quod dare debes?"
"Yes indeed. And what is it that you've got to give?"
"Quid est quod didicisti?"
"What is it that you've learned?"
"quid facere te posse?"
"what you're able to do?"
"Possum cogitare. Possum exspectare. Possum jejunare"
"I can think. I can wait. I can fast"
"Hoc est omnia?" interrogavit Kamaswami
"That's everything?" asked Kamaswami
"Credo quod omne est!"

"I believe that is everything there is!"
"Et quid opus illius?"
"And what's the use of that?"
"Eg, jejunium. Quid est bonum?"
"For example; fasting. What is it good for?"
"Est valde bonus, domine";
"It is very good, sir"
"Sunt temporibus homini nihil manducare"
"there are times a person has nothing to eat"
"Ieiunium ergo cultissima est facere potest"
"then fasting is the smartest thing he can do"
"Fuit tempus quo Siddhartha non didicit jejunare"
"there was a time where Siddhartha hadn't learned to fast"
"in hoc tempore quodlibet servitium debebat accipere".
"in this time he had to accept any kind of service"
"quia fames cogeret ad servitium accipiendum".
"because hunger would force him to accept the service"
"Sed ut hoc, Siddhartha placide expectare potest".
"But like this, Siddhartha can wait calmly"
"Impatientiam non novit, nihil subitis scit".
"he knows no impatience, he knows no emergency"
" diu potest famem oppugnare.
"for a long time he can allow hunger to besiege him"
"et famem deridebit".
"and he can laugh about the hunger"
"Hoc est, domine, quod bonum est ieiunio";
"This, sir, is what fasting is good for"
"Recte dicis, Samana" recognovit Kamaswami
"You're right, Samana" acknowledged Kamaswami
"Exspecta paulisper" hospitem interrogavit
"Wait for a moment" he asked of his guest
Kamaswami reliquerat cubiculum et rediit in librum
Kamaswami left the room and returned with a scroll
librum Siddhartha tradidit et interrogavit eum legere
he handed Siddhartha the scroll and asked him to read it
Siddhartha intuens librum sibi traditum

Siddhartha looked at the scroll handed to him
in librum venditionum contractus scriptum erat
on the scroll a sales-contract had been written
coepit perlegere librum contenta
he began to read out the scroll's contents
Kamaswami valde placebat Siddhartha
Kamaswami was very pleased with Siddhartha
"Vis scribere aliquid mihi in hac charta?"
"would you write something for me on this piece of paper?"
chartam et calamum ei tradidit
He handed him a piece of paper and a pen
Siddhartha scripsit et chartam reddidit
Siddhartha wrote, and returned the paper
Kamaswami legitur, "Bona est scriptura, melior est cogitatio";
Kamaswami read, "Writing is good, thinking is better"
"Enim dolor bonus est, patiens est melior".
"Being smart is good, being patient is better"
"Praeclarum est quam scribere possis" mercator eum laudavit
"It is excellent how you're able to write" the merchant praised him
"Multa de re adhuc habebimus inter se disputare".
"Many a thing we will still have to discuss with one another"
"Hodie te rogo ut sis hospes".
"For today, I'm asking you to be my guest"
"Veni ad habitandum in hac domo"
"please come to live in this house"
Siddhartha gratias egit Kamaswami et accepit oblatio
Siddhartha thanked Kamaswami and accepted his offer
et habitabat in mangone scriptor domum posthac
he lived in the dealer's house from now on
Vestimenta ei allata sunt et calceamentis
Clothes were brought to him, and shoes
et per singulos dies servus balneum paravit ei
and every day, a servant prepared a bath for him

Bis in die multa cena apposita est
Twice a day, a plentiful meal was served
sed Siddhartha semel tantum die comedit
but Siddhartha only ate once a day
et neque cibum comedit neque vinum bibit
and he ate neither meat, nor did he drink wine
Kamaswami ei de commercia sua
Kamaswami told him about his trade
ostendit ei negotiationem et conclavia
he showed him the merchandise and storage-rooms
ostendit ei quomodo factae sint rationes
he showed him how the calculations were done
Siddhartha obtinuit multis novis rebus
Siddhartha got to know many new things
audivit multum et modicum locutus est
he heard a lot and spoke little
sed non oblitus verborum Kamala
but he did not forget Kamala's words
ideo numquam mercatori serviebat
so he was never subservient to the merchant
cogebat ut pari
he forced him to treat him as an equal
fortasse eum etiam plus aequo tractare cogebat
perhaps he forced him to treat him as even more than an equal
Kamaswami rem suam cum cura
Kamaswami conducted his business with care
et de negotiis suis valde iratus est
and he was very passionate about his business
Siddhartha autem haec omnia intuebatur quasi ludus
but Siddhartha looked upon all of this as if it was a game
praecepta ludi diligenter discere conatus est
he tried hard to learn the rules of the game precisely
sed contenta ludi cor eius non attigit
but the contents of the game did not touch his heart
Non diu in Kamaswami domo fuerat

He had not been in Kamaswami's house for long
mox tamen in domini negotiis interfuit
but soon he took part in his landlord's business

cotidie pulchra Kamala visitavit
every day he visited beautiful Kamala
Kamala hora constituta conventibus
Kamala had an hour appointed for their meetings
illa induta satis vestibus et calceamentis
she was wearing pretty clothes and fine shoes
moxque ei dona pertulit
and soon he brought her gifts as well
Multum a rubro et callido ore didicerat
Much he learned from her red, smart mouth
Multum a teneris didicerat , manibus
Much he learned from her tender, supple hand
de amore, Siddhartha adhuc puer erat
regarding love, Siddhartha was still a boy
et in amore caeca tendit
and he had a tendency to plunge into love blindly
incidit in concupiscentiam quasi in foveam profundam
he fell into lust like into a bottomless pit
docuit eum, incipiens a basics
she taught him thoroughly, starting with the basics
delectatio non potest esse sine delectatione
pleasure cannot be taken without giving pleasure
omnis gestus, omnis blanditia, omnis tactus, omnis aspectus
every gesture, every caress, every touch, every look
omnis macula corporis, quamvis parva, occultum habebat
every spot of the body, however small it was, had its secret
mysteria laetitiam scientibus
the secrets would bring happiness to those who know them
amantes non debent ab invicem discedere post amorem
lovers must not part from one another after celebrating love
non debent sine admiratione alterius
they must not part without one admiring the other

ut victi vicerint
they must be as defeated as they have been victorious
nec amans satus sentiens saturi aut fastidio
neither lover should start feeling fed up or bored
ut non male affectum of having been ablative
they should not get the evil feeling of having been abusive
et non sentiant abusi sunt
and they should not feel like they have been abused
Mira horas consumpsit cum pulchris et callidis artificibus
Wonderful hours he spent with the beautiful and smart artist
eius factus est discipulus, amator, amicus eius
he became her student, her lover, her friend
Hic apud Kamala fuit pretium et propositum vitae praesentis
Here with Kamala was the worth and purpose of his present life
propositum non negotium Kamaswami
his purpose was not with the business of Kamaswami

Siddhartha magni momenti litteris et contractibus
Siddhartha received important letters and contracts
Kamaswami de omnibus rebus magnis cum eo disserebat
Kamaswami began discussing all important affairs with him
Mox vidit Siddhartha parum scire de oryza et lana
He soon saw that Siddhartha knew little about rice and wool
sed videbat se facere feliciter
but he saw that he acted in a fortunate manner
et Siddhartha eum tranquillitate et aequo animo superavit
and Siddhartha surpassed him in calmness and equanimity
eum arte intellegendi antea ignotis anteibat
he surpassed him in the art of understanding previously unknown people
Kamaswami locutus est de Siddhartha ad amicum
Kamaswami spoke about Siddhartha to a friend
"Hanc Brahman mercator yeram est"
"This Brahman is no proper merchant"

"Nunquam mercator erit"
"he will never be a merchant"
"Nunquam enim negocium est aliqua passio in anima".
"for business there is never any passion in his soul"
"Sed arcanum qualitatem habet de eo"
"But he has a mysterious quality about him"
"Qualitas haec omnia per se prospera"
"this quality brings success about all by itself"
" posset esse de bona stella natiuitatis " ;
"it could be from a good Star of his birth"
"aut posset aliquid didicerit apud Samanas";
"or it could be something he has learned among Samanas"
"Semper videtur mere ludere cum negotiis nostris".
"He always seems to be merely playing with our business-affairs"
"suum negotium numquam plene pars eius fit".
"his business never fully becomes a part of him"
"Sua res nunquam dominatur ei"
"his business never rules over him"
"Ipse numquam timet defectum"
"he is never afraid of failure"
"Nunquam damnum perturbetur"
"he is never upset by a loss"
Amicus mercatori consilium
The friend advised the merchant
" Da ei tertiam partem fructuum , quam facit tibi " ;
"Give him a third of the profits he makes for you"
sed et ille teneatur cum damna fuerint.
"but let him also be liable when there are losses"
"Inde studiosior fiet".
"Then, he'll become more zealous"
Kamaswami curiosus erat et consilium secutus
Kamaswami was curious, and followed the advice
Sed Siddhartha parum curabat de amissis vel proficuis
But Siddhartha cared little about loses or profits
Is cum lucrum faceret, aequo animo accepit

When he made a profit, he accepted it with equanimity
cum damna fecit, risit
when he made losses, he laughed it off
Videbatur quidem, quasi non curaret negotium
It seemed indeed, as if he did not care about the business
Uno tempore ad vicum iter fecit
At one time, he travelled to a village
profectus est ut emeret messem magnam oryzae
he went there to buy a large harvest of rice
Sed cum illuc venisset, oryza iam vendita est
But when he got there, the rice had already been sold
alius mercator ad villas ante eum
another merchant had gotten to the village before him
Nihilominus Siddhartha aliquot dies in eo pago mansit
Nevertheless, Siddhartha stayed for several days in that village
agricolae ad potum
he treated the farmers for a drink
nummos aeris liberis dedit
he gave copper-coins to their children
in celebratione nuptiarum copulavit
he joined in the celebration of a wedding
et rediit valde contentus de itinere suo
and he returned extremely satisfied from his trip
Kamaswami iratus Siddhartha vastaverat pecuniam
Kamaswami was angry that Siddhartha had wasted time and money
Siddhartha respondit "Carissime increpare desine!"
Siddhartha answered "Stop scolding, dear friend!"
"Nihil unquam obiurgatio".
"Nothing was ever achieved by scolding"
"Si acciderit damnum, feram id damnum".
"If a loss has occurred, let me bear that loss"
"Ego sum contentus hoc itinere"
"I am very satisfied with this trip"
"Ego multa genera hominum cognovi"

"I have gotten to know many kinds of people"
"A Brahman factus est amicus meus"
"a Brahman has become my friend"
"Pueri sederunt super genua mea".
"children have sat on my knees"
" agricolae ostenderunt mihi agros suos ".
"farmers have shown me their fields"
"nemo sciebat me esse mercatorem"
"nobody knew that I was a merchant"
"Quod omnia valde nice" Kamaswami indignanter exclamavit
"That's all very nice," exclaimed Kamaswami indignantly
"sed re vera es mercator post omnes".
"but in fact, you are a merchant after all"
"An tantum iter ad delectationem habuisti?"
"Or did you have only travel for your amusement?"
"Sane me delectationis causa confeci" Siddhartha risit
"of course I have travelled for my amusement" Siddhartha laughed
"Quid enim aliud volui iter facere?"
"For what else would I have travelled?"
"Et loca mea cognovi et loca"
"I have gotten to know people and places"
"Accepi misericordiam et fidem";
"I have received kindness and trust"
" amicitias inveni in hoc pago ".
"I have found friendships in this village"
"Si Kamaswami fuissem, angebatur iter facturus".
"if I had been Kamaswami, I would have travelled back annoyed"
"Fuisset festinans quam primum mea emptio defuit"
"I would have been in hurry as soon as my purchase failed"
"et tempus et pecunia perdita fuisset"
"and time and money would indeed have been lost"
"Sed hoc sic habui, paucos dies bonos".
"But like this, I've had a few good days"

"Non didici tempus meum est"
"I've learned from my time there"
" et ab experientia gavisus sum ";
"and I have had joy from the experience"
Nec mihi nec aliis molestia et festinatione nocui.
"I've neither harmed myself nor others by annoyance and hastiness"
" si unquam rediero amicas , me receperint "
"if I ever return friendly people will welcome me"
"si redeo ad negotia facienda amicae populi, me quoque recipiet"
"if I return to do business friendly people will welcome me too"
"Ego me laudo, quod non festinationem aliquam aut offensam ostendo";
"I praise myself for not showing any hurry or displeasure"
"Sic discede, ut dictum est, amice";
"So, leave it as it is, my friend"
"et increpando non noceas te"
"and don't harm yourself by scolding"
"Si videris Siddhartha nocere sibi, loquere mecum".
"If you see Siddhartha harming himself, then speak with me"
"et Siddhartha ibit in viam suam".
"and Siddhartha will go on his own path"
"Sed adhuc, invicem contenti simus".
"But until then, let's be satisfied with one another"
mercatoris conatus ad persuadendum Siddhartha futiles erant
the merchant's attempts to convince Siddhartha were futile
Siddhartha non potuit comedere panem suum
he could not make Siddhartha eat his bread
Siddhartha panem suum comedit
Siddhartha ate his own bread
immo ambo panes alienos comederunt
or rather, they both ate other people's bread
Siddhartha non audiebat Kamaswami curarum

Siddhartha never listened to Kamaswami's worries
et Kamaswami multas curas voluit communicare
and Kamaswami had many worries he wanted to share
erant negotia agitur periculum deficiendi
there were business-deals going on in danger of failing
portarentur mercium amissae videbantur
shipments of merchandise seemed to have been lost
debitores videbantur solvendo non posse
debtors seemed to be unable to pay
Kamaswami numquam arguere Siddhartha dicere verba anxietas
Kamaswami could never convince Siddhartha to utter words of worry
Kamaswami non potuit sentire Siddhartha iram in negotiis
Kamaswami could not make Siddhartha feel anger towards business
non potuit eum habere in fronte rugas
he could not get him to to have wrinkles on the forehead
non potuit Siddhartha dormire male
he could not make Siddhartha sleep badly

olim Kamaswami loqui conatus Siddhartha
one day, Kamaswami tried to speak with Siddhartha
"Siddhartha, nihil novi addidisti".
"Siddhartha, you have failed to learn anything new"
sed rursus Siddhartha derisit hoc
but again, Siddhartha laughed at this
"An non placeas mihi talibus iocis cape"
"Would you please not kid me with such jokes"
"Quid a te didici quantum sit canistrum piscium constat"
"What I've learned from you is how much a basket of fish costs"
"et didici quantum usurarii sit oneris creditae pecuniae".
"and I learned how much interest may be charged on loaned money"
"Haec areas peritiae sunt tuae"

"These are your areas of expertise"
"Non didici cogitare a te, mi Kamaswami"
"I haven't learned to think from you, my dear Kamaswami"
" debet esse quaerens a me discere ".
"you ought to be the one seeking to learn from me"
Anima enim eius non erat cum commercio
Indeed his soul was not with the trade
Negotium satis erat ei pecuniam praebere pro Kamala
The business was good enough to provide him with money for Kamala
et demeruit eum multo plus quam necesse erat
and it earned him much more than he needed
Praeter Kamala, Siddhartha curiositas erat apud populum
Besides Kamala, Siddhartha's curiosity was with the people
eorum negotia, artes, curas et voluptates
their businesses, crafts, worries, and pleasures
haec omnia aliena esse ab eo
all these things used to be alien to him
stultitia eorum ut longius luna
their acts of foolishness used to be as distant as the moon
facile peruicit omnibus loqueretur
he easily succeeded in talking to all of them
posset vivere cum omnibus illis
he could live with all of them
et posset ab omnibus discere
and he could continue to learn from all of them
sed aliquid erat quod eum ab eis separaret
but there was something which separated him from them
dividere inter eum et populum
he could feel a divide between him and the people
hoc elementum separatum erat eum esse Samana
this separating factor was him being a Samana
Hominem vidit vitam euntem in puerili modo
He saw mankind going through life in a childlike manner
in multis viis vivebant animalia vivunt
in many ways they were living the way animals live

dilexit et contempsit eorum conversationem
he loved and also despised their way of life
Laborem et dolorem vidit
He saw them toiling and suffering
canae fiebant pro indignis hoc pretio
they were becoming gray for things unworthy of this price
res pecunias parvasque voluptates fecerunt
they did things for money and little pleasures
fecerunt pro leviter honorati
they did things for being slightly honoured
Vidit eos increpare et insultare
he saw them scolding and insulting each other
Vidit conquerentes de dolore
he saw them complaining about pain
dolores quos Samana non ridere
pains at which a Samana would only smile
et vidit eos privatio laborantes
and he saw them suffering from deprivations
privationes quas Samana non sentiunt
deprivations which a Samana would not feel
His omnibus patuit iter
He was open to everything these people brought his way
Gratus erat mercator, qui ei linteamina venalia obtulit
welcome was the merchant who offered him linen for sale
Gratus erat debitor qui mutuo quaesivit
welcome was the debtor who sought another loan
Gratus erat mendicus qui narravit ei paupertatis suae historiam
welcome was the beggar who told him the story of his poverty
mendicus qui non erat semivivus inops sicut quivis Samana
the beggar who was not half as poor as any Samana
Non tractavit locupletem mercatorem et servum suum
He did not treat the rich merchant and his servant different
platea-venditor eum deciperet emit aliquet
he let street-vendor cheat him when buying bananas
Kamaswami saepe queri de curarum eius ei

Kamaswami would often complain to him about his worries
aut de negotiis suis increparet eum
or he would reproach him about his business
audiebat curiose ac feliciter
he listened curiously and happily
sed haesitabat ab amico suo
but he was puzzled by his friend
voluit intelligere
he tried to understand him
et quod rectum erat usque ad certum punctum fassus est
and he admitted he was right, up to a certain point
multi sunt qui petierunt Siddhartha
there were many who asked for Siddhartha
Multi negotium cum eo facere voluerunt
many wanted to do business with him
multi sunt qui eum fallere volebant
there were many who wanted to cheat him
multi aliquid secretum ex eo haurire voluerunt
many wanted to draw some secret out of him
multi provocare volebant ad eius misericordiam
many wanted to appeal to his sympathy
multi voluerunt ut eius consilium
many wanted to get his advice
Consilium dedit his qui volebant
He gave advice to those who wanted it
misertus est eorum qui misericordia indigebant
he pitied those who needed pity
dona his qui probaverunt munera fecit
he made gifts to those who liked presents
et dimisit eum partem aliquam fallere
he let some cheat him a bit
hoc ludum, quo omnes ludentes occupabant cogitationes suas
this game which all people played occupied his thoughts
de hoc ludo quantum habuit de Diis

he thought about this game just as much as he had about the Gods
alto pectore sensit morientem
deep in his chest he felt a dying voice
Haec vox eum secreto admonuit
this voice admonished him quietly
et vocem intra se vix percepit
and he hardly perceived the voice inside of himself
Et tunc per horam aliquid sensit
And then, for an hour, he became aware of something
sensit alienam vitam ducebat
he became aware of the strange life he was leading
intellexit hanc vitam tantum ludus
he realized this life was only a game
interdum felicitatem et gaudium perciperet
at times he would feel happiness and joy
sed vita vera adhuc transiens
but real life was still passing him by
et praeteriens non tangendo illum
and it was passing by without touching him
Siddhartha ludunt cum negotiis agit
Siddhartha played with his business-deals
Siddhartha invenit oblectationem in circuitu eius
Siddhartha found amusement in the people around him
cor autem suum non erat cum eis
but regarding his heart, he was not with them
Fons alicubi cucurrit, longe ab eo
The source ran somewhere, far away from him
et cucurrit invisibiliter
it ran and ran invisibly
nihil ad suam vitam habuit amplius
it had nothing to do with his life any more
aliquoties ob tales cogitationes expavit
at several times he became scared on account of such thoughts
voluit se omnes istos pueriles ludos participare posse
he wished he could participate in all of these childlike games

vere voluit vivere
he wanted to really live
in theatro agere voluit
he wanted to really act in their theatre
vere voluit suis voluptatibus frui
he wanted to really enjoy their pleasures
et voluit vivere, non modo spectator
and he wanted to live, instead of just standing by as a spectator

Sed iterum atque iterum venit ad pulchram Kamala
But again and again, he came back to beautiful Kamala
artem didicit amoris
he learned the art of love
cultumque luxuriae exercuit
and he practised the cult of lust
luxuria, in qua dare et accipere fit unum
lust, in which giving and taking becomes one
fabulabatur cum ea et didicit ab ea
he chatted with her and learned from her
ei consilium dedit et consilium eius accepit
he gave her advice, and he received her advice
Melius eum intellexit quam Govinda eum intelligere solebat
She understood him better than Govinda used to understand him
erat ei similior quam Govinda fuerat
she was more similar to him than Govinda had been
dixit ei: "Tu es similis mei"
"You are like me," he said to her
"Tu es diversus a plerisque"
"you are different from most people"
"Kamala es, nihil aliud"
"You are Kamala, nothing else"
"et intra te est pax et refugium".
"and inside of you, there is a peace and refuge"
"refugium ad quod ire potes omni hora diei"

"a refuge to which you can go at every hour of the day"
"Domi apud te esse potes"
"you can be at home with yourself"
"Hoc quoque possum facere"
"I can do this too"
" Pauci homines hunc locum habent ";
"Few people have this place"
et tamen omnes habere potuerunt.
"and yet all of them could have it"
"Non omnes homines sapiunt" dixit Kamala
"Not all people are smart" said Kamala
"Non," inquit Siddhartha, "non est causa quare"
"No," said Siddhartha, "that's not the reason why"
"Kamaswami dolor est sicut et ego"
"Kamaswami is just as smart as I am"
"sed ipse in se non habet refugium".
"but he has no refuge in himself"
"Alii habent, quamvis puerorum animos habeant".
"Others have it, although they have the minds of children"
"Plures homines, Kamala, sunt sicut folium cadens".
"Most people, Kamala, are like a falling leaf"
"folium quod inflatur et volvitur per aerem".
"a leaf which is blown and is turning around through the air"
"Folium quod vacillat et decidit in terram".
"a leaf which wavers, and tumbles to the ground"
"Alii autem pauci sunt sicut stellae".
"But others, a few, are like stars"
"Procedunt certo"
"they go on a fixed course"
"Nullus ventus attingit eos"
"no wind reaches them"
"in se habent suam legem et cursum suum"
"in themselves they have their law and their course"
"Inter omnes viros doctos quos vidi talis erat unus".
"Among all the learned men I have met, there was one of this kind"

« vere perfectus erat ».
"he was a truly perfected one"
"Numquam potero eum oblivisci".
"I'll never be able to forget him"
"Ille est Gotama, excelsus";
"It is that Gotama, the exalted one"
"Milia sectatorum quotidie audiunt dicta eius".
"Thousands of followers are listening to his teachings every day"
"Sequuntur per singulas horas mandata".
"they follow his instructions every hour"
sed omnia folia caduca sunt.
"but they are all falling leaves"
"non in se ipsis habent doctrinam et legem";
"not in themselves they have teachings and a law"
Kamala intuens risus
Kamala looked at him with a smile
"Iterum de eo loqueris"
"Again, you're talking about him," she said
"Iterum es habens cogitationes Samana"
"again, you're having a Samana's thoughts"
Siddhartha nihil dixit, et lusum amoris lusit
Siddhartha said nothing, and they played the game of love
inter triginta vel quadraginta ludos diversos Kamala sciens
one of the thirty or forty different games Kamala knew
Corpus eius flexibile erat sicut in quadro
Her body was flexible like that of a jaguar
flexibile sicut arcus venatoris
flexible like the bow of a hunter
qui didicerat ab ea quomodo amare
he who had learned from her how to make love
multarum libidinis gnarus erat
he was knowledgeable of many forms of lust
qui autem ab ea didicit multa secreta sciebat
he that learned from her knew many secrets
Diu lusit cum Siddhartha

For a long time, she played with Siddhartha
decepit et rejecit illum
she enticed him and rejected him
Coegit eum et amplexatus est eum
she forced him and embraced him
illa fruebatur magister artes
she enjoyed his masterful skills
donec victus et fessus quievit ab ea parte
until he was defeated and rested exhausted by her side
Meretrix incubuit super eum
The courtesan bent over him
et tulit diu vultus in faciem suam
she took a long look at his face
oculis aspexit, quae defatigata erat
she looked at his eyes, which had grown tired
"Optimus es amans me umquam" dixit cogitabundus
"You are the best lover I have ever seen" she said thoughtfully
"Tu es aliis fortior, mollioribus, promptioribus".
"You're stronger than others, more supple, more willing"
"Tu meam artem bene didicisti, Siddhartha".
"You've learned my art well, Siddhartha"
"Aliquo tempore, cum maior ero, vellem puerum tuum ferre".
"At some time, when I'll be older, I'd want to bear your child"
"Et tamen, mi, Samana mansisti".
"And yet, my dear, you've remained a Samana"
"et tamen hoc non amas me".
"and despite this, you do not love me"
"nemo est quem amas"
"there is nobody that you love"
"Nonne ita est?" interrogavit Kamala
"Isn't it so?" asked Kamala
"Optime factum est ita", Siddhartha dixit fesse
"It might very well be so," Siddhartha said tiredly
"similis sum tui, quia tu quoque non amas".
"I am like you, because you also do not love"

"Quomodo enim aliud amare potuisti sicut artem?"
"how else could you practise love as a craft?"
"Fortasse homines nostri generis amare non possunt".
"Perhaps, people of our kind can't love"
"Populus puerilis amare potest, id est secretum suum".
"The childlike people can love, that's their secret"

Sansara

Diu Siddhartha in mundo et libidine vixerat
For a long time, Siddhartha had lived in the world and lust
sic tamen sine parte vixit
he lived this way though, without being a part of it
hunc occidisse, cum Samana fuisset
he had killed this off when he had been a Samana
nunc iterum evigilantes
but now they had awoken again
divitias, libidinem, potentiam
he had tasted riches, lust, and power
diu permansit Samana in corde suo
for a long time he had remained a Samana in his heart
Kamala, cum sapias, hoc satis bene intellexit
Kamala, being smart, had realized this quite right
cogitans, expectans et ieiunans adhuc vitam suam regebat
thinking, waiting, and fasting still guided his life
puerili aliena manserunt ei
the childlike people remained alien to him
et mansit alienus a parvulis hominibus
and he remained alien to the childlike people
Anni transierunt; circumfusa vita
Years passed by; surrounded by the good life
Siddhartha vix sensit annos evacuatur
Siddhartha hardly felt the years fading away
Dives factus est, et possedit domum suam;
He had become rich and possessed a house of his own
habuit etiam suos servos
he even had his own servants
hortum habuit ante urbem iuxta fluvium
he had a garden before the city, by the river
Amavit eum populus et venit ad eum pecunia vel consilium
The people liked him and came to him for money or advice
sed nemo ei proximus erat praeter Kamala .
but there was nobody close to him, except Kamala

clara statu vigilandi
the bright state of being awake
Sensus, quem in juventute expertus erat
the feeling which he had experienced at the height of his youth
in diebus illis postquam Gotama in sermone
in those days after Gotama's sermon
post separationem a Govinda
after the separation from Govinda
temporis exspectatione vitae
the tense expectation of life
superbus statum stans solus
the proud state of standing alone
esse sine doctrina vel magistris
being without teachings or teachers
promptum ad audiendum vocem divinam in corde suo
the supple willingness to listen to the divine voice in his own heart
haec omnia tardius in memoriam
all these things had slowly become a memory
memoria fugae, longinquae et quietae
the memory had been fleeting, distant, and quiet
sanctum fontem, qui prope esse solebat, modo murmurabat
the holy source, which used to be near, now only murmured
fons sanctus, qui intra se murmurabat
the holy source, which used to murmur within himself
multa tamen a Samanis didicerat
Nevertheless, many things he had learned from the Samanas
didicerat Gotama
he had learned from Gotama
a patre Brahman didicerat
he had learned from his father the Brahman
pater eius diu manserat
his father had remained within his being for a long time
modicus vitae, laetitia cogitationis, horae meditationis
moderate living, the joy of thinking, hours of meditation

secreta sui ipsius cognitio; aeternum suum
the secret knowledge of the self; his eternal entity
se neque corpus neque conscientiam
the self which is neither body nor consciousness
Multa pars eius adhuc habuit
Many a part of this he still had
sed una pars post aliam submersus fuit
but one part after another had been submerged
et tandem utraque pars pulvis congregentur
and eventually each part gathered dust
rota figuli semel in motu diu convertetur
a potter's wheel, once in motion, will turn for a long time
vigorem amittit tantum tardius
it loses its vigour only slowly
et finitur post tempus
and it comes to a stop only after time
Anima Siddhartha servaverat rotam ascetismi vertendo
Siddhartha's soul had kept on turning the wheel of asceticism
rota cogitationis converterat diutius
the wheel of thinking had kept turning for a long time
differentiae rota diu adhuc versa
the wheel of differentiation had still turned for a long time
sed lente et cunctanter convertit
but it turned slowly and hesitantly
et prope stabat
and it was close to coming to a standstill
Tarde, ut humiditas morientis truncum intrat
Slowly, like humidity entering the dying stem of a tree
implens radicem lente ac putrescere
filling the stem slowly and making it rot
de mundo et desidia intraverat Siddhartha's anima
the world and sloth had entered Siddhartha's soul
tardius implevit animam suam et aggravavit eam
slowly it filled his soul and made it heavy
fecit animam suam lassus et dormivit
it made his soul tired and put it to sleep

Contra, sensus eius vivus factus est
On the other hand, his senses had become alive
multum sensus eius didicerat
there was much his senses had learned
multaque sensus eius experti erant
there was much his senses had experienced
Siddhartha didicerat ad mercaturam
Siddhartha had learned to trade
didicerat uti potestate populi
he had learned how to use his power over people
didicerat gaudere se muliere
he had learned how to enjoy himself with a woman
pulcherrima veste didicerat uti
he had learned how to wear beautiful clothes
didicerat imperare servis
he had learned how to give orders to servants
lavari didicerat aquis odoratis
he had learned how to bathe in perfumed waters
Didicerat teneris ac diligenter cibum manducare
He had learned how to eat tenderly and carefully prepared food
pisces etiam, carnes et gallinas comedit
he even ate fish, meat, and poultry
aromata et dulcia et vinum, quod causat desidiam et oblivionem
spices and sweets and wine, which causes sloth and forgetfulness
Didicerat ludere cum tesseris et in tabula latrunculorum
He had learned to play with dice and on a chess-board
didicerat spectare chorum puellarum
he had learned to watch dancing girls
didicerat se in lectica circumferri
he learned to have himself carried about in a sedan-chair
didicit dormire in molli lecto
he learned to sleep on a soft bed
Sed tamen aliud sentiebat ab aliis

But still he felt different from others
adhuc prae ceteris sentitur
he still felt superior to the others
semper observabat eos aliquo ludibrio
he always watched them with some mockery
semper quidam derisor fuit quomodo de illis sentiret
there was always some mocking disdain to how he felt about them
idem despectus Samana pro plebe mundi
the same disdain a Samana feels for the people of the world

Kamaswami aegrotantem sensit angebatur
Kamaswami was ailing and felt annoyed
sensit contumeliam Siddhartha
he felt insulted by Siddhartha
et angebatur a sollicitudinibus suis quasi mercator
and he was vexed by his worries as a merchant
Siddhartha semper haec ludibrio spectaverat
Siddhartha had always watched these things with mockery
sed magis defessus ludibrio fuerat
but his mockery had become more tired
superior factus quietior
his superiority had become more quiet
sensim insensibile ac pluviale transitum
as slowly imperceptible as the rainy season passing by
tardius, Siddhartha sumpserat aliquid de puerili moribus
slowly, Siddhartha had assumed something of the childlike people's ways
ceperat quidam ex infantia sua
he had gained some of their childishness
et ex timore aliquo
and he had gained some of their fearfulness
atqui, quanto magis illis similes essemus, magis eis invidebat
And yet, the more be become like them the more he envied them

Invidebat illis unum quod illi defuit
He envied them for the one thing that was missing from him
momentum vitae possent apponere
the importance they were able to attach to their lives
quantum passionis in suis gaudiis et timoribus
the amount of passion in their joys and fears
timidis sed dulcem felicitatem perpetuo amore
the fearful but sweet happiness of being constantly in love
Hi amabant se omni tempore
These people were in love with themselves all of the time
mulieres suos liberos, honores vel pecunias
women loved their children, with honours or money
homines se consiliis aut spe dilexerunt
the men loved themselves with plans or hopes
Sed hoc ex eis non didicit
But he did not learn this from them
non didicit gaudium liberorum
he did not learn the joy of children
et non didicit stultitiam eorum
and he did not learn their foolishness
quae maxime cognita erant incommoda
what he mostly learned were their unpleasant things
et despexit haec
and he despised these things
in mane, postquam habuit comitatum
in the morning, after having had company
magis ac magis in lecto diu mansit
more and more he stayed in bed for a long time
sentiebat cogitare et lassata est
he felt unable to think, and was tired
Iratusque est iratus et impatiens cum Kamaswami taeduit eum sollicitudinibus suis
he became angry and impatient when Kamaswami bored him with his worries
risit clarior nimium , cum ludum talorum perdidit
he laughed just too loud when he lost a game of dice

Vultus eius adhuc subtilior et spiritalis ceteris erat
His face was still smarter and more spiritual than others
sed vultus ejus raro risit amplius
but his face rarely laughed anymore
lente, vultus positis aliis notis
slowly, his face assumed other features
et features saepe in faciem dives populus
the features often found in the faces of rich people
voltus tristitiae, aegritudinis, mali humoris
features of discontent, of sickliness, of ill-humour
lineamenta desidiae et amoris defectus
features of sloth, and of a lack of love
morbus animae quem divites habent
the disease of the soul which rich people have
Tarde, hic morbus apprehendit eum
Slowly, this disease grabbed hold of him
sicut tenuis caligo, languor invasit Siddhartha
like a thin mist, tiredness came over Siddhartha
tardius, haec caligo cotidie densius obtinuit aliquid
slowly, this mist got a bit denser every day
obtinuit aliquantulus murkier omnis mensis
it got a bit murkier every month
et omni anno obtinuit aliquid gravius
and every year it got a bit heavier
vestes veterescent cum tempore
dresses become old with time
vestes amittunt pulchro colore in tempore
clothes lose their beautiful colour over time
maculas accipiunt, rugis attrita rimis
they get stains, wrinkles, worn off at the seams
incipiunt ostendere maculis detrita passim
they start to show threadbare spots here and there
Hoc modo Siddhartha scriptor novae vitae erat
this is how Siddhartha's new life was
vita, quam post discessum a Govinda inceperat

the life which he had started after his separation from
Govinda
suam vitam consenuisse et amisso colore
his life had grown old and lost colour
Minus decoris erat ei quam anni praeteriti
there was less splendour to it as the years passed by
rugas colligebat et maculas vitae suae
his life was gathering wrinkles and stains
et abscondita in fundo, dolore et fastidio, exspectabant
and hidden at bottom, disappointment and disgust were
waiting
ostendebant turpitudinem
they were showing their ugliness
Siddhartha non animadvertit haec
Siddhartha did not notice these things
clara et certa voce intra eum recordatus est
he remembered the bright and reliable voice inside of him
animadvertit vocem tacuisse
he noticed the voice had become silent
vox quae in eo tempore excitavit
the voice which had awoken in him at that time
vox quae optimis temporibus eum duxerat
the voice that had guided him in his best times
se captum a mundo
he had been captured by the world
captus libidine, avaritia, desidia
he had been captured by lust, covetousness, sloth
postremo a vilissimis vitiis captus
and finally he had been captured by his most despised vice
quod vitium maxime elusit
the vice which he mocked the most
stultissimus omnium vitiorum
the most foolish one of all vices
avaritiam miserat in corde suo
he had let greed into his heart
Res, possessiones, opes etiam tandem captae sunt

Property, possessions, and riches also had finally captured him
res habens iam ludus ei
having things was no longer a game to him
facta sunt ei omnia in compedibus et oneribus
his possessions had become a shackle and a burden
Mirum ac devium factum erat
It had happened in a strange and devious way
Siddhartha hoc vitium ex ludo taxillorum repperit
Siddhartha had gotten this vice from the game of dice
Samana desisset in corde suo
he had stopped being a Samana in his heart
deinde coepit ludere pecuniam
and then he began to play the game for money
primum ludum cum risu
first he joined the game with a smile
tum casu tantum lusit
at this time he only played casually
volebat iungere mores puerili populo
he wanted to join the customs of the childlike people
nunc vero cum ira et ira increscit
but now he played with an increasing rage and passion
aleator metuendus inter ceteros mercatores erat
He was a feared gambler among the other merchants
sudes tam audacis erant ut pauci eum capere auderent
his stakes were so audacious that few dared to take him on
Ludum lusit propter dolorem cordis sui
He played the game due to a pain of his heart
perdens et perdens pecuniam miseram attulit ei laetitiam iratam
losing and wasting his wretched money brought him an angry joy
non aliter opum fastidium demonstrare potuit
he could demonstrate his disdain for wealth in no other way
non potuit meliore modo falsus mercator deridere
he could not mock the merchants' false god in a better way

Itaque lusit alta sudes
so he gambled with high stakes
inclementer se oderat et se ipsum illusit
he mercilessly hated himself and mocked himself
millia vicit, abjecit millia
he won thousands, threw away thousands
pecuniam, ornamenta, domum ruri amisit
he lost money, jewellery, a house in the country
vicit iterum et iterum amisit
he won it again, and then he lost again
amavit timorem , dum volvens sortem
he loved the fear he felt while he was rolling the dice
amavit affectum sollicitos de amissis quod lusit
he loved feeling worried about losing what he gambled
semper hunc timorem leviter altius assequi cupiebat
he always wanted to get this fear to a slightly higher level
tantum aliquid felicitatis sensit, cum hunc timorem sensit
he only felt something like happiness when he felt this fear
factum est quasi ebrietas
it was something like an intoxication
aliquid simile vitae formam elevatum
something like an elevated form of life
quid lucidius in medio vita sua hebetata
something brighter in the midst of his dull life
Et post magnum uniuscuiusque detrimentum, novis divitiis mens intenta est
And after each big loss, his mind was set on new riches
mercaturam studiosius prosecutus est
he pursued the trade more zealously
debitores suos arctius solvere coegit
he forced his debtors more strictly to pay
quia voluit permanere alea
because he wanted to continue gambling
volebat pergere spargens
he wanted to continue squandering
voluit ostendere fastidium divitiarum permanere

he wanted to continue demonstrating his disdain of wealth
Siddhartha amisit tranquillitatem cum damna facta
Siddhartha lost his calmness when losses occurred
patientiam amisit, cum in tempore non esset
he lost his patience when he was not paid on time
erga mendicos misericordiam amisit
he lost his kindness towards beggars
decem milia lusit in uno volumine taxillorum
He gambled away tens of thousands at one roll of the dice
in negotiis suis arctior et pusillus factus est
he became more strict and more petty in his business
interdum de pecunia nocte somniabat!
occasionally, he was dreaming at night about money!
quotiens ex turpi carmine evigilavit, fugiens
whenever he woke up from this ugly spell, he continued fleeing
quotiens faciem in speculo senuit, novum ludum invenit
whenever he found his face in the mirror to have aged, he found a new game
quotienscumque illi pudor et fastidium accessit, torpebat animum
whenever embarrassment and disgust came over him, he numbed his mind
torpescit mente sexus et vino
he numbed his mind with sex and wine
inde in stimulum struere et obtinere possessiones
and from there he fled back into the urge to pile up and obtain possessions
In hoc inani cyclo cucurrit
In this pointless cycle he ran
e vita lassatur, senex et male
from his life he grow tired, old, and ill

Tunc advenit tempus, quo somnium eum admonuit
Then the time came when a dream warned him
Horas vespertinas cum Kamala

He had spent the hours of the evening with Kamala
quod in pulchrae voluptatis horto
he had been in her beautiful pleasure-garden
Sub arboribus sedebant, colloquentes
They had been sitting under the trees, talking
et Kamala dixit cogitationibus verbis
and Kamala had said thoughtful words
verba post quae tristitia et languor latebat
words behind which a sadness and tiredness lay hidden
Quaesivit ut nuntiaret sibi de Gotama
She had asked him to tell her about Gotama
non poterat audire satis ab eo
she could not hear enough of him
quam dilexit eam purgare oculos eius
she loved how clear his eyes were
quam adhuc et amavit pulchra os suum
she loved how still and beautiful his mouth was
amavit misericordiam risus
she loved the kindness of his smile
et amavit quam pacificus in deambulatio fuerat
she loved how peaceful his walk had been
Diu narrare ei de praecelso Buddha
For a long time, he had to tell her about the exalted Buddha
et Kamala ingemuit et locutus est
and Kamala had sighed, and spoke
"Olim fortasse mox, Buddha etiam sequar"
"One day, perhaps soon, I'll also follow that Buddha"
"Dabo illi hortum meum pro munere".
"I'll give him my pleasure-garden for a gift"
et in doctrinis eius sperabo.
"and I will take my refuge in his teachings"
Post haec autem eum excitavit
But after this, she had aroused him
ligaverat eum sibi in actu venereorum
she had tied him to her in the act of making love
cum dolore dolorosa, mordens et lacrimans

with painful fervour, biting and in tears
quasi ex hoc vino stillam dulcem exprimere vellet
it was as if she wanted to squeeze the last sweet drop out of this wine
Numquam antea tam mirum in modum patuit Siddhartha
Never before had it become so strangely clear to Siddhartha
sensit quam arcta libido morti propinquior
he felt how close lust was akin to death
iuxta eam posuit, et facies Kamala ei iuncta erat
he laid by her side, and Kamala's face was close to him
sub oculis eius et iuxta angulos oris eius
under her eyes and next to the corners of her mouth
fuit sicut patet quod numquam prius
it was as clear as never before
ibi legitur pavidum inscriptum
there read a fearful inscription
tituli lineolae et tenues striati
an inscription of small lines and slight grooves
epigramma simile autumni et senectutis
an inscription reminiscent of autumn and old age
passim cani inter nigras
here and there, gray hairs among his black ones
Ipse Siddhartha, qui tantum in suis forties erat, idem animadvertit
Siddhartha himself, who was only in his forties, noticed the same thing
Tedium scriptum est in pulchra facie Kamala
Tiredness was written on Kamala's beautiful face
languor ambulans longam viam
tiredness from walking a long path
per viam quae non habet beatus destination
a path which has no happy destination
languor et principium arescentes
tiredness and the beginning of withering
metu senectutis autumni et mori
fear of old age, autumn, and having to die

Cum gemitu valedicere ei iussisset
With a sigh, he had bid his farewell to her
anima plena pigritiae, plena sollicitudinis occultae
the soul full of reluctance, and full of concealed anxiety

Siddhartha pernoctavit in domo sua cum puellis choris
Siddhartha had spent the night in his house with dancing girls
ut si superior esset
he acted as if he was superior to them
praelatos erga sodales sui ordinis
he acted superior towards the fellow-members of his caste
sed hoc non est verum
but this was no longer true
multo vino illa nocte biberat
he had drunk much wine that night
et dormivit post mediam noctem
and he went to bed a long time after midnight
fessi et tamen excitati ad fletum et desperationem
tired and yet excited, close to weeping and despair
diu quaerebat dormire, sed frustra
for a long time he sought to sleep, but it was in vain
cor eius erat miseriae plenum
his heart was full of misery
diutius se ferre non posse existimabat
he thought he could not bear any longer
ille fastidio plenus, quo totum corpus penetrabat;
he was full of a disgust, which he felt penetrating his entire body
sicut egelidum foedi saporis vini
like the lukewarm repulsive taste of the wine
musica hebes nimium felix fuit paulo
the dull music was a little too happy
Risus puellarum paulo mollior
the smile of the dancing girls was a little too soft
redolet crines pectoraque paulo nimium dulces
the scent of their hair and breasts was a little too sweet

Sed plusquam aliud taedium sibi
But more than by anything else, he was disgusted by himself
taedet unguentis crinibus
he was disgusted by his perfumed hair
odor vini ex ore ejus fastiditus
he was disgusted by the smell of wine from his mouth
taedio cutis inertia
he was disgusted by the listlessness of his skin
Sicut cum aliquis qui comedit et bibit nimis
Like when someone who has eaten and drunk far too much
iterum evomunt dolore cruciabili
they vomit it back up again with agonising pain
sed levari sentiunt vomitus
but they feel relieved by the vomiting
hic insomnis his voluptatibus se liberare voluit
this sleepless man wished to free himself of these pleasures
his moribus carere voluit
he wanted to be rid of these habits
voluit effugere omnes huius inanis vitae
he wanted to escape all of this pointless life
et ex se effugere cupiebat
and he wanted to escape from himself
non usque ad lucem matutinam cum leviter dormierit
it wasn't until the light of the morning when he had slightly fallen sleep
primum actiones in platea iam inciperent
the first activities in the street were already beginning
parumper somnos admonitus invenerat
for a few moments he had found a hint of sleep
His temporibus somnium
In those moments, he had a dream
Kamala parva et rara avis cantus in aurea cavea
Kamala owned a small, rare singing bird in a golden cage
ei semper mane canebat
it always sung to him in the morning
sed tunc somniavit hanc avem obmutuisse

but then he dreamt this bird had become mute
quo facto animum advertit ante caveam
since this arose his attention, he stepped in front of the cage
respexit ad avem intra caveam
he looked at the bird inside the cage
avicula mortua est, et rigens in terra jacuit
the small bird was dead, and lay stiff on the ground
Avem mortuam e cavea tulit
He took the dead bird out of its cage
accepit autem momento ponderis avem mortuam in manu sua
he took a moment to weigh the dead bird in his hand
et proiecit eum foras in platea
and then threw it away, out in the street
eodem momento perculsa sensit
in the same moment he felt terribly shocked
cor ejus dolet quasi proiecisset omnem valorem
his heart hurt as if he had thrown away all value
omne bonum hoc intus fuerat avis mortua
everything good had been inside of this dead bird
Ab hoc somnio excitus, gravi tristitia circumventum sensit
Starting up from this dream, he felt encompassed by a deep sadness
quae videbantur ei viles erant
everything seemed worthless to him
vanus et vanus erat via per quam vita erat
worthless and pointless was the way he had been going through life
nihil quod vivus in manibus relictum erat
nothing which was alive was left in his hands
nihil quod aliquo modo delectabile posset custodiri
nothing which was in some way delicious could be kept
nihil valet observatio maneret
nothing worth keeping would stay
solus ibi stabat, inanis ut litore iectus
alone he stood there, empty like a castaway on the shore

- 153 -

Mente tristis, Siddhartha abiit ad hortum suum
With a gloomy mind, Siddhartha went to his pleasure-garden
Et clausit portam, et sedit sub mango
he locked the gate and sat down under a mango-tree
sensit mortem in corde et horror in pectore
he felt death in his heart and horror in his chest
sensit, quomodo omnia in eo mortua sint et aruit
he sensed how everything died and withered in him
Mox, cogitationem in mente collegit
By and by, he gathered his thoughts in his mind
iterumque per totam vitae suae semitam pertransivit
once again, he went through the entire path of his life
incepit cum primis diebus non recordabor
he started with the first days he could remember
Quando umquam fuit quando veram beatitudinem senserat?
When was there ever a time when he had felt a true bliss?
Immo aliquoties tale expertus erat
Oh yes, several times he had experienced such a thing
Puer in annis eius gustum habuit beatitudinis
In his years as a boy he had had a taste of bliss
quod felicitatem in corde acceperat, cum laudem adeptus est a Brachmans
he had felt happiness in his heart when he obtained praise from the Brahmans
"Est via ante eum qui se ipsum distinxit".
"There is a path in front of the one who has distinguished himself"

..
he had felt bliss reciting the holy verses
senserat beatum disputare cum doctis
he had felt bliss disputing with the learned ones
senserat beatum, cum esset assistens in oblationibus
he had felt bliss when he was an assistant in the offerings
Tunc sensit in corde suo
Then, he had felt it in his heart

"Est iter in conspectu tuo"
"There is a path in front of you"
"Hoc iter destinati estis"
"you are destined for this path"
"dii te exspectant"
"the gods are awaiting you"
Et iterum, sicut iuvenis, beatitudinem sensit
And again, as a young man, he had felt bliss
cum separaverunt eum a cogitationibus suis
when his thoughts separated him from those thinking on the same things
cum luctaretur in dolore ad Brahman
when he wrestled in pain for the purpose of Brahman
cum omnis scientia parta nova in eo sitim accenderet
when every obtained knowledge only kindled new thirst in him
hoc ipsum in medio dolore sensit
in the midst of the pain he felt this very same thing
"Age! Invocatus es!"
"Go on! You are called upon!"
Hanc vocem audivit cum domo exisset
He had heard this voice when he had left his home
hanc vocem audivit, cum eum vitam Samana elegisset
he heard heard this voice when he had chosen the life of a Samana
et iterum hanc vocem audivit, cum exiret Samanas
and again he heard this voice when left the Samanas
audierat vocem quando ivit ad videndum perfectum
he had heard the voice when he went to see the perfected one
et cum ab perfecto discessisset, audivit vocem
and when he had gone away from the perfected one, he had heard the voice
vocem audierat, cum in incertam vocem ibat
he had heard the voice when he went into the uncertain
Quamdiu enim non audierat hanc vocem amplius?
For how long had he not heard this voice anymore?

quousque enim non pervenit amplius altitudo?
for how long had he reached no height anymore?
quam par erat et hebes, quomodo vita transierit?
how even and dull was the manner in which he went through life?
per multos annos diu sine fine magno
for many long years without a high goal
fuisset sine siti vel elevatione
he had been without thirst or elevation
parvis libidinibus contentum fuisse
he had been content with small lustful pleasures
et tamen numquam fuit contentus!
and yet he was never satisfied!
Per hos omnes annos conatus est difficile fieri sicut caeteri
For all of these years he had tried hard to become like the others
cupiebat unus ex parvulis populus
he longed to be one of the childlike people
sed nesciebat id quod vere voluit
but he didn't know that that was what he really wanted
vita sua multo miserior et pauperior illis fuerat
his life had been much more miserable and poorer than theirs
quia metas et sollicitudines non his
because their goals and worries were not his
universum mundum Kamaswami-populus solus ei ludus fuerat
the entire world of the Kamaswami-people had only been a game to him
vita eorum chorus esset observaturus
their lives were a dance he would watch
comoediam fecerunt ut se oblectare posset
they performed a comedy he could amuse himself with
Tantum Kamala carus ac pretiosus
Only Kamala had been dear and valuable to him
sed erat adhuc pretiosus?
but was she still valuable to him?

Etiamne opus est ea?
Did he still need her?
An adhuc eo opus erat?
Or did she still need him?
Nonne sine fine ludunt?
Did they not play a game without an ending?
an propter hoc necesse erat vivere?
Was it necessary to live for this?
Non, necesse erat!
No, it was not necessary!
Nomen huius ludi erat Sansara
The name of this game was Sansara
ludus puerorum, qui fortasse aliquando iucundus fuit
a game for children which was perhaps enjoyable to play once
fortasse bis
maybe it could be played twice
fortasse potes illud decies
perhaps you could play it ten times
sed tu eam ludis in saecula saeculorum?
but should you play it for ever and ever?
Tum Siddhartha scivit ludum esse nimis
Then, Siddhartha knew that the game was over
sciebat se amplius agere non posse
he knew that he could not play it any more
Currens corpus eius intus tremiscit
Shivers ran over his body and inside of him
sentiebat quod mortuus esset
he felt that something had died

Toto die ille sedit sub mango
That entire day, he sat under the mango-tree
cogitabat patris
he was thinking of his father
Govinda cogitabat
he was thinking of Govinda
et Gotama cogitabat

and he was thinking of Gotama
Nonne eas relinquere fecit ut Kamaswami fierent?
Did he have to leave them to become a Kamaswami?
Sedebat ibi cum nox cecidisset
He was still sitting there when the night had fallen
stellas conspexit, et cogitabat sibi
he caught sight of the stars, and thought to himself
"**Hic sedeo sub mango meo in horto meo**".
"Here I'm sitting under my mango-tree in my pleasure-garden"
Subridens sibi paulum
He smiled a little to himself
an vere necessarium erat hortum habere?
was it really necessary to own a garden?
nonne ludus stultus?
was it not a foolish game?
numquid opus est habere mango-arborem?
did he need to own a mango-tree?
Etiam huic finem imposuit
He also put an end to this
et hoc in ipso mortuus est
this also died in him
Qui surgens valedicens mango
He rose and bid his farewell to the mango-tree
ad viridarium suum valedicere iubet
he bid his farewell to the pleasure-garden
Cum hodie cibo caruisset, magnam famem sensit
Since he had been without food this day, he felt strong hunger
et cogitavit domum suam in civitate
and he thought of his house in the city
thalamum , cubile
he thought of his chamber and bed
putabat mensae cibum in eo
he thought of the table with the meals on it
subridens lassus ipse valefaciensque ad haec se quatiebat

He smiled tiredly, shook himself, and bid his farewell to these things
Eadem hora noctis Siddhartha hortum suum reliquit
In the same hour of the night, Siddhartha left his garden
ex urbe numquam rediit
he left the city and never came back

Diu Kamaswami homines exspectant eum
For a long time, Kamaswami had people look for him
in latrones incidisse putabant
they thought he had fallen into the hands of robbers
Kamala neminem exspectamus
Kamala had no one look for him
non obstupefactus ablatione sua
she was not astonished by his disappearance
Nonne semper expectat?
Did she not always expect it?
non erat Samana?
Was he not a Samana?
homo domi nusquam, peregrinus
a man who was at home nowhere, a pilgrim
sensit hoc ultimum tempus fuisse
she had felt this the last time they had been together
fuit felix non obstante omni amissionis dolore
she was happy despite all the pain of the loss
beatus erat cum eo unum extremum tempus
she was happy she had been with him one last time
laeta erat quae tam amanter ad cor traxit eum
she was happy she had pulled him so affectionately to her heart
illa laeta erat quae ab eo penitus possessa et penetrata sensit
she was happy she had felt completely possessed and penetrated by him
Quae cum accepisset nuntium, ivit ad fenestram
When she received the news, she went to the window
per fenestram tenuit rara avis

at the window she held a rare singing bird
avem aurea cavea captivus
the bird was held captive in a golden cage
Ea cavea ostium aperuit
She opened the door of the cage
et tulit eam avem et volare
she took the bird out and let it fly
Diu intuebatur eam
For a long time, she gazed after it
Ex hoc die amplius visitatores non accepit
From this day on, she received no more visitors
et clausa domum suam custodivit
and she kept her house locked
Post aliquod autem tempus concepit eam concepisse
But after some time, she became aware that she was pregnant
gravida ab ultimo tempore fuit cum Siddhartha
she was pregnant from the last time she was with Siddhartha

Ad flumen
By the River

Siddhartha ambulavit per silvam
Siddhartha walked through the forest
iam procul urbe
he was already far from the city
et nihil sciebat nisi unum
and he knew nothing but one thing
non est reversus ad eum
there was no going back for him
vita, quam multos annos vixerat, supererat
the life that he had lived for many years was over
gustaverat omnes vitae
he had tasted all of this life
omnia ex hac vita suxerat
he had sucked everything out of this life
donec fastidiens
until he was disgusted with it
cantus avem quam viderat mortuus est
the singing bird he had dreamt of was dead
et avem in corde suo mortua est
and the bird in his heart was dead too
penitus impeditus Sansarae
he had been deeply entangled in Sansara
fastidium et mortem in corpus suxit
he had sucked up disgust and death into his body
spongia sugit aquam donec sit plenum
like a sponge sucks up water until it is full
erat enim miseriae et mortis plenus
he was full of misery and death
nihil erat in hoc mundo quod eum attrahere posset
there was nothing left in this world which could have attracted him
nihil ei laetitiae vel consolationis dare potuit
nothing could have given him joy or comfort

nihil de se amplius scire cupiebat
he passionately wished to know nothing about himself anymore
habere requiem voluit et mortuus est
he wanted to have rest and be dead
fulmen voluit fuisse ut eum mortuum feriret.
he wished there was a lightning-bolt to strike him dead!
Utinam esset tigris ut devoraret eum!
If there only was a tiger to devour him!
Vinum si venenatum, quod sensus obstupefacit
If there only was a poisonous wine which would numb his senses
vinum, quod ei oblivionem et somnum attulit
a wine which brought him forgetfulness and sleep
vinum unde non evigilabit
a wine from which he wouldn't awake from
Ecquis adhuc erat qui se sordibus inquinaret?
Was there still any kind of filth he had not soiled himself with?
an erat peccatum aut stulte factum, quod non commiserat?
was there a sin or foolish act he had not committed?
an intimitas animae nesciebat?
was there a dreariness of the soul he didn't know?
ecquisnam ipse non attulisset?
was there anything he had not brought upon himself?
adhuc vivere poterat?
Was it still at all possible to be alive?
Potuitne iterum atque iterum respirare?
Was it possible to breathe in again and again?
Poteratne adhuc spirare?
Could he still breathe out?
Potuitne famem ferre?
was he able to bear hunger?
ecquis iter ad manducandum recepit?
was there any way to eat again?
iterum dormire potuit?

was it possible to sleep again?
potuit dormire cum muliere adhuc?
could he sleep with a woman again?
Nonne hic cyclus defatigatus est?
had this cycle not exhausted itself?
non ad exitum perducta sunt?
were things not brought to their conclusion?

Siddhartha pervenit ad magnum flumen in silva
Siddhartha reached the large river in the forest
idem amnis, cum adhuc adulescens fuisset, traiecit
it was the same river he crossed when he had still been a young man
idem flumen transiit ab oppido Gotamana
it was the same river he crossed from the town of Gotama
recordatus est portitor qui eum trans fluvium duxerat
he remembered a ferryman who had taken him over the river
Hoc flumine constitit, et cunctanter ad ripam constitit
By this river he stopped, and hesitantly he stood at the bank
Taedium et fames infirmaverat eum
Tiredness and hunger had weakened him
"Quid ambulo pro?"
"what should I walk on for?"
"quorsum ibi relictum eat?"
"to what goal was there left to go?"
Immo nihil amplius proposita
No, there were no more goals
nihil supererat nisi laboriosus ad excutiendum hoc somnium
there was nothing left but a painful yearning to shake off this dream
desiderabat exspue hoc vinum
he yearned to spit out this stale wine
huic miserae ac turpissimae vitae finem imponere voluit
he wanted to put an end to this miserable and shameful life
Cocoes arbor super ripam fluminis
a coconut-tree bent over the bank of the river

Siddhartha innixa trunco suo umero
Siddhartha leaned against its trunk with his shoulder
amplexus truncum brachio
he embraced the trunk with one arm
et despexit in aquam viridem
and he looked down into the green water
aqua sub eo
the water ran under him
despexit et invenit se totum velle dimittere
he looked down and found himself to be entirely filled with the wish to let go
in his aquis mergere voluit
he wanted to drown in these waters
meticulosa inanitate aquae reflectitur ad eum
the water reflected a frightening emptiness back at him
respondit aqua magnae vanitati animae suae
the water answered to the terrible emptiness in his soul
Etiam ad finem pervenerat
Yes, he had reached the end
nihil sibi relictum, nisi ut deleret
There was nothing left for him, except to annihilate himself
voluit frangere defectum in quo vitam suam formaverat
he wanted to smash the failure into which he had shaped his life
animam suam voluit proicere ante pedes deorum irridentium
he wanted to throw his life before the feet of mockingly laughing gods
Hic magnus vomitus desideratus est; mortem
This was the great vomiting he had longed for; death
frena formae oderat
the smashing to bits of the form he hated
Sit cibus piscibus et crocodilis
Let him be food for fishes and crocodiles
Siddhartha canis, lunaticus
Siddhartha the dog, a lunatic

corpus pravum et corruptum; infirmata et abusa anima!
a depraved and rotten body; a weakened and abused soul!
a daemonibus concisus sit
let him be chopped to bits by the daemons
Vultu distorto, aspiciens in aquam
With a distorted face, he stared into the water
vidit imaginem vultus sui et exspuit ad illum
he saw the reflection of his face and spat at it
In alta tedia tulit bracchium de trunco arboris
In deep tiredness, he took his arm away from the trunk of the tree
vertit aliquantulum, ut se in directum demitteret
he turned a bit, in order to let himself fall straight down
ut tandem demergat in flumine
in order to finally drown in the river
Occisis oculis, ad mortem lapsus est
With his eyes closed, he slipped towards death
Deinde, e longinquis locis animae, sonus excitatur
Then, out of remote areas of his soul, a sound stirred up
sonus excitatus ex praeteritis vitae suae temporibus
a sound stirred up out of past times of his now weary life
Verbum singulare, una syllaba
It was a singular word, a single syllable
sine cogitatione vocem sibi dixit
without thinking he spoke the voice to himself
initium finemque omnium orationum Brachmanarum aggressus est
he slurred the beginning and the end of all prayers of the Brahmans
sanctus Om . locutus est
he spoke the holy Om
id quod perfectum est seu perfectio;
"that what is perfect" or "the completion"
Et statim cognovit stultitiam operum suorum
And in the moment he realized the foolishness of his actions
sonitus Om tetigit Siddhartha in aurem

the sound of Om touched Siddhartha's ear
sopitam spiritum repente expergefactus
his dormant spirit suddenly woke up
Siddhartha valde abhorrent
Siddhartha was deeply shocked
hoc videbat quomodo se haberet
he saw this was how things were with him
sic erat moriturus ut mortem quaerere posset
he was so doomed that he had been able to seek death
tantum amiserat ut finem vellet
he had lost his way so much that he wished the end
voluntas puerilis in eo crescere potuisset
the wish of a child had been able to grow in him
quiescere voluisset exstincto corpore.
he had wished to find rest by annihilating his body!
omnibus doloribus recentibus temporibus
all the agony of recent times
omnem vitam suam creaverat sobrietate
all sobering realizations that his life had created
omnem desperationem quam senserat
all the desperation that he had felt
Haec non hoc tempore
these things did not bring about this moment
Cum autem Om in conscientiam suam intrasset, se ipsum sensit
when the Om entered his consciousness he became aware of himself
intellexit suam miseriam et errorem suum
he realized his misery and his error
Om! locutus est ad se
Om! he spoke to himself
Om! et iterum sciebat de Brahman
Om! and again he knew about Brahman
Om! sciebat de incorruptibilitate vitae
Om! he knew about the indestructibility of life
Om! noverat omnia divina, quae oblitus erat

Om! he knew about all that is divine, which he had forgotten
Sed hoc momentum fuit quod coram eo emicuit
But this was only a moment that flashed before him
Ad pedem arboris Cocoes Siddhartha corruit
By the foot of the coconut-tree, Siddhartha collapsed
per languorem percussus est
he was struck down by tiredness
sono "Om", imposuit caput super radicem arboris
mumbling "Om", he placed his head on the root of the tree
et incidit in soporem;
and he fell into a deep sleep
Profundus somnus erat et sine somniis
Deep was his sleep, and without dreams
diu talem somnum non noverat amplius
for a long time he had not known such a sleep any more

Evigilans post multas horas, sensit quasi decem annos elapsos
When he woke up after many hours, he felt as if ten years had passed
audivit aquam quiete fluentem
he heard the water quietly flowing
nesciebat unde esset
he did not know where he was
nec sciebat quis eum huc adduxisset
and he did not know who had brought him here
aperuit oculos suos et vidit stuporem
he opened his eyes and looked with astonishment
ibi erant arbores et caelum sursum
there were trees and the sky above him
recordatus est ubi esset et quomodo hic
he remembered where he was and how he got here
Sed diu hoc eum cepit
But it took him a long while for this
praeterita videbantur ei velo
the past seemed to him as if it had been covered by a veil

in infinitum, in infinitum, in infinitum, in infinitum, in infinitum, in infinitum
infinitely distant, infinitely far away, infinitely meaningless
Solus scivit priorem vitam relictam esse
He only knew that his previous life had been abandoned
haec anteacta vita quasi antiquissimum, ante incarnationem ei videbatur
this past life seemed to him like a very old, previous incarnation
haec vita anteacta sentitur quasi prae-nascentis sui ipsius
this past life felt like a pre-birth of his present self
offensionibus et miseriis destinaverat vitam abicere
full of disgust and wretchedness, he had intended to throw his life away
resipiscat per flumen sub arbore Cocoes
he had come to his senses by a river, under a coconut-tree
sanctum verbum "Om" erat in ore ejus
the holy word "Om" was on his lips
dormierat et iam excitatus est
he had fallen asleep and had now woken up
hoc spectabat mundum ut novum hominem
he was looking at the world as a new man
Quiete verbum "Om" ad se locutus est
Quietly, he spoke the word "Om" to himself
the "Om" loquebatur cum obdormisset
the "Om" he was speaking when he had fallen asleep
eius somnus nihil aliud sensit quam longam meditationem recitationis "Om"
his sleep felt like nothing more than a long meditative recitation of "Om"
totus dormiens cogitabat "Om"
all his sleep had been a thinking of "Om"
submergence et integram introitum "Om"
a submergence and complete entering into "Om"
ingressus in perfecto et perfecto
a going into the perfected and completed

Quantus hic fuit somnus mirabilis!
What a wonderful sleep this had been!
numquam ante ita somno refectus est
he had never before been so refreshed by sleep
Fortasse vere mortuus erat
Perhaps, he really had died
forte submersus et renatus in corpore novo?
maybe he had drowned and was reborn in a new body?
Sed non ipsum quis erat
But no, he knew himself and who he was
sciebat manus et pedes
he knew his hands and his feet
sciebat locum ubi iacebat
he knew the place where he lay
hoc sciebat se in pectore suo
he knew this self in his chest
Siddhartha eccentricus, fatum one
Siddhartha the eccentric, the weird one
sed haec Siddhartha nihilominus transfigurata est
but this Siddhartha was nevertheless transformed
mirum in modum quievit
he was strangely well rested and awake
et gavisus et curiosus
and he was joyful and curious

Siddhartha erecta et circumspiciebat
Siddhartha straightened up and looked around
Et vidit hominem sedentem contra eum
then he saw a person sitting opposite to him
monachus in pallio luteo cum rasa capite
a monk in a yellow robe with a shaven head
sedebat in loco cogitans
he was sitting in the position of pondering
Hominem observavit, qui neque capillum habebat neque caput barbatum

He observed the man, who had neither hair on his head nor a beard
non diu eum observaverat, cum hunc monachum agnovisset
he had not observed him for long when he recognised this monk
erat Govinda, amicus iuventutis suae
it was Govinda, the friend of his youth
Govinda, qui cum praecelso Buddha confugit
Govinda, who had taken his refuge with the exalted Buddha
Sicut Siddhartha, Govinda etiam senex
Like Siddhartha, Govinda had also aged
sed vultus etiamnum eadem voltus gestabat
but his face still bore the same features
vultus tamen exprimit zelum et fidem
his face still expressed zeal and faithfulness
videres eum adhuc quaerere, sed timide
you could see he was still searching, but timidly
Govinda eius intuitum persensit, oculos aperuit, et eum aspexit
Govinda sensed his gaze, opened his eyes, and looked at him
Siddhartha vidit Govinda eum non agnovisse
Siddhartha saw that Govinda did not recognise him
Govinda beatus erat ut eum excitaret
Govinda was happy to find him awake
videtur hic diu sedisse
apparently, he had been sitting here for a long time
exspectaverat eum excitare
he had been waiting for him to wake up
exspectavit, licet eum ignoraret
he waited, although he did not know him
"Dormivi" dixit Siddhartha
"I have been sleeping" said Siddhartha
"Quomodo huc venisti?"
"How did you get here?"
"Dormivisti" respondit Govinda
"You have been sleeping" answered Govinda

"Non est bonum in talibus locis dormire".
"It is not good to be sleeping in such places"
" Serpentes et bestiae silvarum tramites hic habent " .
"snakes and the animals of the forest have their paths here"
« Ego, o domine, Gotama excelsi imitator sum ».
"I, oh sir, am a follower of the exalted Gotama"
"In hac via fui peregrinatus".
"I was on a pilgrimage on this path"
"Vidi te iacentem et dormientem in loco ubi periculosum est dormire"
"I saw you lying and sleeping in a place where it is dangerous to sleep"
"Ergo volui te excitare".
"Therefore, I sought to wake you up"
"sed vidi quod somnus tuus profundus erat".
"but I saw that your sleep was very deep"
"mansi post e sodalitate"
"so I stayed behind from my group"
"et sedebam vobiscum donec expergefactus es"
"and I sat with you until you woke up"
"Et tunc, ut videtur, ego ipse dormivi".
"And then, so it seems, I have fallen asleep myself"
"Ego, qui somnum tuum servare volui, obdormivi."
"I, who wanted to guard your sleep, fell asleep"
"Male, tibi parui".
"Badly, I have served you"
"tedium me oppresserat"
"tiredness had overwhelmed me"
"Sed quia vigilas, permitte me adsequi cum fratribus meis".
"But since you're awake, let me go to catch up with my brothers"
"Gratias tibi ago, Samana, quod per somnum meum vigilans" locutus est Siddhartha .
"I thank you, Samana, for watching out over my sleep" spoke Siddhartha
« Vos amici estis, sectatores excelsi ».

"You're friendly, you followers of the exalted one"
"Nunc eas adeas".
"Now you may go to them"
"Eo, domine. Sit tibi semper bene valere"
"I'm going, sir. May you always be in good health"
"Gratias tibi ago, Samana"
"I thank you, Samana"
Govinda salutationis verba fecit et dixit "Vale".
Govinda made the gesture of a salutation and said "Farewell"
"Vale Govinda" Siddhartha . dixit
"Farewell, Govinda" said Siddhartha
Monachus sistitur quasi de caelo tacta
The monk stopped as if struck by lightning
"Permitte me quaerere, domine, unde nosti nomen meum?"
"Permit me to ask, sir, from where do you know my name?"
Siddhartha risit, "Novi te, o Govinda, ex casa patris tui".
Siddhartha smiled, "I know you, oh Govinda, from your father's hut"
"et scio te e schola Brachmanarum".
"and I know you from the school of the Brahmans"
et ego novi vos de oblationibus.
"and I know you from the offerings"
"et scio te ex itinere nostro ad Samanas".
"and I know you from our walk to the Samanas"
"et scio te ex quo confugisti cum excelso".
"and I know you from when you took refuge with the exalted one"
"Tu Siddhartha es", Govinda magna voce exclamavit, "Nunc te agnosco".
"You're Siddhartha," Govinda exclaimed loudly, "Now, I recognise you"
"Non comprehendo quomodo non possum te statim agnoscere"
"I don't comprehend how I couldn't recognise you right away"
"Siddhartha, gaudium meum magnum est te videre iterum"
"Siddhartha, my joy is great to see you again"

"Hoc quoque mihi gaudium dat, ut te iterum videam" locutus est Siddhartha .
"It also gives me joy, to see you again" spoke Siddhartha
"Tu fuisti custodia somni mei"
"You've been the guard of my sleep"
" iterum gratias ago tibi pro hoc "
"again, I thank you for this"
"sed ego nullam custodiam requirebam".
"but I wouldn't have required any guard"
"Quo tenditis, o amice?"
"Where are you going to, oh friend?"
"Nusquam vado", Govinda respondit
"I'm going nowhere," answered Govinda
"Monachi sumus semper iter"
"We monks are always travelling"
"quoties tempus pluvium non est, ex uno loco in alium transferemus".
"whenever it is not the rainy season, we move from one place to another"
"vivimus secundum praecepta doctrinarum quae nobis tradita sunt".
"we live according to the rules of the teachings passed on to us"
" eleemosynas accipimus, et tunc movemur ".
"we accept alms, and then we move on"
"Semper sic est"
"It is always like this"
"At tu, Siddhartha, quo tendis?"
"But you, Siddhartha, where are you going to?"
"Mecum est sicut apud te"
"for me it is as it is with you"
"Eo nusquam, Im 'iustus iter"
"I'm going nowhere; I'm just travelling"
"Ego quoque in peregrinatione sum".
"I'm also on a pilgrimage"

Govinda locutus est "Tu dicis te esse in peregrinatione et credo te".
Govinda spoke "You say you're on a pilgrimage, and I believe you"
"At, ignosce mihi, o Siddhartha, peregrinus non videris".
"But, forgive me, oh Siddhartha, you do not look like a pilgrim"
"Vestem divitis geris".
"You're wearing a rich man's garments"
"calceatis viri egregii"
"you're wearing the shoes of a distinguished gentleman"
et coma tua in odore unguenti non est coma peregrina.
"and your hair, with the fragrance of perfume, is not a pilgrim's hair"
"capillum Samanae non habes"
"you do not have the hair of a Samana"
"Recte dicis, mi"
"you are right, my dear"
"Quae bene observasti"
"you have observed things well"
"Oculi tui acuti vident omnia"
"your keen eyes see everything"
"Sed non dixi vobis Samana me esse"
"But I haven't said to you that I was a Samana"
"Dixi me in peregrinatione"
"I said I'm on a pilgrimage"
"Et sic est: Ego peregrinor".
"And so it is, I'm on a pilgrimage"
"In peregrinatione es" dixit Govinda .
"You're on a pilgrimage" said Govinda
"Sed pauci in talibus vestibus peregrinantur".
"But few would go on a pilgrimage in such clothes"
"pauci in tali calceis pilger"
"few would pilger in such shoes"
"et pauci peregrini tales habent capillos."
"and few pilgrims have such hair"

"Nunquam talem peregrinum conveni".
"I have never met such a pilgrim"
"et peregrinatus sum multis annis".
"and I have been a pilgrim for many years"
"Credo tibi, mi Govinda".
"I believe you, my dear Govinda"
"Sed nunc hodie peregrinum hoc modo convenisti".
"But now, today, you've met a pilgrim just like this"
"Peregrinus has species calceos et amictus".
"a pilgrim wearing these kinds of shoes and garment"
"Memento, karissime, mundus apparentiarum non est aeternus";
"Remember, my dear, the world of appearances is not eternal"
" Calceamenta et vestimenta nostra nihil aliud sunt quam aeterna."
"our shoes and garments are anything but eternal"
"crines et corpora non sunt aeterna".
"our hair and bodies are not eternal either"
Divitis vestimenta gero"
I'm wearing a rich man's clothes"
"Vidi hoc satis"
"you've seen this quite right"
"eos gero, quia dives sum".
"I'm wearing them, because I have been a rich man"
"et comam gero sicut homines seculares et luxuriosi".
"and I'm wearing my hair like the worldly and lustful people"
"quia unus ex illis fui"
"because I have been one of them"
"Et quid nunc es, Siddhartha?" Govinda interrogavit
"And what are you now, Siddhartha?" Govinda asked
"Nescio, sicut tu"
"I don't know it, just like you"
"Dives fui et iam non sum dives ultra"
"I was a rich man, and now I am not a rich man anymore"
"et quid cras ero, nescio"
"and what I'll be tomorrow, I don't know"

"Amisisti divitias tuas?" interrogavit Govinda
"You've lost your riches?" asked Govinda
" Divitias perdidi aut me amisi ";
"I've lost my riches, or they have lost me"
" Divitiae meae aliquo modo a me dilabuntur".
"My riches somehow happened to slip away from me"
"Rota manifestationes physicarum cito versat, Govinda"
"The wheel of physical manifestations is turning quickly, Govinda"
"Ubi est Siddhartha Brahman?"
"Where is Siddhartha the Brahman?"
"Ubi est Siddhartha Samana?"
"Where is Siddhartha the Samana?"
"Ubi est Siddhartha dives?"
"Where is Siddhartha the rich man?"
"Non aeterna cito mutantur, Govinda, scis"
"Non-eternal things change quickly, Govinda, you know it"
Govinda amicum iuventutis diu aspexit
Govinda looked at the friend of his youth for a long time
dubio oculis aspexit
he looked at him with doubt in his eyes
Deinde ei salutationem, qua quis uteretur, dedit
After that, he gave him the salutation which one would use on a gentleman
et ibat, et iter faciebat
and he went on his way, and continued his pilgrimage
Blando vultu, Siddhartha eum observavit relinquere
With a smiling face, Siddhartha watched him leave
amavit eum adhuc fidelis homo timidus
he loved him still, this faithful, fearful man
quomodo non omnes et omnia hoc tempore amaret?
how could he not have loved everybody and everything in this moment?
in hora gloriosa, post mirificum suum somnum repletum, Om!
in the glorious hour after his wonderful sleep, filled with Om!

incantatio, quae intra eum in somnis acciderat
The enchantment, which had happened inside of him in his sleep
hoc augurium erat omne quod amabat
this enchantment was everything that he loved
. .
he was full of joyful love for everything he saw
prorsus hoc fuerat in infirmitate sua ante
exactly this had been his sickness before
non potuit amare aliorum vel aliquid
he had not been able to love anybody or anything
Blando vultu, Siddhartha monachum relinquentem spectavit
With a smiling face, Siddhartha watched the leaving monk

multum ei somnus confirmaverat
The sleep had strengthened him a lot
sed fames magnum ei dolorem dabat
but hunger gave him great pain
iam non comedisset biduum
by now he had not eaten for two days
tempora longa fuerunt, cum tantam famem posset resistere
the times were long past when he could resist such hunger
Tristitia, sed etiam risu, cogitavit illo
With sadness, and yet also with a smile, he thought of that time
In diebus illis, recordatus est, se de tribus rebus iactasse Kamala .
In those days, so he remembered, he had boasted of three things to Kamala
tria nobilia et invicta facinora facere potuisset
he had been able to do three noble and undefeatable feats
poterat ieiunare, expectare et cogitare
he was able to fast, wait, and think
Haec illi sua fuerant; suam potentiam et fortitudinem
These had been his possessions; his power and strength

haec tria facinora in iuventute versata, laborioso iuventutis anno, didicerat
in the busy, laborious years of his youth, he had learned these three feats
Iamque eius facinora reliquerunt
And now, his feats had abandoned him
nulla facta eius amplius
none of his feats were his any more
neque jejunus, neque exspectans, neque cogitans
neither fasting, nor waiting, nor thinking
eos pro miserrimis rebus dederat
he had given them up for the most wretched things
quid est quod celerrime marcescit?
what is it that fades most quickly?
libido, bona vita, divitiae!
sensual lust, the good life, and riches!
Eius vita mirum quidem fuerat
His life had indeed been strange
Nunc, ut videbatur, vere factus est homo puerilis
And now, so it seemed, he had really become a childlike person
Siddhartha cogitavi de situ suo
Siddhartha thought about his situation
Cogito difficile sibi nunc
Thinking was hard for him now
non vere sentire sicut cogitandi "
he did not really feel like thinking
sed cogit se cogitare
but he forced himself to think
"haec omnia facillime pereunt, quae a me exciderunt".
"all these most easily perishing things have slipped from me"
"Iterum nunc hic sto sub sole".
"again, now I'm standing here under the sun"
"Hic sto sicut puer parvulus"
"I am standing here just like a little child"
"nihil est meum, nihil habeo ingenii".

"nothing is mine, I have no abilities"
"Nihil efficere potui"
"there is nothing I could bring about"
"Nihil didici de vita mea"
"I have learned nothing from my life"
"Quam mira haec omnia!"
"How wondrous all of this is!"
"Mirum est quod iam non sum puer"
"it's wondrous that I'm no longer young"
"Comae iam mediae griseae et vires caducae sunt"
"my hair is already half gray and my strength is fading"
"et nunc iterum ab initio incipio, sicut puer!"
"and now I'm starting again at the beginning, as a child!"
Rursum ridere sibi debuit
Again, he had to smile to himself
Fatum mirum!
Yes, his fate had been strange!
Res proclivi cum eo
Things were going downhill with him
et nunc iterum contra mundum nudum ac stupidum est
and now he was again facing the world naked and stupid
Sed de hoc non potuit contristari
But he could not feel sad about this
imo magnam stimulum ridendi sensit
no, he even felt a great urge to laugh
sensit cupidine ridere de se
he felt an urge to laugh about himself
de hoc novo, stulto mundo, stimulum ridendi sensit
he felt an urge to laugh about this strange, foolish world
"Proclivis eat apud te!" dixit ad se
"Things are going downhill with you!" he said to himself
et risit de situ suo
and he laughed about his situation
forte ut diceret amnem intueri
as he was saying it he happened to glance at the river
et vidit fluvium descensum

and he also saw the river going downhill
cantabat et esse beatus de omnibus
it was singing and being happy about everything
Hoc libuit, et benigne risit ad amnem
He liked this, and kindly he smiled at the river
Nonne hic fluvius in quo se submergere destinaverat?
Was this not the river in which he had intended to drown himself?
olim centum annos
in past times, a hundred years ago
an hoc viderat?
or had he dreamed this?
« Mira quidem vita mea » cogitavit
"Wondrous indeed was my life" he thought
"Miros ambages vita mea capta est"
"my life has taken wondrous detours"
"Puer ego deis tantum et donis egi".
"As a boy, I only dealt with gods and offerings"
"Adolescens, solus asceticismum tractavi".
"As a youth, I only dealt with asceticism"
"Tempus exegi in cogitatione et meditatione"
"I spent my time in thinking and meditation"
"Ego quaerebam Brahman
"I was searching for Brahman
"et adoravi aeternum in Atman".
"and I worshipped the eternal in the Atman"
"Sed adulescens secutus sum paenitentes".
"But as a young man, I followed the penitents"
"Ego in silva vixi et aestum et pruinam pertuli".
"I lived in the forest and suffered heat and frost"
"ibi didici famem vincere"
"there I learned how to overcome hunger"
"et docui corpus meum mortuum fieri".
"and I taught my body to become dead"
"Miro postmodo ad me venit intuitus".
"Wonderfully, soon afterwards, insight came towards me"

"**forma prudentiae magnae doctrinae Buddha**"
"insight in the form of the great Buddha's teachings"
"**Sensit unitatem mundi**";
"I felt the knowledge of the oneness of the world"
"**Sensi in me quasi sanguinem meum**".
"I felt it circling in me like my own blood"
"**At ego quoque relinquere Buddha et magna scientia**"
"But I also had to leave Buddha and the great knowledge"
"**Veni et didici artem amoris apud Kamala**"
"I went and learned the art of love with Kamala"
"**Negotiam et negotiationem didici cum Kamaswami**"
"I learned trading and business with Kamaswami"
Pecuniam cumulavi et iterum desumpsi.
"I piled up money, and wasted it again"
" **Didici amare ventrem et sensus meos placere** "
"I learned to love my stomach and please my senses"
" **Habui per tot annos amisso spiritu meo** ";
"I had to spend many years losing my spirit"
"**et habui dedocere cogitandi iterum**"
"and I had to unlearn thinking again"
"**ibi oblitus sum unitatis**".
"there I had forgotten the oneness"
"**Nonne perinde est ac si tardius ex viro in puerum verterem**"?
"Isn't it just as if I had turned slowly from a man into a child"?
"**Ex excogitatoris in persona puerilis**"
"from a thinker into a childlike person"
"**Atqui valde bona hac via fuit**".
"And yet, this path has been very good"
" **attamen avem in pectore non mortuam** ";
"and yet, the bird in my chest has not died"
"**Quae via haec fuit!**"
"what a path has this been!"
"**Per tantam stultitiam transire habui**";
"I had to pass through so much stupidity"
" **per tanta vitia transire habui** ";

"I had to pass through so much vice"
" Tot me errores facere oportuit " ;
"I had to make so many errors"
"Equidem sentire tantum fastidium et dolorem";
"I had to feel so much disgust and disappointment"
"Id facere oportuit, ut puer iterum fieret";
"I had to do all this to become a child again"
"Et iterum incipere potui"
"and then I could start over again"
"At bene ut facias".
"But it was the right way to do it"
"Cor meum etiam dicit ad eam et oculi mei ridere ad eam"
"my heart says yes to it and my eyes smile to it"
" Habui desperationem experiri "
"I've had to experience despair"
"Ego habui stultum omnium cogitationum subsidere"
"I've had to sink down to the most foolish of all thoughts"
"Ego habui cogitare ad mortem cogitationibus"
"I've had to think to the thoughts of suicide"
"Tantum igitur vellem divinam gratiam experiri".
"only then would I be able to experience divine grace"
"Tunc modo iterum audire potui"
"only then could I hear Om again"
"Tunc demum recte dormire potero et iterum evigilare".
"only then would I be able to sleep properly and awake again"
"Stulte fieri habui, atman in me iterum invenire"
"I had to become a fool, to find Atman in me again"
" Peccare habui, ut possem reviviscere ".
"I had to sin, to be able to live again"
"Quo me ducet ad alium via mea?"
"Where else might my path lead me to?"
"Stultum est, hac calle, quod movetur in loramenta";
"It is foolish, this path, it moves in loops"
"fortasse in gyro ambiens"
"perhaps it is going around in a circle"
"Eat hac via qua vult"

"Let this path go where it likes"
"ubi semper hac via vadit, eam sequi volo".
"where ever this path goes, I want to follow it"
gaudium volvens sicut fluctus in pectore
he felt joy rolling like waves in his chest
Quaesivit cor suum, "unde hanc felicitatem habuisti?"
he asked his heart, "from where did you get this happiness?"
"An forte venit ex illo tempore bonus somnus?"
"does it perhaps come from that long, good sleep?"
"somnus qui me tam multa bona fecit"
"the sleep which has done me so much good"
an ex verbo Om, quod dixi?
"or does it come from the word Om, which I said?"
an ex eo quod fugi?
"Or does it come from the fact that I have escaped?"
"Numquid haec felicitas quasi pueri sub caelo stant?"
"does this happiness come from standing like a child under the sky?"
"O quam fugisse bonum est"
"Oh how good is it to have fled"
"Magnum est liberum facti!"
"it is great to have become free!"
"Quam mundus et pulcher aer hic est"
"How clean and beautiful the air here is"
"Aer bonum est spiritus"
"the air is good to breath"
"ubi ab omni fragrantia unguentorum fugi"
"where I ran away from everything smelled of ointments"
aromata, vinum, excessus, desidia.
"spices, wine, excess, sloth"
"Quam odio habui hunc mundum divitum".
"How I hated this world of the rich"
"Odivi eos qui fine cibo et aleatoribus gaudent!"
"I hated those who revel in fine food and the gamblers!"
"Odisti me tam diu manendi in hoc gravi mundo!
"I hated myself for staying in this terrible world for so long!

"Ego me privavi, toxicum excruciavi".
"I have deprived, poisoned, and tortured myself"
"Senem me feci et malum!"
"I have made myself old and evil!"
"Minime, numquam amplius facere quae tantum probaverunt"
"No, I will never again do the things I liked doing so much"
"Non me deludet sapere Siddhartha."
"I won't delude myself into thinking that Siddhartha was wise!"
"At hoc unum bene feci".
"But this one thing I have done well"
"Hoc placet, hoc laudandum est".
"this I like, this I must praise"
" Placet nunc mihi odium illius in me finis esse ";
"I like that there is now an end to that hatred against myself"
" Finis est istius stultae ac dirae vitae."
"there is an end to that foolish and dreary life!"
" Laudo te, Siddhartha, post tot annos stultitiae".
"I praise you, Siddhartha, after so many years of foolishness"
"Habes semel iterumque ideam"
"you have once again had an idea"
"Avem audivisti in pectore cantus"
"you have heard the bird in your chest singing"
"Et secuta es canere volucris!"
"and you followed the song of the bird!"
his cogitationibus se laudabat
with these thoughts he praised himself
quod in se iterum gaudium invenisset
he had found joy in himself again
stomachum sonantem fame curiose audivit
he listened curiously to his stomach rumbling with hunger
gustaverat et exspuit partem doloris ac miseriae
he had tasted and spat out a piece of suffering and misery
his recentibus temporibus et diebus, hoc modo sensit
in these recent times and days, this is how he felt

usque ad desperationem et mortem devoraverat
he had devoured it up to the point of desperation and death
quomodo omnia contigerunt bona
how everything had happened was good
Kamaswami multo diutius manere potuisset
he could have stayed with Kamaswami for much longer
plus potuit pecuniae facere, deinde eam depopulatus est
he could have made more money, and then wasted it
Potuit impleri ventrem suum et anima eius siti moriatur
he could have filled his stomach and let his soul die of thirst
in molli ascenso inferno multo diutius vivere potuit
he could have lived in this soft upholstered hell much longer
si hoc non accidisset, vita permansisset
if this had not happened, he would have continued this life
tempore desperationis et desperationis
the moment of complete hopelessness and despair
summa cum imminentibus aquis
the most extreme moment when he hung over the rushing waters
interim paratus erat se perdere
the moment he was ready to destroy himself
iam desperatione atque fastidio
the moment he had felt this despair and deep disgust
non cessit ei
he had not succumbed to it
avem adhuc viveret postquam omnia
the bird was still alive after all
quare gavisus est et risit
this was why he felt joy and laughed
hoc erat quod facies ejus sub crine clare ridebat
this was why his face was smiling brightly under his hair
coma quae iam griseo
his hair which had now turned gray
"Bonum est", inquit, "degustare pro se omnia";
"It is good," he thought, "to get a taste of everything for oneself"

"Omne quod opus est scire"
"everything which one needs to know"
"cupiditas mundi et divitiarum non sunt bona".
"lust for the world and riches do not belong to the good things"
"Iam ut puer hoc didici"
"I have already learned this as a child"
" diu notum ";
"I have known it for a long time"
"sed non expertus sum usque nunc"
"but I hadn't experienced it until now"
"Et nunc quod expertus sum id scio".
"And now that I I've experienced it I know it"
"Non solum scio in memoria mea, sed in oculis, corde, et in ventre"
"I don't just know it in my memory, but in my eyes, heart, and stomach"
"Bonum est mihi hoc scire!"
"it is good for me to know this!"

Diu cogitabat suam transformationem
For a long time, he pondered his transformation
audiebat avem, prae gaudio cecinit
he listened to the bird, as it sang for joy
Nonne haec avis in illo mortua est?
Had this bird not died in him?
ni hanc avem mortem sensisset ?
had he not felt this bird's death?
Imo aliud intus in ipso demortui erat
No, something else from within him had died
aliquid, quod cupiebat mori decessisse
something which yearned to die had died
Nonne hoc volebat occidere?
Was it not this that he used to intend to kill?
Nonne pusillus, territus, et superbus moriturus?

Was it not his his small, frightened, and proud self that had died?
cum se per tot annos luctaretur
he had wrestled with his self for so many years
ipse qui vicerat identidem
the self which had defeated him again and again
in se quod erat rursus post omnem occisionem
the self which was back again after every killing
sui, qui vetuit laetitiam et metum percepit?
the self which prohibited joy and felt fear?
Nonne hic ipse qui hodie tandem ad mortem venit?
Was it not this self which today had finally come to its death?
hic in silva, per hoc amabile flumen
here in the forest, by this lovely river
Nonne huic morti debetur, quod iam parvulus erat?
Was it not due to this death, that he was now like a child?
sic plenus fiducia et gaudio sine timore
so full of trust and joy, without fear
Nunc Siddhartha quoque nonnihil accepit cur ipse hoc frustra pugnasset
Now Siddhartha also got some idea of why he had fought this self in vain
sciebat quare non posset pugnare se sicut Brahman
he knew why he couldn't fight his self as a Brahman
Nimia scientia tenuerat eum
Too much knowledge had held him back
nimis multi sacri versiculi, sacrificiorum regulae et propriae castigationes
too many holy verses, sacrificial rules, and self-castigation
haec omnia continuerunt eum
all these things held him back
tantum agendo et scopo ad illud propositum!
so much doing and striving for that goal!
fuerat plenus arrogantiae
he had been full of arrogance
fuit semper cultissima

he was always the smartest
et semper opus maxime
he was always working the most
eum semper unum gradum ante omnes alios fuisse
he had always been one step ahead of all others
semper fuit sciens et spiritualis
he was always the knowing and spiritual one
fuit semper sacerdos vel sapiens
he was always considered the priest or wise one
se ipsum in sacerdotem, arrogantiam et spiritualem se recepisse
his self had retreated into being a priest, arrogance, and spirituality
Ibi sedit firmiter et crevit hoc tempore
there it sat firmly and grew all this time
Et putabat se jejunio posse interficere
and he had thought he could kill it by fasting
Vidit autem suam vitam sicut factum est
Now he saw his life as it had become
vocem secretam iure videbat
he saw that the secret voice had been right
nullus magister salutem suam efficere potuisset
no teacher would ever have been able to bring about his salvation
Ergo debuit exire in mundum
Therefore, he had to go out into the world
Habebat se amittere libidini et potentiae
he had to lose himself to lust and power
Mulieres se perdere pecuniam
he had to lose himself to women and money
mercator fieri debuit, parili-aleator, potator
he had to become a merchant, a dice-gambler, a drinker
et quod homo avarus fieri
and he had to become a greedy person
Hoc autem erat faciendum, donec sacerdos et Samana in eo mortua essent

he had to do this until the priest and Samana in him was dead
Ideo necesse habuit hos annos turpes continuare
Therefore, he had to continue bearing these ugly years
taedio ac doctrinis ferre debuit
he had to bear the disgust and the teachings
tristem ac perditam ferre inanem vitam habuit
he had to bear the pointlessness of a dreary and wasted life
ad extremum finem habuit
he had to conclude it up to its bitter end
debuerat hoc facere, donec Siddhartha libidinosus etiam mori posset
he had to do this until Siddhartha the lustful could also die
Mortuus erat et novus Siddhartha e somno excitatus erat
He had died and a new Siddhartha had woken up from the sleep
hoc Siddhartha esset etiam veterescent
this new Siddhartha would also grow old
vellet etiam aliquando mori
he would also have to die eventually
Siddhartha adhuc mortalis erat, sicut omnis corporis forma
Siddhartha was still mortal, as is every physical form
Hodie autem erat iuvenis et puer et gaudio plenus
But today he was young and a child and full of joy
Haec secum
He thought these thoughts to himself
audiebat subridens stomachum
he listened with a smile to his stomach
stridoribus apis grato animo audiebat
he listened gratefully to a buzzing bee
libens in rapidum amnem respexit
Cheerfully, he looked into the rushing river
numquam antea quantum iste aquae probaverunt
he had never before liked a water as much as this one
numquam antea vocem tam fortiorem perceperat
he had never before perceived the voice so stronger

nunquam tam vehementer intellexisse parabolam aquae vivae
he had never understood the parable of the moving water so strongly
numquam antea quam pulchre moverit
he had never before noticed how beautifully the river moved
Visum est ei, quasi flumen haberet aliquid speciale indicare ei
It seemed to him, as if the river had something special to tell him
adhuc aliquid non noverat, quod eum adhuc exspectabat;
something he did not know yet, which was still awaiting him
In hoc fluvio Siddhartha se mergere in animo habuit
In this river, Siddhartha had intended to drown himself
in hoc flumine vetus fessus et desperatus Siddhartha hodie submersus est
in this river the old, tired, desperate Siddhartha had drowned today
Sed nova Siddhartha sensit altam amorem huius aquae rapidae
But the new Siddhartha felt a deep love for this rushing water
Statuit sibi, ne quam primum discederet
and he decided for himself, not to leave it very soon

Partitor
The Ferryman

"Per hunc fluvium manere volo", Siddhartha putavit
"By this river I want to stay," thought Siddhartha
"Idem amnis est quem olim transivi".
"it is the same river which I have crossed a long time ago"
"Me deducatis usque ad puerilem populum"
"I was on my way to the childlike people"
"Amicus portitor trans flumen me deduxerat"
"a friendly ferryman had guided me across the river"
"Ille est ille volo ire"
"he is the one I want to go to"
"Proficiscens e tugurio suo, semita mea me duxit ad vitam novam".
"starting out from his hut, my path led me to a new life"
"viam quae senuerat et nunc mortua est"
"a path which had grown old and is now dead"
"Mea via praesens etiam ibi initium capiet".
"my present path shall also take its start there!"
Leniter, rapidas prospexit aquas
Tenderly, he looked into the rushing water
perlucidos lineas viridis aqua hausit
he looked into the transparent green lines the water drew
cristallum lineae aquae erant in secretis
the crystal lines of water were rich in secrets
margaritas splendidas vidit ab alto surgentes
he saw bright pearls rising from the deep
quietam bullae aeris innatant in consideratione superficiei
quiet bubbles of air floating on the reflecting surface
caeruleum aeri depictum in bullis
the blue of the sky depicted in the bubbles
flumen oculis mille intuens
the river looked at him with a thousand eyes
flumine viridi oculos albos oculos
the river had green eyes and white eyes

flumen cristallum oculos caeruleos oculos
the river had crystal eyes and sky-blue eyes
hanc aquam valde amavit, eum delectavit
he loved this water very much, it delighted him
gratus erat aqua
he was grateful to the water
In corde suo audivit vocem loquentem
In his heart he heard the voice talking
"Ama hanc aquam! Mane prope eam!"
"Love this water! Stay near it!"
"Disce ex aqua!" vox eius praecepit ei
"Learn from the water!" his voice commanded him
Immo discere ex eo voluit
Oh yes, he wanted to learn from it
voluit audire aquam
he wanted to listen to the water
Qui huius aquae mysteria intelligeret
He who would understand this water's secrets
etiam plura alia
he would also understand many other things
ita sibi visum est
this is how it seemed to him
Sed ex omnibus fluminis secretis, hodie solus vidit
But out of all secrets of the river, today he only saw one
arcanum hoc animae tetigit
this secret touched his soul
aqua cucurrit et cucurrit indesinenter
this water ran and ran, incessantly
aqua cucurrit, sed tamen semper fuit
the water ran, but nevertheless it was always there
aqua semper, omni tempore idem fuit
the water always, at all times, was the same
et simul nova fuit omni momento
and at the same time it was new in every moment
qui id capere posset, magnus esset
he who could grasp this would be great

sed non intelligere vel capere
but he didn't understand or grasp it
tantum sentiebam aliquam ideam movendi
he only felt some idea of it stirring
quasi memoriam longinquam, divinas voces
it was like a distant memory, a divine voices

Siddhartha resurrexit sicut operatio famis in corpore intolerabilis facta est
Siddhartha rose as the workings of hunger in his body became unbearable
Attonitus longius ab urbe ambulavit
In a daze he walked further away from the city
ambulavit in via fluminis ripae
he walked up the river along the path by the bank
et audiebat aquam
he listened to the current of the water
commotionem famem audiebat in corpore suo
he listened to the rumbling hunger in his body
Cum porttitor attigisset, navi adveniens
When he reached the ferry, the boat was just arriving
idem portitor qui iuvenem Samana transvexit amnem
the same ferryman who had once transported the young Samana across the river
ipse in navi stetit et Siddhartha agnovit eum
he stood in the boat and Siddhartha recognised him
et senex valde
he had also aged very much
portitor mirabatur talem virum elegantem pedibus incedere
the ferryman was astonished to see such an elegant man walking on foot
"Vis me vada?" interrogavit
"Would you like to ferry me over?" he asked
et apprehensum eum in navim proiecit
he took him into his boat and pushed it off the bank
"Est pulchra vita, quam elegisti tibi" viatoribus locutus est

"It's a beautiful life you have chosen for yourself" the passenger spoke
"Decet pulchrum esse ex hac aqua cotidie vivere"
"It must be beautiful to live by this water every day"
"et oportet lecythus super flumine pulcher esse".
"and it must be beautiful to cruise on it on the river"
Subridens homo ad remum latus ad latus movetur
With a smile, the man at the oar moved from side to side
"Est pulchra ut dicis, domine"
"It is as beautiful as you say, sir"
"Sed non omnis vita et omne opus pulchrum est?"
"But isn't every life and all work beautiful?"
"Hoc verum sit", respondit Siddhartha
"This may be true" replied Siddhartha
"Sed invideo tibi pro vita tua"
"But I envy you for your life"
"Ah, mox desine frui"
"Ah, you would soon stop enjoying it"
"Hoc non est opus hominibus subtilibus vestibus indutum".
"This is no work for people wearing fine clothes"
Siddhartha risit observatione
Siddhartha laughed at the observation
"Quondam ante, hodie propter vestimenta mea visus sum".
"Once before, I have been looked upon today because of my clothes"
"Respectus sum in diffidentia"
"I have been looked upon with distrust"
"sunt molesti mihi"
"they are a nuisance to me"
"Nonne tu, portitor, has vestes accipere velim"
"Wouldn't you, ferryman, like to accept these clothes"
"quia scire debes, pecuniam non habeo quod ad victum tuum".
"because you must know, I have no money to pay your fare"
"Iocaris, domine," risit portitor
"You're joking, sir," the ferryman laughed

"**Non iocari, amice**"
"I'm not joking, friend"
"**semel antequam hanc aquam in navi tua transvexisti**"
"once before you have ferried me across this water in your boat"
"**pro immaterialibus boni operis praemio fecistis**"
"you did it for the immaterial reward of a good deed"
"**me trans flumen portate et vestimenta mea pro eo accipite**".
"ferry me across the river and accept my clothes for it"
"**Et tu, domine, sine vestibus pergere iter facis?**"
"And do you, sir, intent to continue travelling without clothes?"
"**Ah, maxime omnium nolo iter omnino pergere**".
"Ah, most of all I wouldn't want to continue travelling at all"
"**Malo mihi vetus lumbare dedistis**";
"I would rather you gave me an old loincloth"
"**Vellem id si me tibi adiutorem haberes**".
"I would like it if you kept me with you as your assistant"
"**Immo velim si me in tuum DISCIPLINARUM susceperis**.
"or rather, I would like if you accepted me as your trainee"
"**quia prius discere debeam navem tractandam**".
"because first I'll have to learn how to handle the boat"
Diu portitor advena respexit
For a long time, the ferryman looked at the stranger
in memoria eius quaerebat hunc hominem alienum
he was searching in his memory for this strange man
"**Nunc te agnosco**" **dixit tandem**
"Now I recognise you," he finally said
"**Uno tempore in casa mea dormivisti**"
"At one time, you've slept in my hut"
"**Hoc olim fuit, fortasse plus quam viginti annos**".
"this was a long time ago, possibly more than twenty years"
"**et tu a me transvectus es flumen**"
"and you've been ferried across the river by me"
"**Illo die discessimus sicut amici boni**"
"that day we parted like good friends"

"Nonne tu Samana fuisti?"
"Haven't you been a Samana?"
"Non possum amplius cogitare de nomine tuo"
"I can't think of your name anymore"
"Meum nomen est Siddhartha, et ego Samana".
"My name is Siddhartha, and I was a Samana"
"Eram adhuc Samana cum me novissime viderunt"
"I had still been a Samana when you last saw me"
"Ita salve, Siddhartha. Nomen meum Vasudeva est".
"So be welcome, Siddhartha. My name is Vasudeva"
"Vis, ut spero, hospes hodie quoque esto".
"You will, so I hope, be my guest today as well"
"et tu in casa mea dormias"
"and you may sleep in my hut"
et dic mihi unde venis.
"and you may tell me, where you're coming from"
"et dicas mihi quare haec pulcherrimae vestes sunt hoc nocumentum tibi".
"and you may tell me why these beautiful clothes are such a nuisance to you"
medium flumen perventum est
They had reached the middle of the river
Vasudeva remum plus viribus impulit
Vasudeva pushed the oar with more strength
ut superare hodiernam
in order to overcome the current
Placide, lacertis
He worked calmly, with brawny arms
Oculi eius in fronte navi
his eyes were fixed in on the front of the boat
Siddhartha sedebat et custodiebant eum
Siddhartha sat and watched him
recordatus est tempus Samana
he remembered his time as a Samana
et recordatus est quomodo amor iste in corde suo commotus est

he remembered how love for this man had stirred in his heart
Grato animo invitavit Vasudeva
Gratefully, he accepted Vasudeva's invitation
Cum autem ad ripam perventum esset, eum navim ad palos religandam adiuvit
When they had reached the bank, he helped him to tie the boat to the stakes
Post haec, portitor eum rogavit ut tugurium intraret
after this, the ferryman asked him to enter the hut
obtulit ei panem et aquam , et comedit Siddhartha
he offered him bread and water, and Siddhartha ate with eager pleasure
et ipse quoque mango fructuum Vasudeva prebebat avidissime comedebat
and he also ate with eager pleasure of the mango fruits Vasudeva offered him

Postea erat fere tempus solis occasum
Afterwards, it was almost the time of the sunset
sederunt super truncum ad ripam
they sat on a log by the bank
Siddhartha dixit portitor ubi primum ab
Siddhartha told the ferryman about where he originally came from
dixit ei de vita sua sicut hodie viderat
he told him about his life as he had seen it today
Viam vidit in illa hora desperationis
the way he had seen it in that hour of despair
fabula vitae suae in multam noctem duravit
the tale of his life lasted late into the night
Vasudeva attente audiebat
Vasudeva listened with great attention
Audiens diligenter, omnia in mentem intromisit
Listening carefully, he let everything enter his mind
nativitas et pueritia, omnis doctrina
birthplace and childhood, all that learning

omnis inquisitio, omnis gaudium, omnis angustia
all that searching, all joy, all distress
Hic fuit unus portitor virtutes maximas
This was one of the greatest virtues of the ferryman
sicut pauci, sciebat audire
like only a few, he knew how to listen
non habere verbum loqui
he did not have to speak a word
sed persensit disertus quomodo Vasudeva verba ejus in mentem intret
but the speaker sensed how Vasudeva let his words enter his mind
mens quieta, aperta, et exspectans
his mind was quiet, open, and waiting
non amisit unum verbum
he did not lose a single word
nullum verbum impatienter expectabat
he did not await a single word with impatience
non addidit laudem vel increpationem suam
he did not add his praise or rebuke
sicut erat auditum, et nihil aliud
he was just listening, and nothing else
Siddhartha sensit quid sit felix fortuna tali auditore confiteri
Siddhartha felt what a happy fortune it is to confess to such a listener
felix sensit animam suam sepelire in corde suo
he felt fortunate to bury in his heart his own life
sepelivit inquisitionem suam et dolorem
he buried his own search and suffering
dixit fabula de vita Siddhartha
he told the tale of Siddhartha's life
cum de arbore iuxta flumen
when he spoke of the tree by the river
cum dixit de lapsu suo
when he spoke of his deep fall
cum de sancto Om

when he spoke of the holy Om
cum diceret quomodo talem fluminis amorem sensisset
when he spoke of how he had felt such a love for the river
haec portitor bis tanto attentione auscultat
the ferryman listened to these things with twice as much attention
totus et totus absorptus
he was entirely and completely absorbed by it
audiebat clausis oculis
he was listening with his eyes closed
Cum Siddhartha obticuit longum silentium factum
when Siddhartha fell silent a long silence occurred
tunc Vasudeva locutus est, "Est sicut cogitavi".
then Vasudeva spoke "It is as I thought"
"Fluvius locutus est tibi".
"The river has spoken to you"
"Fluvius est amicus tuus tum"
"the river is your friend as well"
"Fluvius tecum quoque loquitur"
"the river speaks to you as well"
"Quod bonum est, id est ipsum bonum".
"That is good, that is very good"
"Mane mecum, Siddhartha, amicus meus"
"Stay with me, Siddhartha, my friend"
"Uxorem habere solebat"
"I used to have a wife"
"Iuxta lectum meum"
"her bed was next to mine"
"sed diu abhinc mortuus est"
"but she has died a long time ago"
"Diu solus vixi"
"for a long time, I have lived alone"
"Nunc vives mecum".
"Now, you shall live with me"
"Satis spatium et cibus ambobus"
"there is enough space and food for both of us"

"Gratias tibi ago", inquit Siddhartha
"I thank you," said Siddhartha
" Gratias tibi ago et accipio " ;
"I thank you and accept"
"Et etiam tibi gratias ago pro hoc, Vasudeva".
"And I also thank you for this, Vasudeva"
"Gratias ago tibi, quia tam bene me audiendo"
"I thank you for listening to me so well"
"populi qui sciunt audire rara"
"people who know how to listen are rare"
"Non occurrit unum hominem qui scivit sicut tu"
"I have not met a single person who knew it as well as you do"
" Discam etiam in hac parte a te."
"I will also learn in this respect from you"
"disces" locutus est Vasudeva
"You will learn it," spoke Vasudeva
"sed non discis a me".
"but you will not learn it from me"
"Fluvius me docuit audire";
"The river has taught me to listen"
"Disces a flumine tum audire".
"you will learn to listen from the river as well"
« Novit omnia, flumen »;
"It knows everything, the river"
" flumine omnia cognosci possunt "
"everything can be learned from the river"
"Ecce iam ex aqua etiam hoc didicisti".
"See, you've already learned this from the water too"
"Dixisti quod bonum est deorsum contendere";
"you have learned that it is good to strive downwards"
" Submergere et profundum quaerere didiceris "
"you have learned to sink and to seek depth"
"Dives et elegans Siddhartha remi servus decet".
"The rich and elegant Siddhartha is becoming an oarsman's servant"
"Doctum Brahman Siddhartha fit portitor"

"the learned Brahman Siddhartha becomes a ferryman"
" Hoc etiam dictum est tibi per fluvium ".
"this has also been told to you by the river"
" Rem aliam ex eo etiam disces " .
"You'll learn the other thing from it as well"
Siddhartha locutus est post longum spatium
Siddhartha spoke after a long pause
"Quae alia discam, Vasudeva?"
"What other things will I learn, Vasudeva?"
Vasudeva resurrexit. "Sero est", inquit
Vasudeva rose. "It is late," he said
et Vasudeva proposuit somnum
and Vasudeva proposed going to sleep
"Nescio quod aliud, o amice".
"I can't tell you that other thing, oh friend"
" Rem aliam disces, aut fortasse iam scies ".
"You'll learn the other thing, or perhaps you know it already"
"Ecce nullus sum doctus homo".
"See, I'm no learned man"
"Nihil habeo singularem dicendi facultatem";
"I have no special skill in speaking"
"Ego quoque nullam singularem cogitandi peritiam habeo"
"I also have no special skill in thinking"
"Omnia possum audire et pius esse".
"All I'm able to do is to listen and to be godly"
"Nihil aliud didici"
"I have learned nothing else"
"Si possem dicere et docere, sapiens essem".
"If I was able to say and teach it, I might be a wise man"
"sed sic sum solus portitor".
"but like this I am only a ferryman"
"et mihi opus est vada trans flumen"
"and it is my task to ferry people across the river"
"Multa hominum milia transportavi";
"I have transported many thousands of people"

"et omnibus eorum flumen nihil aliud fuit quam obstaculum".
"and to all of them, my river has been nothing but an obstacle"
"Est aliquid quod in via peregrinationis eorum obtinuit".
"it was something that got in the way of their travels"
"Iter ad quaerendam pecuniam et negotiationem"
"they travelled to seek money and business"
"pro nuptiis et peregrinationibus peregrinati sunt"
"they travelled for weddings and pilgrimages"
"et flumen impediret iter suum"
"and the river was obstructing their path"
"Procuratoris officium erat ut eos celeriter per illud impedimentum acciperet".
"the ferryman's job was to get them quickly across that obstacle"
"Sed aliquot inter milia, paucos, flumen obstare desiit";
"But for some among thousands, a few, the river has stopped being an obstacle"
vocem ejus audiverunt, et vocem ejus audiverunt;
"they have heard its voice and they have listened to it"
et fluvius factus est eis sacer.
"and the river has become sacred to them"
"Eis sacer fit ut mihi sacer";
"it become sacred to them as it has become sacred to me"
"iam, Siddhartha quiescamus".
"for now, let us rest, Siddhartha"

Siddhartha mansit apud portitor et didicit navem operari
Siddhartha stayed with the ferryman and learned to operate the boat
cum nihil ad vada faciendum esset, cum Vasudeva in oryza elaboravit
when there was nothing to do at the ferry, he worked with Vasudeva in the rice-field
ligna collegit et decerpsit fructum Musarum
he gathered wood and plucked the fruit off the banana-trees

Remum aedificare didicit et navem emendare
He learned to build an oar and how to mend the boat
cophinos texere et tuguriolum reddidit
he learned how to weave baskets and repaid the hut
et gavisus est propter omnia quae didicit
and he was joyful because of everything he learned
dies et menses cito
the days and months passed quickly
Sed plusquam Vasudeva eum docere potuit, a flumine edoctus est
But more than Vasudeva could teach him, he was taught by the river
Incessanter a flumine didicit
Incessantly, he learned from the river
Maxime, audire didicit
Most of all, he learned to listen
didicit adtendat placido corde
he learned to pay close attention with a quiet heart
exspectationem servare didicit, aperta anima
he learned to keep a waiting, open soul
et didicit audire sine passione
he learned to listen without passion
didicit sine velle
he learned to listen without a wish
didicit sine iudicio audire
he learned to listen without judgement
didicit sine sententia
he learned to listen without an opinion

Amice degebat cum Vasudeva .
In a friendly manner, he lived side by side with Vasudeva
interdum mutavit aliqua verba
occasionally they exchanged some words
tum demum de verbis cogitaverunt
then, at length, they thought about the words
Vasudeva non erat amicus verborum

Vasudeva was no friend of words
Raro Siddhartha potuit suadere loqui
Siddhartha rarely succeeded in persuading him to speak
"Numquid etiam secretum de flumine disces?"
"did you too learn that secret from the river?"
" Arcanum quod tempus non est?"
"the secret that there is no time?"
Vasudeva facies impleta est splendida risu
Vasudeva's face was filled with a bright smile
"Ita, Siddhartha," dixit
"Yes, Siddhartha," he spoke
"Flumen ubique simul didici"
"I learned that the river is everywhere at once"
"est in fonte et in ostio fluminis"
"it is at the source and at the mouth of the river"
"Est apud cataracta et porttitor"
"it is at the waterfall and at the ferry"
"est in rapidis et in mari".
"it is at the rapids and in the sea"
est in montibus et ubique simul.
"it is in the mountains and everywhere at once"
"et didici solum tempus fluminis esse".
"and I learned that there is only the present time for the river"
"non habet umbram praeteritum"
"it does not have the shadow of the past"
et non habet futuri umbram.
"and it does not have the shadow of the future"
"Hoc est quod vis?" interrogavit
"is this what you mean?" he asked
"Hoc est quod dixi", Siddhartha
"This is what I meant," said Siddhartha
"Et cum cognovissem, vidi vitam meam".
"And when I had learned it, I looked at my life"
" et vita mea fuit etiam fluvius " .
"and my life was also a river"

"puer Siddhartha solum ab homine Siddhartha per umbram separatus est"
"the boy Siddhartha was only separated from the man Siddhartha by a shadow"
"et umbra separavit hominem Siddhartha a sene Siddhartha"
"and a shadow separated the man Siddhartha from the old man Siddhartha"
umbra separantur res, non res verae.
"things are separated by a shadow, not by something real"
"Item, partus Siddharthae priores non fuerunt".
"Also, Siddhartha's previous births were not in the past"
"et eius mors et reditus ad Brahmam in futuro non est".
"and his death and his return to Brahma is not in the future"
" nihil fuit , nihil erit , sed omnia sunt " .
"nothing was, nothing will be, but everything is"
" omnia habet existentia et est praesens " ;
"everything has existence and is present"
Siddhartha locutus est cum excessu
Siddhartha spoke with ecstasy
Haec illustratio penitus eum delectaverat
this enlightenment had delighted him deeply
"Nonne omnis tribulatio temporis?"
"was not all suffering time?"
"nonne omnes formae temporis se affligunt?"
"were not all forms of tormenting oneself a form of time?"
"nonne omnia dura et inimica a tempore sunt?"
"was not everything hard and hostile because of time?"
"Nonne omne malum vincitur, cum vincit tempus?"
"is not everything evil overcome when one overcomes time?"
"ut primum animum deserit tempus, an dolor etiam deserit?"
"as soon as time leaves the mind, does suffering leave too?"
Siddhartha fuerat in gaudio
Siddhartha had spoken in ecstatic delight
sed Vasudeva risit ei clare et adnuit in confirmatione
but Vasudeva smiled at him brightly and nodded in confirmation

tacite adnuit et manum super humero Siddhartha remisit
silently he nodded and brushed his hand over Siddhartha's shoulder
et reversus est ad opus suum
and then he turned back to his work

Et Siddhartha Vasudeva iterum alio tempore interrogavit
And Siddhartha asked Vasudeva again another time
flumen modo augebat fluxus pluviæ
the river had just increased its flow in the rainy season
et sonitum magnum
and it made a powerful noise
"Nonne ita est, o amice, multas voces habet fluvius?"
"Isn't it so, oh friend, the river has many voices?"
"Num vox regis et bellatoris?"
"Hasn't it the voice of a king and of a warrior?"
"Nonne vox tauri et avis noctis?"
"Hasn't it the voice of of a bull and of a bird of the night?"
"Nonne vox parturientis et gemitus?"
"Hasn't it the voice of a woman giving birth and of a sighing man?"
"etne etiam voces mille alias?"
"and does it not also have a thousand other voices?"
"est ut dicis" Vasudeva adnuit
"it is as you say it is," Vasudeva nodded
"Omnes creaturarum voces in voce sua sunt"
"all voices of the creatures are in its voice"
"Et scis..." Siddhartha continued
"And do you know..." Siddhartha continued
"quid vox loquitur, cum omnes simul audiendo efficis voces?"
"what word does it speak when you succeed in hearing all of voices at once?"
Laete facies Vasudeva ridebat
Happily, Vasudeva's face was smiling

ad Siddhartha inclinavit se, et locutus est sanctum Om in aurem suam
he bent over to Siddhartha and spoke the holy Om into his ear
Fuerat autem hoc ipsum quod audierat Siddhartha
And this had been the very thing which Siddhartha had also been hearing

Post tempus, risus eius similior factus est portitoro
time after time, his smile became more similar to the ferryman's
in risu factus est fere tam clara quam portitor
his smile became almost just as bright as the ferryman's
erat propemodum ualde fausta
it was almost just as thoroughly glowing with bliss
mille rugae lucent
shining out of thousand small wrinkles
sicut risus de puero
just like the smile of a child
sicut risus senis
just like the smile of an old man
Multi viatores videntes duos vectores, putaverunt se esse fratres
Many travellers, seeing the two ferrymen, thought they were brothers
Saepe simul ad ripam vesperi sedebant
Often, they sat in the evening together by the bank
nihil dixerunt et ambo audiverunt aquam
they said nothing and both listened to the water
aqua, non aqua
the water, which was not water to them
non aqua sed vox vitae
it wasn't water, but the voice of life
vox existit et quod aeterna figuratur
the voice of what exists and what is eternally taking shape
Accidit subinde ut idem uterque senserit

it happened from time to time that both thought of the same thing
putabant colloquii Pridie
they thought of a conversation from the day before
putabant viatorum
they thought of one of their travellers
cogitabant de morte et pueritia sua
they thought of death and their childhood
audientes flumen idem dicere
they heard the river tell them the same thing
et de eadem quaestione delectatus est
both delighted about the same answer to the same question
Aliquid erat de duobus portitoribus qui aliis transmissi sunt
There was something about the two ferrymen which was transmitted to others
aliquid quod multi viatores senserunt
it was something which many of the travellers felt
interdum viatores vultus ad vectores
travellers would occasionally look at the faces of the ferrymen
et narraverunt fabulam vitae suae
and then they told the story of their life
omnia mala confessi
they confessed all sorts of evil things
et rogaverunt consolationem et consilium
and they asked for comfort and advice
interdum aliquis poposcit licentiam manere per noctem
occasionally someone asked for permission to stay for a night
ipsi etiam flumen audire volebant
they also wanted to listen to the river
Accidit etiam, ut curiosus populus veniret
It also happened that curious people came
Quibus dictum est duos viros sapientes
they had been told that there were two wise men
aut duo maleficos sibi dictos fuisse
or they had been told there were two sorcerers
Curiosus populus quaesivit multas quaestiones

The curious people asked many questions
sed nihil respondetur ad quaestiones
but they got no answers to their questions
nec magos nec sapientes invenerunt
they found neither sorcerers nor wise men
modo duos amicos parvos senes invenerunt, qui mutus esse videbatur
they only found two friendly little old men, who seemed to be mute
quasi aliena in silva facti viderentur
they seemed to have become a bit strange in the forest by themselves
Et deridebant curiosi quod audierant
And the curious people laughed about what they had heard
vulgus stulte dixit rumores inanes evulgare
they said common people were foolishly spreading empty rumours

anni praeterierunt et nemo numeravit eos
The years passed by, and nobody counted them
Vno deinde tempore monachi peregrini uenerunt
Then, at one time, monks came by on a pilgrimage
Gotamae Buddha sectatores erant
they were followers of Gotama, the Buddha
petierunt ut trans flumen ferri
they asked to be ferried across the river
dixeruntque illis festinantes redire ad sapientissimum magistrum
they told them they were in a hurry to get back to their wise teacher
nuntium divulgaverat exaltatum erat infirmum mortiferum
news had spread the exalted one was deadly sick
mox moriturum suum ultimam hominis mortem
he would soon die his last human death
ut una cum salute fiant
in order to become one with the salvation

Non ita multo ante venit novus monachorum grex
It was not long until a new flock of monks came
erant etiam in peregrinatione sua
they were also on their pilgrimage
plerique peregrini nihil aliud dixerunt quam Gotama
most of the travellers spoke of nothing other than Gotama
de morte eius omnibus cogitabant
his impending death was all they thought about
si bellum fuisset, as many would travel
if there had been war, just as many would travel
totidem venturi ad coronationem regis
just as many would come to the coronation of a king
congregentur sicut formicae catervatim
they gathered like ants in droves
confluebant, ut magico carmine traherentur
they flocked, like being drawn onwards by a magic spell
ubi magna Buddha mortem eius opperiebatur
they went to where the great Buddha was awaiting his death
perfecti temporis unus erat cum gloria
the perfected one of an era was to become one with the glory
Saepe Siddhartha cogitavit in diebus illis sapientis morientis
Often, Siddhartha thought in those days of the dying wise man
magnus magister cuius vox gentes monuerat
the great teacher whose voice had admonished nations
ille qui excitavit centena millia
the one who had awoken hundreds of thousands
vir, cujus vocem etiam semel audivit
a man whose voice he had also once heard
doctorem, cuius vultum sanctum etiam reverenter viderat
a teacher whose holy face he had also once seen with respect
Benigne cogitabat de eo
Kindly, he thought of him
ante oculos suos perfectionis viam vidit
he saw his path to perfection before his eyes

et recordatus est subridens verba illa quae dixerat ei
and he remembered with a smile those words he had said to him
cum esset adulescens et locutus est ad praecelsum
when he was a young man and spoke to the exalted one
Fuerant, ut sibi videbantur, superbis et pretiosis verbis
They had been, so it seemed to him, proud and precious words
subridens recordatus verborum
with a smile, he remembered the the words
sciebat nihil esse inter Gotamam et eum amplius
he knew that there was nothing standing between Gotama and him any more
iam diu sciverat
he had known this for a long time already
quamvis non posset accipere eius doctrinam
though he was still unable to accept his teachings
non fuit doctrina de inquisitione vere hominem
there was no teaching a truly searching person
aliquis qui vere invenire volebat, posset accipere
someone who truly wanted to find, could accept
Sed is qui responsum invenerat, nullam doctrinam probare poterat
But he who had found the answer could approve of any teaching
omnis semita, omnis meta, omnes idem erant
every path, every goal, they were all the same
nihil inter ipsum et alios millenos amplius
there was nothing standing between him and all the other thousands any more
milia qui in aeternum
the thousands who lived in that what is eternal
ad millia, qui inspiravit divina
the thousands who breathed what is divine

Uno autem horum dierum, Kamala quoque perrexit ad eum

On one of these days, Kamala also went to him
illa meretricum esse solebat pulcherrimus
she used to be the most beautiful of the courtesans
Iampridem recesserat a vita priore
A long time ago, she had retired from her previous life
hortum suum monachis de Gotama pro dono dederat
she had given her garden to the monks of Gotama as a gift
eam confugit ad doctrinam
she had taken her refuge in the teachings
erat inter amicos et benefactores peregrinorum
she was among the friends and benefactors of the pilgrims
erat una cum Siddhartha, puero
she was together with Siddhartha, the boy
Siddhartha puer erat filius eius
Siddhartha the boy was her son
iverat in itinere propter famam propinquae mortis Gotamae
she had gone on her way due to the news of the near death of Gotama
erat in simplicibus vestibus et in pede
she was in simple clothes and on foot
et erat cum filiolo suo
and she was With her little son
illa iter ad flumen
she was travelling by the river
sed puer mox lassavit
but the boy had soon grown tired
volebat ire domum
he desired to go back home
cupiebat requiescere et manducare
he desired to rest and eat
et factus est incredulus et incepit plorare
he became disobedient and started whining
Kamala saepe habuit ad quietem cum eo
Kamala often had to take a rest with him
solitus erat questus quod vellet
he was accustomed to getting what he wanted

quae habebat ut pasceret eum et consolaretur eum
she had to feed him and comfort him
quae erat obiurgare eum ad mores suos
she had to scold him for his behaviour
Non comprehendit, cur in hanc fatigationem proficisceretur
He did not comprehend why he had to go on this exhausting pilgrimage
nesciebat quid haberet ad locum ignotum
he did not know why he had to go to an unknown place
sciret cur sanctum peregrinum morientem videret
he did know why he had to see a holy dying stranger
"Quid ergo, si mortuus?" conquestus est
"So what if he died?" he complained
quid ad eum pertinet?
why should this concern him?
Peregrini prope Cumas Vasudeva porttitor
The pilgrims were getting close to Vasudeva's ferry
modicum Siddhartha iterum coactus matrem suam quiescere
little Siddhartha once again forced his mother to rest
Kamala etiam lassata est
Kamala had also become tired
dum musa puer mandendo, procubuit humi
while the boy was chewing a banana, she crouched down on the ground
et clausit oculos eius a frenum et requievit
she closed her eyes a bit and rested
Sed subito emisit ululatus
But suddenly, she uttered a wailing scream
puer intuens eam in timore
the boy looked at her in fear
vidit faciem pallescere ab horrore
he saw her face had grown pale from horror
et sub veste parva, niger, anguis
and from under her dress, a small, black snake fled
coluber quo percussus Kamala
a snake by which Kamala had been bitten

Cito currebant per viam, ut ad populum pervenirent
Hurriedly, they both ran along the path, to reach people
accedunt ad porttitor ac Kamala concidit
they got near to the ferry and Kamala collapsed
et ultra ire non potuit
she was not able to go any further
puer incepit misere flere
the boy started crying miserably
clamores modo intermisso matris osculatur
his cries were only interrupted when he kissed his mother
illa quoque iunxit voce clamoribus auxilium
she also joined his loud screams for help
clamavit usque ad aures Vasudeva sonus pervenit
she screamed until the sound reached Vasudeva's ears
Vasudeva cito venit et mulierem in ulnas accepit
Vasudeva quickly came and took the woman on his arms
eam in navim portavit et puer una cucurrerunt
he carried her into the boat and the boy ran along
mox ad tugurium, ubi stabat Siddhartha iuxta focum
soon they reached the hut, where Siddhartha stood by the stove
mox accensis ignis
he was just lighting the fire
Suspexit ac primum vidit faciem pueri
He looked up and first saw the boy's face
mirum in modum admonitus aliquid
it wondrously reminded him of something
quasi commonitionem meminisse quod oblitus esset
like a warning to remember something he had forgotten
Tum Kamala vidit, quem statim agnovit
Then he saw Kamala, whom he instantly recognised
nescia iacebat in arma portitor
she lay unconscious in the ferryman's arms
nunc filium suum esse sciebat
now he knew that it was his own son
filius cuius facies talis fuerat ei commonitorium

his son whose face had been such a warning reminder to him
et cor in pectore
and the heart stirred in his chest
vulnus Kamala lotum est, sed iam nigrum vertitur
Kamala's wound was washed, but had already turned black
et corpus eius intumuit
and her body was swollen
et facta est ad bibendum medicinam
she was made to drink a healing potion
Conscientia rediit et in lecto Siddhartha iacuit
Her consciousness returned and she lay on Siddhartha's bed
Siddhartha stetit super Kamala, qui tantum amabat
Siddhartha stood over Kamala, who he used to love so much
Visum est ei sicut somnium
It seemed like a dream to her
subridens, vultum amici aspexit
with a smile, she looked at her friend's face
tardius cognovit eam condicionem
slowly she realized her situation
Recordatus est morsus fuerat
she remembered she had been bitten
et timide vocavit filium suum
and she timidly called for her son
"Tecum est, ne solliciti," dixit Siddhartha
"He's with you, don't worry," said Siddhartha
Kamala intuens oculos
Kamala looked into his eyes
Haec locuta est lingua gravi, veneno exanimata
She spoke with a heavy tongue, paralysed by the poison
"Vos factus es senex, mi", inquit
"You've become old, my dear," she said
"canescere factus es" addidit
"you've become gray," she added
"Sed vos estis sicut pueri Samana, qui sine vestibus venit".
"But you are like the young Samana, who came without clothes"

"sicut Samana es, quae pulverulentis pedibus in hortum meum venit"
"you're like the Samana who came into my garden with dusty feet"
" Multo similior es quam tu cum a me discessisti " ;
"You are much more like him than you were when you left me"
"In oculis es similis ei, Siddhartha".
"In the eyes, you're like him, Siddhartha"
"Heu, etiam consenui".
"Alas, I have also grown old"
"Potesne me adhuc agnoscere?"
"could you still recognise me?"
Siddhartha risit, "Ilico te cognovi, Kamala, mea carissima".
Siddhartha smiled, "Instantly, I recognised you, Kamala, my dear"
Kamala ostendit sibi puero
Kamala pointed to her boy
"Nonne tu eum quoque agnovisti?"
"Did you recognise him as well?"
" Filius tuus est ", confirmavit
"He is your son," she confirmed
Oculi eius confusi sunt et clausi
Her eyes became confused and fell shut
Puer flevit et Siddhartha genuflexit eum
The boy wept and Siddhartha took him on his knees
fleat et tangi comam
he let him weep and petted his hair
, viso faciei infantis, oratio Brahman ad mentem venit
at the sight of the child's face, a Brahman prayer came to his mind
orationem, quam olim didicerat
a prayer which he had learned a long time ago
quando ipse puerulus fuerat
a time when he had been a little boy himself
lente voce canora loqui coepit

Slowly, with a singing voice, he started to speak
ab anteacta pueritia, verba ad eum profluebant
from his past and childhood, the words came flowing to him
Et cum cantu illo, factus est puer tranquillus
And with that song, the boy became calm
tantum interdum gemitum edere
he was only now and then uttering a sob
et tandem obdormivit
and finally he fell asleep
Siddhartha posuit eum in lecto Vasudeva
Siddhartha placed him on Vasudeva's bed
Vasudeva stabat camini et oryza cocta
Vasudeva stood by the stove and cooked rice
Siddhartha vultu ei dedit, qui subridens rediit
Siddhartha gave him a look, which he returned with a smile
"Morietur" Siddhartha tacite dixit
"She'll die," Siddhartha said quietly
Vasudeva sciebat verum esse et adnuit
Vasudeva knew it was true, and nodded
super faciem amica currit lumen camini ignis
over his friendly face ran the light of the stove's fire
iterum, Kamala rediit ad conscientiam
once again, Kamala returned to consciousness
dolor veneni distorta facie
the pain of the poison distorted her face
Oculi Siddhartha legunt dolorem in ore suo
Siddhartha's eyes read the suffering on her mouth
pallentes genas videre patiebatur
from her pale cheeks he could see that she was suffering
Quiete legit in oculis dolorem
Quietly, he read the pain in her eyes
attente, exspectans, mens una cum dolore sua fiet
attentively, waiting, his mind become one with her suffering
Kamala sentiebat et oculorum eius intuitus quaesivit
Kamala felt it and her gaze sought his eyes
Intuitus eum, dixit

Looking at him, she spoke
"Iam video etiam oculos tuos mutatos esse".
"Now I see that your eyes have changed as well"
"Fiunt omnino alia"
"They've become completely different"
"quid adhuc agnosco in te quod est Siddhartha?
"what do I still recognise in you that is Siddhartha?"
"Est te, et non est tibi"
"It's you, and it's not you"
Siddhartha nihil dixit, tacite oculos eius aspexit
Siddhartha said nothing, quietly his eyes looked at hers
"Perfecisti eam?" rogavit
"You have achieved it?" she asked
"Invenimus pacem?"
"You have found peace?"
Subridens manum suam
He smiled and placed his hand on hers
"Video" inquit
"I'm seeing it" she said
"Ego quoque pacem inveniam".
"I too will find peace"
"Invenimus" Siddhartha in susurro locutus est
"You have found it," Siddhartha spoke in a whisper
Kamala destitit vultus in oculis eius
Kamala never stopped looking into his eyes
Cogitavit de peregrinatione sua ad Gotamam
She thought about her pilgrimage to Gotama
peregrinationem quam capere voluit
the pilgrimage which she wanted to take
ut videas faciem perfecti
in order to see the face of the perfected one
ut respirare pacem
in order to breathe his peace
sed in alio loco iam invenerat
but she had now found it in another place
et hoc putavit nimium esse bonum

and this she thought that was good too
hoc tam bonum est quam si alterum viderit
it was just as good as if she had seen the other one
Hoc voluit indicare ei
She wanted to tell this to him
sed lingua eius iam non oboedivit voluntati
but her tongue no longer obeyed her will
Sine loquendo vidit eum
Without speaking, she looked at him
vidit vitam evacuatur ab oculis eius
he saw the life fading from her eyes
dolor finalis implevit oculos suos et obscuravit eos
the final pain filled her eyes and made them grow dim
tremere ultima per membra cucurrit
the final shiver ran through her limbs
digitus eius palpebras clausit
his finger closed her eyelids

Diu sedit et eam pacifice mortuam faciem aspexit
For a long time, he sat and looked at her peacefully dead face
Diu os eius observavit
For a long time, he observed her mouth
os illi fessum vetus, labris illis, quae extenuata erant
her old, tired mouth, with those lips, which had become thin
Recordatus est os comparare cum ficu recenter findi
he remembered he used to compare this mouth with a freshly cracked fig
hoc erat in vere aetatis suae
this was in the spring of his years
Diu residens legit pallida facie
For a long time, he sat and read the pale face
defessam legit rugas
he read the tired wrinkles
hoc visu se implevit
he filled himself with this sight
faciem suam videbat eodem modo

he saw his own face in the same manner
vidit faciem eius sicut alba
he saw his face was just as white
vidit faciem suam sicut exstinguitur
he saw his face was just as quenched out
Vidit simul os et iuvenem
at the same time he saw his face and hers being young
ora rubea et ignea
their faces with red lips and fiery eyes
affectum utriusque rei simul
the feeling of both being real at the same time
aeternitatis affectum complet omnem rationem suae essentiae
the feeling of eternity completely filled every aspect of his being
hac hora altius quam umquam antea senserat
in this hour he felt more deeply than than he had ever felt before
sensit incorruptibilitatem omnis vitae
he felt the indestructibility of every life
omne momentum aeternitatem sensit
he felt the eternity of every moment
Cum resurrexit, Vasudeva oryza ei paraverat
When he rose, Vasudeva had prepared rice for him
Sed Siddhartha illa nocte non comedit
But Siddhartha did not eat that night
In stabulo stabat capra eorum
In the stable their goat stood
duo senes stramenta sibi stramenta paraverunt
the two old men prepared beds of straw for themselves
Vasudeva obdormivit
Vasudeva laid himself down to sleep
Siddhartha autem egressus foras sedit ante tugurium
But Siddhartha went outside and sat before the hut
flumine audito cingitur
he listened to the river, surrounded by the past

omni tempore vitae suae tactus et redimitus est
he was touched and encircled by all times of his life at the same time
interdum surrexit et ad ostio casae
occasionally he rose and he stepped to the door of the hut
audivit an puer dormiens
he listened whether the boy was sleeping

antequam sol cerneretur, Vasudeva e stabulo prodiit
before the sun could be seen, Vasudeva came out of the stable
ambulavit ad amicum
he walked over to his friend
"Non dormivi", inquit
"You haven't slept," he said
"Non, Vasudeva. sedi hic"
"No, Vasudeva. I sat here"
"Flumen audiebam"
"I was listening to the river"
"Fluvius multum mihi dixit"
"the river has told me a lot"
« me penitus replevit unitatem cogitationis sanationis ».
"it has deeply filled me with the healing thought of oneness"
"Dolor expertus es, Siddhartha".
"You've experienced suffering, Siddhartha"
"sed nullam video tristitiam intrasse cor tuum".
"but I see no sadness has entered your heart"
"Minime mi, quomodo tristis sim?"
"No, my dear, how should I be sad?"
" Ego, qui dives sum et felix " ;
"I, who have been rich and happy"
"Ditior factus sum et nunc beatior";
"I have become even richer and happier now"
"Filius meus mihi datus est";
"My son has been given to me"
" Filius tuus bene mihi erit ".
"Your son shall be welcome to me as well"

"Sed nunc, Siddhartha, ad laborem veniamus"
"But now, Siddhartha, let's get to work"
"multum fieri"
"there is much to be done"
"Kamala mortua est in eodem lecto quo uxor mea mortua est".
"Kamala has died on the same bed on which my wife had died"
"Faciamus rogum Kamala in monte"
"Let us build Kamala's funeral pile on the hill"
"mons in quo me uxoris rogus est".
"the hill on which I my wife's funeral pile is"
Puero adhuc dormiente, rogum construxerunt
While the boy was still asleep, they built the funeral pile

Filius
The Son

Puer timidus et flens funus matris frequentavit
Timid and weeping, the boy had attended his mother's funeral
tristis et fugax audivisset Siddhartha
gloomy and shy, he had listened to Siddhartha
Siddhartha salutavit eum ut filium suum
Siddhartha greeted him as his son
excepit eum in casa sua Vasudevae
he welcomed him at his place in Vasudeva's hut
Pallidus, per multos dies sedit in tumulo
Pale, he sat for many days by the hill of the dead
nolebat manducare
he did not want to eat
at quis non
he did not look at anyone
non aperiens cor suum
he did not open his heart
fortunam suam repugnante et negatione obvium habuit
he met his fate with resistance and denial
Siddhartha pepercit ei lectionibus
Siddhartha spared giving him lessons
et faciat sicut voluit
and he let him do as he pleased
Siddhartha honoravit filii luctus
Siddhartha honoured his son's mourning
filium suum non noverat
he understood that his son did not know him
intellexit non posse eum amare patrem
he understood that he could not love him like a father
Tarde etiam intellexit puerum undecim annos natum esse delicatum
Slowly, he also understood that the eleven-year-old was a pampered boy
vidit quod erat puer matris

he saw that he was a mother's boy
videbat se crevisse in divitum moribus
he saw that he had grown up in the habits of rich people
lautior cibus et molli strato solitus erat
he was accustomed to finer food and a soft bed
solitus erat imperare servis
he was accustomed to giving orders to servants
puer maerens non poterat subito contenta vita inter alienos
the mourning child could not suddenly be content with a life among strangers
Siddhartha intellexit puerum delicatum noluisse libenter in paupertate esse
Siddhartha understood the pampered child would not willingly be in poverty
Ad haec eum non coegit
He did not force him to do these these things
Siddhartha fecit multos chores ad puerum
Siddhartha did many chores for the boy
semper optimum frustum prandium servavit eum
he always saved the best piece of the meal for him
Tarde eum conciliare sperabat amica patientia
Slowly, he hoped to win him over, by friendly patience
Dives et laetus se vocaverat, cum puer ad eum venisset
Rich and happy, he had called himself, when the boy had come to him
Cum aliquando transisset
Since then some time had passed
puer autem peregrinus et tristis manebat
but the boy remained a stranger and in a gloomy disposition
cor superbum et contumaciter inobedientem ostendit
he displayed a proud and stubbornly disobedient heart
non vis ad operandum
he did not want to do any work
non senibus reverentiam suam
he did not pay his respect to the old men
Vasudeva de arboribus fructiferis furatus est

he stole from Vasudeva's fruit-trees
filius non adduxit ei felicitatem et pacem
his son had not brought him happiness and peace
puer ferens ei dolorem et anxietatem
the boy had brought him suffering and worry
tardius Siddhartha coepit intelligere hoc
slowly Siddhartha began to understand this
Sed diligebat eum, quantumcumque pertulisset
But he loved him regardless of the suffering he brought him
praetulit dolorem et sollicitudinem amoris in laetitiam et gaudium sine puero
he preferred the suffering and worries of love over happiness and joy without the boy
ex iuvene Siddhartha in tugurio senes scindebant opus
from when young Siddhartha was in the hut the old men had split the work
Vasudeva iterum officium portitor
Vasudeva had again taken on the job of the ferryman
et Siddhartha, ut esset cum filio suo, fecit opus in casa et agro
and Siddhartha, in order to be with his son, did the work in the hut and the field

Siddhartha diu menses exspectavit filium suum ut intelligeret eum
for long months Siddhartha waited for his son to understand him
exspectavit ut acciperet amorem suum
he waited for him to accept his love
et exspectavit filium fortasse amorem suum reciprocum
and he waited for his son to perhaps reciprocate his love
Diu menses Vasudeva expectavit, vigilantes
For long months Vasudeva waited, watching
expectavit et dixit nihil
he waited and said nothing

Quadam die iuvenis Siddhartha patrem suum valde torquebat
One day, young Siddhartha tormented his father very much
tum phialas oryza fregisset
he had broken both of his rice-bowls
Vasudeva amici sui secessit et loquebatur ei
Vasudeva took his friend aside and talked to him
"Ignosce", dixit Siddhartha .
"Pardon me," he said to Siddhartha
"Ex corde benigno, ad te loquor"
"from a friendly heart, I'm talking to you"
"Video quod te ipsum crucias".
"I'm seeing that you are tormenting yourself"
"Video te esse in dolore".
"I'm seeing that you're in grief"
"Filius tuus, carissime, solicitat te";
"Your son, my dear, is worrying you"
"et me etiam affligit".
"and he is also worrying me"
"Ille avis alia vita solet"
"That young bird is accustomed to a different life"
"In alio nido est usus vivere"
"he is used to living in a different nest"
"non, ut tu, a divitiis et urbe fugit".
"he has not, like you, run away from riches and the city"
"non fastidit et satur est cum vita in Sansara".
"he was not disgusted and fed up with the life in Sansara"
"Hc omnia fecit invitus".
"he had to do all these things against his will"
"Ille quod post haec omnia relinquere"
"he had to leave all this behind"
"Flumen quaesivi, o amice";
"I asked the river, oh friend"
"Toties fluvium petii"
"many times I have asked the river"
"Sed de hoc flumine ridet".

"But the river laughs at all of this"
"Me deridet et deridet te"
"it laughs at me and it laughs at you"
Risus tremit fluvius ad stultitiam nostram.
"the river is shaking with laughter at our foolishness"
"Aqua vult iungere aquam, sicut puer vult iuvenem iungere"
"Water wants to join water as youth wants to join youth"
"filius tuus non est in loco ubi prosperari potest".
"your son is not in the place where he can prosper"
" tu quoque fluvium petas "
"you too should ask the river"
"Tu quoque illud audi!"
"you too should listen to it!"
Conturbatus, Siddhartha inspexit amicas facies
Troubled, Siddhartha looked into his friendly face
rugas multas aspexit, in quibus hilaritas continua fuit
he looked at the many wrinkles in which there was incessant cheerfulness
"Quomodo cum eo dimittam?" dixit quiete, pudefactus
"How could I part with him?" he said quietly, ashamed
"Da mihi tempus aliquod, mi carissime";
"Give me some more time, my dear"
"Ecce ego pro eo pugno".
"See, I'm fighting for him"
"Quaero cor eius"
"I'm seeking to win his heart"
" cum amore et cum patientia amicabili eam capere intendo ".
"with love and with friendly patience I intend to capture it"
"Quando die etiam loquetur ei fluvius".
"One day, the river shall also talk to him"
"invocatur etiam";
"he also is called upon"
Vasudeva scriptor risus ardentius viguit
Vasudeva's smile flourished more warmly
"Ah vero, et ipse invocatus est".

"Oh yes, he too is called upon"
ipse est vitae aeternae.
"he too is of the eternal life"
"Sed nos, et me, quid vocatus est?"
"But do we, you and me, know what he is called upon to do?"
"scimus qua via capiendi et quid agendi ad faciendum".
"we know what path to take and what actions to perform"
"scimus quem dolorem pati debemus".
"we know what pain we have to endure"
"sed scit haec?"
"but does he know these things?"
"Non levis, dolor erit"
"Not a small one, his pain will be"
« Superbum et durum est cor eius ».
"after all, his heart is proud and hard"
"populi tales habent multum pati et errare"
"people like this have to suffer and err a lot"
"Habent facere multam iniustitiam"
"they have to do much injustice"
"et se gravant multo peccato".
"and they have burden themselves with much sin"
"Dic mihi, mi", interrogavit Siddhartha .
"Tell me, my dear," he asked of Siddhartha
"Non es imperium filii tui educatio?"
"you're not taking control of your son's upbringing?"
"Non vis eum, tu verberas, an punis?"
"You don't force him, beat him, or punish him?"
"Imo, Vasudeva, nihil horum facio".
"No, Vasudeva, I don't do any of these things"
"Sciebam. Tu eum non opprimere"
"I knew it. You don't force him"
"Non verberas eum et non ei imperare"
"you don't beat him and you don't give him orders"
"Quia scis mollitiem fortius quam difficile"
"because you know softness is stronger than hard"
"Tu scis aquam fortiorem quam saxa"

"you know water is stronger than rocks"
"et scis amor fortior quam vis"
"and you know love is stronger than force"
"Optime laudo te in hoc".
"Very good, I praise you for this"
"Sed non aliquo modo fallis?"
"But aren't you mistaken in some way?"
"nonne tibi videtur eum cogere?"
"don't you think that you are forcing him?"
"ecquid aliter punis fortasse?"
"don't you perhaps punish him a different way?"
"Nonne illum amore tuo alligabis?"
"Don't you shackle him with your love?"
"Nonne sentis eum quotidie inferiorem facere?"
"Don't you make him feel inferior every day?"
"Nonne tua humanitas et patientia id ei durius facit?"
"doesn't your kindness and patience make it even harder for him?"
"Nonne cogis eum in tugurio vivere cum duobus vetulis Musarum ficedulis?"
"aren't you forcing him to live in a hut with two old banana-eaters?"
"senes quibus et rice est in deliciis"
"old men to whom even rice is a delicacy"
"senes quorum cogitationes non possunt esse ejus"
"old men whose thoughts can't be his"
"senes quorum corda senex et quies"
"old men whose hearts are old and quiet"
"senes, quorum corda alio pede plangunt, quam sua";
"old men whose hearts beat in a different pace than his"
"Nonne in his omnibus coactus et punitus est?"
"Isn't he forced and punished by all this?""
Turbatus Siddhartha respexit ad terram
Troubled, Siddhartha looked to the ground
Quielam quaesivit, "Quid censes facere?"
Quietly, he asked, "What do you think should I do?"

Vasudeva dixit: Adducite eum in civitatem.
Vasudeva spoke, "Bring him into the city"
"Adduc eum in domum matris suae"
"bring him into his mother's house"
"Erunt servi tui, da eis".
"there'll still be servants around, give him to them"
"Et si non sunt servi, adduc eum ad magistrum".
"And if there aren't any servants, bring him to a teacher"
"sed non propter doctrinam eum ad magistrum"
"but don't bring him to a teacher for teachings' sake"
"adduc eum ad magistrum ut sit inter alios filios".
"bring him to a teacher so that he is among other children"
et perducat eum in mundum, qui est eius.
"and bring him to the world which is his own"
"Numquam hoc cogitasti?"
"have you never thought of this?"
"Visis in corde meo" Siddhartha tristis locutus est
"you're seeing into my heart," Siddhartha spoke sadly
"Saepe de hoc cogitavi".
"Often, I have thought of this"
"quomodo autem eum possum in hunc mundum mittere?"
"but how can I put him into this world?"
"Numquid ille exuberet?"
"Won't he become exuberant?"
"nonne se voluptatibus et potestati perdet?"
"won't he lose himself to pleasure and power?"
"Nonne omnia errata patris repetet?"
"won't he repeat all of his father's mistakes?"
"nonne ille fortasse in Sansara funditus peribit?"
"won't he perhaps get entirely lost in Sansara?"
Splendide porttitor risus accendit
Brightly, the ferryman's smile lit up
molliter tetigit Siddhartha brachium
softly, he touched Siddhartha's arm
"Fluvium de eo pete, mi amice!"
"Ask the river about it, my friend!"

"Audi flumen ride."
"Hear the river laugh about it!"
"Velles credere te stulta fecisse?"
"Would you actually believe that you had committed your foolish acts?"
" ut parcas filio tuo, ne eas committas "
"in order to spare your son from committing them too"
"Et tu potes aliquo modo tueri filium tuum a Sansara?"
"And could you in any way protect your son from Sansara?"
"Quomodo eum a Sansara defendes?"
"How could you protect him from Sansara?"
"Per doctrinam, orationem, admonitionem?"
"By means of teachings, prayer, admonition?"
"Carissima, esne plane oblitus es istius fabulae?"
"My dear, have you entirely forgotten that story?"
"Fabulam continet tot Lectiones"
"the story containing so many lessons"
"Fabulam de Siddhartha, Brahman filio"
"the story about Siddhartha, a Brahman's son"
"Quam rem mihi quondam narrasti hoc ipso loco?"
"the story which you once told me here on this very spot?"
"Quis Samana Siddhartha a Sansara incolumem servavit?"
"Who has kept the Samana Siddhartha safe from Sansara?"
quis eum a peccato, avaritia, et stultitia prohibuit?
"who has kept him from sin, greed, and foolishness?"
"Numquid pietas paterna eum incolumem servare potuit?
"Were his father's religious devotion able to keep him safe?"
"Numquid monita magistri sui eum salvum facere poterant?"
"were his teacher's warnings able to keep him safe?"
numquid sua scientia potuit eum custodire.
"could his own knowledge keep him safe?"
"Numquid sua quaesitio salvam servare potuit?"
"was his own search able to keep him safe?"
"Quis pater filium tueri potuit?"
"What father has been able to protect his son?"
"Quis pater filium suum, ne sibi vitam ferret?".

"what father could keep his son from living his life for himself?"
"Quis magister discipulum suum tueri potuit?"
"what teacher has been able to protect his student?"
"Quis magister discipulum suum prohibere potest ne se vita polluat?"
"what teacher can stop his student from soiling himself with life?"
"Quis eum prohibere potest quominus culpae se oneret?"
"who could stop him from burdening himself with guilt?"
"Quis illum amarum sibi potionem potare prohiberet?"
"who could stop him from drinking the bitter drink for himself?"
"Quis eum prohibere potuit quominus sibi viam inveniret?"
"who could stop him from finding his path for himself?"
"Putasne quemquam hac via parcendum esse?"
"did you think anybody could be spared from taking this path?"
"Fortasse parvulum filium tuum parcendum putasti?"
"did you think that perhaps your little son would be spared?"
"Tu putas amorem facere omnia illa?"
"did you think your love could do all that?"
"Tu putes amorem posse eum a dolore retinere"
"did you think your love could keep him from suffering"
"Tune putas amorem posse eum a dolore et dolore defendere?
"did you think your love could protect him from pain and disappointment?
"Potestis pro eo mori decies"
"you could die ten times for him"
"Sed nullam partem sortis in te potuisti".
"but you could take no part of his destiny upon yourself"
Nunquam ante, Vasudeva tot verba locutus est
Never before, Vasudeva had spoken so many words
Benigne, Siddhartha gratias egit
Kindly, Siddhartha thanked him

turbatus est in tuguriolum
he went troubled into the hut

non diu dormire potuit
he could not sleep for a long time
Vasudeva nihil ei dixerat quod nisi prius cogitaverat et scivit
Vasudeva had told him nothing he had not already thought and known
Sed hoc scire non potuit
But this was a knowledge he could not act upon
plus quam scientia erat amor pueri
stronger than knowledge was his love for the boy
plus quam scientia pietatis suae
stronger than knowledge was his tenderness
plusquam scientia timoris amittere
stronger than knowledge was his fear to lose him
num umquam ad aliquid tantum animum amisi?
had he ever lost his heart so much to something?
ecquis umquam tam temere amaverat?
had he ever loved any person so blindly?
si umquam pro aliquo tam infeliciter passus est?
had he ever suffered for someone so unsuccessfully?
quis umquam tanta sacrificia et tam infelix fecerat?
had he ever made such sacrifices for anyone and yet been so unhappy?
Siddhartha non potuit audire consilium amici sui
Siddhartha could not heed his friend's advice
non potuit cedere puero
he could not give up the boy
Iussit ei puero
He let the boy give him orders
contemnat eum
he let him disregard him
Nihil dixit et expectavit
He said nothing and waited
quotidie amicitiae certamen tentabat

daily, he attempted the struggle of friendliness
patientiae tacitum bellum initiavit
he initiated the silent war of patience
Vasudeva etiam tacuit et expectavit
Vasudeva also said nothing and waited
Erant ambo domini patientiae
They were both masters of patience

olim facies pueri admonuit eum valde Kamala
one time the boy's face reminded him very much of Kamala
Siddhartha subito habuit cogitare aliquid Kamala quondam dixit
Siddhartha suddenly had to think of something Kamala had once said
"Non potes amare" dixerat ei
"You cannot love" she had said to him
et convenerit cum ea
and he had agreed with her
et se comparaverat cum stella
and he had compared himself with a star
et cum foliis caducis parvulis comparaverat
and he had compared the childlike people with falling leaves
sed tamen in eo quoque crimen sensisse
but nevertheless, he had also sensed an accusation in that line
nunquam enim amare potuit
Indeed, he had never been able to love
numquam se totum alteri devovere potuisse
he had never been able to devote himself completely to another person
numquam se oblivisci potuit
he had never been able to to forget himself
nunquam se pro alterius amore facere potuisse stulta
he had never been able to commit foolish acts for the love of another person
eo tempore eum a puerili populo segregare visum est

at that time it seemed to set him apart from the childlike people
Sed ex quo hic filius eius fuit, Siddhartha etiam persona puerilis facta est
But ever since his son was here, Siddhartha also become a childlike person
patiebatur pro alio
he was suffering for the sake of another person
amabat alium hominem
he was loving another person
ille amissus est amor aliquis
he was lost to a love for someone else
ille stultus propter amorem
he had become a fool on account of love
Is quoque omnium passionum fortissimum et mirabilem sensit
Now he too felt the strongest and strangest of all passions
ex hac passione misere
he suffered from this passion miserably
et tamen erat in beatitudine
and he was nevertheless in bliss
Renovatus tamen est in uno
he was nevertheless renewed in one respect
hoc uno ditatus est
he was enriched by this one thing
Valde bene sentiebat amorem hunc caecum erga filium suum esse passionem
He sensed very well that this blind love for his son was a passion
sciebat esse aliquid valde humanum
he knew that it was something very human
sciebat Sansarae
he knew that it was Sansara
sciebat quod esset fons tenebrosus et tenebrosus
he knew that it was a murky source, dark waters
sed sentiebat non inutile, sed necessarium

but he felt it was not worthless, but necessary
hoc est ab essentia sui ipsius
it came from the essence of his own being
Haec voluptas etiam expiari debuit
This pleasure also had to be atoned for
hic dolor etiam tolerandus erat
this pain also had to be endured
haec quoque stulta perpetrari oportuit
these foolish acts also had to be committed
In omnibus his filius committat sua opera
Through all this, the son let him commit his foolish acts
dimittat eum pro affectione sua
he let him court for his affection
se humiliet cotidie
he let him humiliate himself every day
dedit ad modos filii sui
he gave in to the moods of his son
pater nihil habuit quod eum delectare posset
his father had nothing which could have delighted him
et nihil, quod timuit puer
and he nothing that the boy feared
Vir bonus, hic pater
He was a good man, this father
bonus, benignus, mollis
he was a good, kind, soft man
forte fuit vir valde devotus
perhaps he was a very devout man
fortasse sanctus fuit, puer cogitabat
perhaps he was a saint, the boy thought
Sed haec omnia non poterant vincere puerum
but all these attributes could not win the boy over
Ab hoc patre fastidiosus, qui eum incarceratum servaverat
He was bored by this father, who kept him imprisoned
vinctus in hac misera tuguriolo suo
a prisoner in this miserable hut of his
perforaretur ab omni malitia risu

he was bored of him answering every naughtiness with a smile
non bene iniurias respondit per amicitiam
he didn't appreciate insults being responded to by friendliness
Nolebat vitiositas rediit in misericordiam
he didn't like viciousness returned in kindness
hoc ipsum erat invisa fraudis veteris obreptionis
this very thing was the hated trick of this old sneak
multo magis puer voluisset, si ei comminatus esset
Much more the boy would have liked it if he had been threatened by him
abusi vellet
he wanted to be abused by him

Dies venit, cum iuvenis Siddhartha satis habuit
A day came when young Siddhartha had had enough
quid animo erumperet?
what was on his mind came bursting forth
et palam contra patrem
and he openly turned against his father
Siddhartha dederat ei negotium
Siddhartha had given him a task
dixerat ei se colligentes Brushwood
he had told him to gather brushwood
Sed puer casa non relinquit
But the boy did not leave the hut
in contumacia inoboedientiae et irae, mansit ubi erat
in stubborn disobedience and rage, he stayed where he was
tundebat humi pedibus
he thumped on the ground with his feet
Et exclamavit in pugnis vehementi
he clenched his fists and screamed in a powerful outburst
odium et contemptum in faciem patris
he screamed his hatred and contempt into his father's face
"Habe tibi virgulta!" clamavit, spumans

"Get the brushwood for yourself!" he shouted, foaming at the mouth
"Non sum servus tuus"
"I'm not your servant"
"Scio te non me ferire, non audebis".
"I know that you won't hit me, you wouldn't dare"
"Scio te assidue me punire velle"
"I know that you constantly want to punish me"
"Vis deponere me cum vestra pietate et indulgentia vestra".
"you want to put me down with your religious devotion and your indulgence"
"Vis me sicut tu"
"You want me to become like you"
"Vis me iustum esse devotum, mollem et sapientem sicut tu".
"you want me to be just as devout, soft, and wise as you"
"sed non faciam, modo ut te patiar".
"but I won't do it, just to make you suffer"
"Malo latrocinari fieri quam mollis esse quam tu".
"I would rather become a highway-robber than be as soft as you"
"Malo homicida esse quam sapiens esse sicut tu".
"I would rather be a murderer than be as wise as you"
"Malo ire ad infernum, quam similis esse tibi."
"I would rather go to hell, than to become like you!"
"Odi te, non es pater meus"
"I hate you, you're not my father
"etsi decies cum matre mea dormivisti, pater meus non es!"
"even if you've slept with my mother ten times, you are not my father!"
Furor et dolor in eo coquitur
Rage and grief boiled over in him
centum spumat patremque nefandum
he foamed at his father in a hundred savage and evil words
Tum puer in silvam fugit
Then the boy ran away into the forest

Erat autem nocte multa cum puer rediret
it was late at night when the boy returned
Sequenti autem mane disparuit
But the next morning, he had disappeared
Quod etiam evanuit erat cophinus?
What had also disappeared was a small basket
canistrum in quo portitores aerarii et argentei
the basket in which the ferrymen kept those copper and silver coins
denarios quos in victu
the coins which they received as a fare
Etiam in navi disparuit
The boat had also disappeared
Siddhartha vidit navem iacentem ad alteram ripam
Siddhartha saw the boat lying by the opposite bank
Siddhartha fuerat horrore
Siddhartha had been shivering with grief
verba sonantia puer tetigerat
the ranting speeches the boy had made touched him
"Sequere eum" dixit Siddhartha
"I must follow him," said Siddhartha
"Per silvam solus non potest puer ire, peribit".
"A child can't go through the forest all alone, he'll perish"
"Rem aedificare oportet, Vasudeva, ut aquam transgrediamur".
"We must build a raft, Vasudeva, to get over the water"
"Rem aedificabimus" dixit Vasudeva .
"We will build a raft" said Vasudeva
"Edificabimus eam ad navem nostram redire"
"we will build it to get our boat back"
"Sed non fugies post puerum tuum, mi amice".
"But you shall not run after your child, my friend"
"Puer non est amplius"
"he is no child anymore"
"Qui sciat quam impetro circum"
"he knows how to get around"

- 239 -

"Viam ad urbem quaerit"
"He's looking for the path to the city"
"et rectus est, noli oblivisci"
"and he is right, don't forget that"
"Agat quod te facere te ipsum"
"he's doing what you've failed to do yourself"
"Ille curae se"
"he's taking care of himself"
"Ille cursum suum sibi sumit"
"he's taking his course for himself"
"Heu, Siddhartha, video te laborare".
"Alas, Siddhartha, I see you suffering"
"sed dolorem doles quo quis rideat".
"but you're suffering a pain at which one would like to laugh"
"dolorem feres in quo mox te ridebis".
"you're suffering a pain at which you'll soon laugh yourself"
Siddhartha non responde suo
Siddhartha did not answer his friend
Iam securim in manibus tenebat
He already held the axe in his hands
ratis Bamboo facere coepit
and he began to make a raft of bamboo
Vasudeva eum adiuvit ut cannas funibus graminis ligaret
Vasudeva helped him to tie the canes together with ropes of grass
Cum flumen transgressi erant, procul ibant cursum suum
When they crossed the river they drifted far off their course
ratis adversa upriver extraxerunt ripam
they pulled the raft upriver on the opposite bank
"Cur securim pertulisti?" interrogavit Siddhartha
"Why did you take the axe along?" asked Siddhartha
"Poterat fieri ut remus navis nostrae amissae".
"It might have been possible that the oar of our boat got lost"
Sed Siddhartha noverat quid cogitaret amicus eius
But Siddhartha knew what his friend was thinking
Putabat puer remum proiecisse

He thought, the boy would have thrown away the oar
ut aliquam vindictae genus
in order to get some kind of revenge
et ne sequatur
and in order to keep them from following him
Remus in navi relictus non erat
And in fact, there was no oar left in the boat
Vasudeva ostendit in fundo navi
Vasudeva pointed to the bottom of the boat
et respexit ad amicum suum subridens
and he looked at his friend with a smile
subridens quasi aliquid dicere vellet
he smiled as if he wanted to say something
"Nonne vides quid filius tuus tibi dicere conatur?"
"Don't you see what your son is trying to tell you?"
"Nonne vides quod sequi nolit?"
"Don't you see that he doesn't want to be followed?"
Sed hoc verbis non dixit
But he did not say this in words
Remum novum incepit facere
He started making a new oar
At Siddhartha suum valedicere iussit, ut fugientem quaereret
But Siddhartha bid his farewell, to look for the run-away
Vasudeva non obstitit eum ab infante suo quaerere
Vasudeva did not stop him from looking for his child

Siddhartha diu per silvam ambulaverat
Siddhartha had been walking through the forest for a long time
occurrebat ei cogitatio inutilis
the thought occurred to him that his search was useless
Aut puer ille longe ante erat et iam in urbem pervenerat
Either the boy was far ahead and had already reached the city
aut se ab eo celaret
or he would conceal himself from him

adhuc cogitabat de filio
he continued thinking about his son
invenit se non curare filium
he found that he was not worried for his son
sciebat penitus non periisse
he knew deep inside that he had not perished
neque in ullo periculo silvae
nor was he in any danger in the forest
attamen sine intermissione cucurrit
Nevertheless, he ran without stopping
non currit servare eum
he was not running to save him
ille currit ut impleat desiderium suum
he was running to satisfy his desire
fortasse unum tempus videre voluit
he wanted to perhaps see him one more time
Et cucurrit ad solum extra civitatem
And he ran up to just outside of the city
Cum prope urbem latam viam pervenisset
When, near the city, he reached a wide road
substitit ad introitum pulchrae viridariae
he stopped, by the entrance of the beautiful pleasure-garden
hortus qui pertinebat ad Kamala
the garden which used to belong to Kamala
ubi hortus eam primum viderat
the garden where he had seen her for the first time
cum sedebat in sella sella
when she was sitting in her sedan-chair
Praeterita resurrexit in animam
The past rose up in his soul
iterum vidit se ibi stantem
again, he saw himself standing there
puer barbatus, nudus Samana
a young, bearded, naked Samana
comae comae plenae pulveris
his hair hair was full of dust

Diu, Siddhartha stabat
For a long time, Siddhartha stood there
portam apertam in hortum perspexit
he looked through the open gate into the garden
vidit monachos flavis stolas ambulantes inter pulchras arbores
he saw monks in yellow robes walking among the beautiful trees
Ibi diu stetit, cogitans
For a long time, he stood there, pondering
imagines vidit et vitae suae historiam auscultavit
he saw images and listened to the story of his life
Ibi diu stetit ad monachos
For a long time, he stood there looking at the monks
vidit iuvenem Siddhartha in loco suo
he saw young Siddhartha in their place
vidit iuvenem Kamala ambulantem in altissimis arboribus
he saw young Kamala walking among the high trees
Plane vidit se cibo et potu a Kamala ministrari
Clearly, he saw himself being served food and drink by Kamala
Vidit se primum osculum ab illa
he saw himself receiving his first kiss from her
se videbat superbe et superbe in vitam suam retractantem Brahman
he saw himself looking proudly and disdainfully back on his life as a Brahman
videbat se mundanam vitam inchoans, superbe et desiderii plenus
he saw himself beginning his worldly life, proudly and full of desire
Vidit Kamaswami, servos, orgia
He saw Kamaswami, the servants, the orgies
aleatores vidit cum aleis
he saw the gamblers with the dice
vidit Kamala scriptor avis in cavea

he saw Kamala's song-bird in the cage
iterum vixit per omnia haec
he lived through all this again
inspiravit Sansara et olim iterum senex et defessus
he breathed Sansara and was once again old and tired
fastidium sensit et iterum se velle exstinguere
he felt the disgust and the wish to annihilate himself again
et iterum sanatus est a sancto Om .
and he was healed again by the holy Om
diu Siddhartha adfuerat porta
for a long time Siddhartha had stood by the gate
desiderium intellexit stultum
he realised his desire was foolish
intellexit stultitiam esse quae eum ad locum istum ascendere fecerat
he realized it was foolishness which had made him go up to this place
intellexit se non iuvare filium suum
he realized he could not help his son
et intellexit sibi non licere
and he realized that he was not allowed to cling to him
Sensit amor pro-fugienti penitus in corde suo
he felt the love for the run-away deeply in his heart
amor in filium sensit vulnus
the love for his son felt like a wound
sed id vulnus ei datum non erat, ut gladium in eo converteret
but this wound had not been given to him in order to turn the knife in it
quod vulnus erat florere
the wound had to become a blossom
et vulnus habebat lucere
and his wound had to shine
Hoc vulnus non florere nec lucere sed tristem fecit
That this wound did not blossom or shine yet made him sad
Pro desiderato fine, vanitas erat

Instead of the desired goal, there was emptiness
traxerat hie inanitas, moesta sedit
emptiness had drawn him here, and sadly he sat down
sensit aliquid mori in corde suo
he felt something dying in his heart
vidit inanem et non vidit amplius gaudium
he experienced emptiness and saw no joy any more
nullus finis quo intendere
there was no goal for which to aim for
Sedit in cogitatione et expectavit
He sat lost in thought and waited
Hoc flumine didicerat
This he had learned by the river
exspectans, patientiam habens, attente audiendo
waiting, having patience, listening attentively
Et sedebat et audiebat in pulvere viae
And he sat and listened, in the dust of the road
et ad cor suum audiebat, graviter tundens et maerens
he listened to his heart, beating tiredly and sadly
et expectavit vocem
and he waited for a voice
Multae horae cubavit, audiendo
Many an hour he crouched, listening
nullas imagines vidit amplius
he saw no images any more
in vacuum cecidit et ipse cadens
he fell into emptiness and let himself fall
nullam viam videre potuit coram eo
he could see no path in front of him
Utque ardentem vulnus sensit, tacite locutus est Om
And when he felt the wound burning, he silently spoke the Om
om se implevit
he filled himself with Om
Monachi in horto viderunt eum
The monks in the garden saw him

pulvis colligebat in canities
dust was gathering on his gray hair
cum per multas horas cubaret, unus ex monachis duas aliquet ante se posuit
since he crouched for many hours, one of monks placed two bananas in front of him
Senex non videbat eum
The old man did not see him

Ex hac saxea civitate excitatus est manu tangens humerum suum
From this petrified state, he was awoken by a hand touching his shoulder
Protinus agnovit tactum hunc tenerum verecunde
Instantly, he recognised this tender bashful touch
Vasudeva sequebantur eum et expectabant
Vasudeva had followed him and waited
resipuit et surrexit ad Vasudevam
he regained his senses and rose to greet Vasudeva
Vasudeva amica inspexit faciem
he looked into Vasudeva's friendly face
rugis inspexerat
he looked into the small wrinkles
rugae erant quasi nihil nisi risu repleti
his wrinkles were as if they were filled with nothing but his smile
oculos laetos inspexit et subridens quoque
he looked into the happy eyes, and then he smiled too
Nunc aliquet ante ipsum iacentem vidit
Now he saw the bananas lying in front of him
aliquet sustulit et unum dedit portitori
he picked the bananas up and gave one to the ferryman
Postquam aliquet comederunt, taciti in silvam reversi sunt
After eating the bananas, they silently went back into the forest
Reversi sunt in domum suam ad portitor

they returned home to the ferry
Nec quisquam de iis, quae illo die acciderant, loquebatur
Neither one talked about what had happened that day
neuter nomen pueri
neither one mentioned the boy's name
nec quisquam de eo fugiens locutus est
neither one spoke about him running away
nec quisquam de vulnere locutus est
neither one spoke about the wound
Siddhartha in tugurio iacebat in lecto suo
In the hut, Siddhartha lay down on his bed
Post aliquantum Vasudeva venit ad eum
after a while Vasudeva came to him
pateram lactis Cocoes
he offered him a bowl of coconut-milk
sed iam dormiebat
but he was already asleep

Om

Diu vulnus ardebat
For a long time the wound continued to burn
Siddhartha habebat multos viatores trans flumen vada
Siddhartha had to ferry many travellers across the river
multi viatores comitabantur filium vel filiam
many of the travellers were accompanied by a son or a daughter
et neminem eorum vidit sine invidia
and he saw none of them without envying them
non poterat videre sine cogitatione amissum filium
he couldn't see them without thinking about his lost son
" Tot milia fortunarum dulcissima possident " ;
"So many thousands possess the sweetest of good fortunes"
"cur non ego quoque hanc teneo fortunam?"
"why don't I also possess this good fortune?"
"etiam fures et latrones liberos habent et eos amant."
"even thieves and robbers have children and love them"
"et amantur a liberis".
"and they are being loved by their children"
"amantur omnes a liberis praeter me".
"all are loved by their children except for me"
nunc quasi puerili, sine causa
he now thought like the childlike people, without reason
factus est unus ex parvulis hominibus
he had become one of the childlike people
aliter quam prius aspexit
he looked upon people differently than before
ille minus dolor et minus superbus sui
he was less smart and less proud of himself
sed erat calidior et curiosior
but instead, he was warmer and more curious
cum iter faceret, plus implicatus quam ante
when he ferried travellers, he was more involved than before
puerili homines, negotiatores, bellatores, mulieres

childlike people, businessmen, warriors, women
isti non videntur ab eo aliena, sicut solebant
these people did not seem alien to him, as they used to
intellexit eos vitae suae participes
he understood them and shared their life
vita, quae non cogitata et scientia ducitur
a life which was not guided by thoughts and insight
sed vita sola urgentibus et votis ducitur
but a life guided solely by urges and wishes
sensit ut puerili populo
he felt like the the childlike people
extremum vulnus ferebat
he was bearing his final wound
appropinquaret perfectum
he was nearing perfection
sed adhuc populus parvulus videbatur sicut fratres eius
but the childlike people still seemed like his brothers
eorum vanitates, cupiditates possessionis non amplius ridiculae sunt
their vanities, desires for possession were no longer ridiculous to him
facti sunt comprehensibile et amabile
they became understandable and lovable
ipsi etiam venerabiles facti sunt
they even became worthy of veneration to him
Caecus amor matris ad prolem
The blind love of a mother for her child
stultorum et caeca superbia patris Unico nato
the stupid, blind pride of a conceited father for his only son
caeca, ferox iuvenis, vanae femina pro jocalibus
the blind, wild desire of a young, vain woman for jewellery
ea vis admirans aspectus ab hominibus
her wish for admiring glances from men
Omnes hi simplices cohortes non sunt pueriles notiones
all of these simple urges were not childish notions
sed erant valde fortes, vivi, et urgentes praevalentes

but they were immensely strong, living, and prevailing urges
vidit homines viventes propter suas angustias
he saw people living for the sake of their urges
Vidit homines ad res raras suas urget
he saw people achieving rare things for their urges
iter, bella, patiens
travelling, conducting wars, suffering
ferebant infinitum doloris
they bore an infinite amount of suffering
et amare potuit pro eo, quia videbat vitam
and he could love them for it, because he saw life
quod vivum erat in singulis passionibus
that what is alive was in each of their passions
quod incorruptibile erat in suadet, Brahman
that what is is indestructible was in their urges, the Brahman
isti amore et admiratione digni
these people were worthy of love and admiration
caeca fide et caeca virtute meruere
they deserved it for their blind loyalty and blind strength
nihil quod deerat
there was nothing that they lacked
Siddhartha nihil habuit quod eum praeponeret praeter unum
Siddhartha had nothing which would put him above the rest, except one thing
parum adhuc erat quod non habebat
there still was a small thing he had which they didn't
sibi consciam cogitationem totius vitae
he had the conscious thought of the oneness of all life
sed Siddhartha etiam dubitavit an haec scientia tanti aestimari debeat
but Siddhartha even doubted whether this knowledge should be valued so highly
posset etiam esse puerilis idea cogitationis hominum
it might also be a childish idea of the thinking people
saeculares pares sapientibus erant

the worldly people were of equal rank to the wise men
animalia etiam quibusdam momentis videntur hominibus esse superiora
animals too can in some moments seem to be superior to humans
superiores sunt in duris et inexorabilis faciendis necessariis
they are superior in their tough, unrelenting performance of what is necessary
ideam tardius floruit in Siddhartha
an idea slowly blossomed in Siddhartha
et notio tardius in eo
and the idea slowly ripened in him
coepit videre quae sapientia erat
he began to see what wisdom actually was
vidit quae sit longae quaestionis meta
he saw what the goal of his long search was
quaesitio eius nihil aliud erat quam animi promptitudo
his search was nothing but a readiness of the soul
occultam artem quovis momento cogitare, dum vitam suam vivit
a secret art to think every moment, while living his life
una cogitatio
it was the thought of oneness
ut possit sentire unitatem
to be able to feel and inhale the oneness
Tarde haec conscientia in eo floruit
Slowly this awareness blossomed in him
relucebat apud eum ex vetere Vasudeva, facie puerili
it was shining back at him from Vasudeva's old, childlike face
concordia et cognitio aeternae perfectionis mundi
harmony and knowledge of the eternal perfection of the world
subridens et pars unitatis
smiling and to be part of the oneness
Vulnus tamen ardet
But the wound still burned
cupide et amare Siddhartha cogitabat filium suum

longingly and bitterly Siddhartha thought of his son
caritatem suam et viscera in corde suo nutrivit
he nurtured his love and tenderness in his heart
dolor corrodere eum permisit
he allowed the pain to gnaw at him
omnia stulta amoris
he committed all foolish acts of love
ipsa flamma non exiret
this flame would not go out by itself

olim vulnus incensum
one day the wound burned violently
anno acti, Siddhartha flumen transiit
driven by a yearning, Siddhartha crossed the river
ille navim emisit et ad civitatem ire voluit
he got off the boat and was willing to go to the city
iterum quaerere voluit filium suum
he wanted to look for his son again
Fluvius molliter et quiete ibat
The river flowed softly and quietly
siccitate erat, sed vox sonabat insolita;
it was the dry season, but its voice sounded strange
constabat audire quod flumen risit
it was clear to hear that the river laughed
clare et clare risit ad senem porttitor
it laughed brightly and clearly at the old ferryman
inclinavit se super aquam, ut magis audiret
he bent over the water, in order to hear even better
et vidit faciem suam in aquis quiete reflexam
and he saw his face reflected in the quietly moving waters
hoc erat in facie reflexo aliquid
in this reflected face there was something
quod monuerat, sed oblitus
something which reminded him, but he had forgotten
cum de eo cogitaret, invenit
as he thought about it, he found it

haec facies erat similis alteri faciei quam sciebat et amare solebat
this face resembled another face which he used to know and love
sed etiam faciem timebat
but he also used to fear this face
Patris vultus similis est, Brahman
It resembled his father's face, the Brahman
recordatus est quomodo eum pater coegit dimittere
he remembered how he had forced his father to let him go
recordatus est quomodo sibi renuntiasset
he remembered how he had bid his farewell to him
recordatus est quomodo abisset et numquam rediret
he remembered how he had gone and had never come back
Nonne etiam pater eius eundem illum dolorem admisit?
Had his father not also suffered the same pain for him?
paterni dolor non dolor Siddhartha nunc laborat?
was his father's pain not the pain Siddhartha is suffering now?
Pater ejus non ita pridem mortuus est?
Had his father not long since died?
an ne iterum filium vidisset?
had he died without having seen his son again?
Nonne ipse sibi eandem exspectet fortunam?
Did he not have to expect the same fate for himself?
Nonne comoedia in circulo fatali?
Was it not a comedy in a fateful circle?
De his omnibus risit fluvius
The river laughed about all of this
omnia reversa sunt quae non sunt passi
everything came back which had not been suffered
omne quod non fuerat solutum
everything came back which had not been solved
idem dolor passus est atque etiam
the same pain was suffered over and over again
Siddhartha reversus est in navi
Siddhartha went back into the boat

et reuersus est ad tugurium
and he returned back to the hut
de patre et filio cogitabat
he was thinking of his father and of his son
ratus deridendum flumine
he thought of having been laughed at by the river
dissidet sibi et tendit ad desperationem
he was at odds with himself and tending towards despair
sed etiam tentatus est risum
but he was also tempted to laugh
se ipsum et mundum rideat
he could laugh at himself and the entire world
Heu, vulnus nondum floruit!
Alas, the wound was not blossoming yet
adhuc erat in corde suo fatum pugnando
his heart was still fighting his fate
laetitia et victoria nondum ex dolore micantes
cheerfulness and victory were not yet shining from his suffering
spem tamen cum desperatione percepit
Nevertheless, he felt hope along with the despair
semel ad tugurium rediit, desiderium inexpugnabile ad Vasudeva aperiendum sensit
once he returned to the hut he felt an undefeatable desire to open up to Vasudeva
omnia voluit ostendere
he wanted to show him everything
omnia dicere voluit magistro auscultandi
he wanted to say everything to the master of listening

Vasudeva in tugurio sedebat, cophinum texens
Vasudeva was sitting in the hut, weaving a basket
Phasellus ut porttitor neque
He no longer used the ferry-boat
oculi eius incipiens ad infirma
his eyes were starting to get weak

bracchia et manus erant debiles
his arms and hands were getting weak as well
modo hilaritas et hilaritas vultus immutabilis erat
only the joy and cheerful benevolence of his face was unchanging
Siddhartha sedit iuxta senem
Siddhartha sat down next to the old man
lente loqui coepit de iis quae numquam locuti sunt
slowly, he started talking about what they had never spoke about
dixit ei de ambulatione sua ad urbem
he told him of his walk to the city
dixit ad eum de vulnere ardenti
he told at him of the burning wound
dixit ei de invidia videndi patres beati
he told him about the envy of seeing happy fathers
scientiam stultitiam talium voluntatum
his knowledge of the foolishness of such wishes
contra voluntatem suam vanam pugnam
his futile fight against his wishes
omnia dicere poterat, etiam gravissima
he was able to say everything, even the most embarrassing parts
dixit ei omnia posset indicare ei
he told him everything he could tell him
ostendit ei omnia monstrare
he showed him everything he could show him
vulnus suum ei obtulit
He presented his wound to him
Item dixit ei quomodo hodie fugerat
he also told him how he had fled today
dixit ei quomodo trans aquam
he told him how he ferried across the water
puerile currunt, volens ambulare in urbem
a childish run-away, willing to walk to the city
et dixit ei quomodo flumen risisset

and he told him how the river had laughed
diu locutus est
he spoke for a long time
Vasudeva cum placida facie audiebat
Vasudeva was listening with a quiet face
Vasudeva auscultatio Siddhartha fortius sensum dedit quam umquam ante
Vasudeva's listening gave Siddhartha a stronger sensation than ever before
sensit dolorem et timores ad eum defluxisse
he sensed how his pain and fears flowed over to him
persensit quomodo super eum fluxit secreta spes eius
he sensed how his secret hope flowed over him
Vulnus auditori ostendere idem fuit ac lavari in flumine
To show his wound to this listener was the same as bathing it in the river
flumen refrigeratum vulnus Siddhartha
the river would have cooled Siddhartha's wound
audire quietam refrigeratum vulnus Siddhartha
the quiet listening cooled Siddhartha's wound
donec una cum flumine eum refrigeravit
it cooled him until he become one with the river
Adhuc eo loquente, adhuc confitens et confitens
While he was still speaking, still admitting and confessing
Siddhartha magis magisque sensit hanc iam non esse Vasudeva
Siddhartha felt more and more that this was no longer Vasudeva
iam non erat homo qui eum audiebat
it was no longer a human being who was listening to him
hic immotus auditor confessionem suam in se trahebat
this motionless listener was absorbing his confession into himself
hic auditor immotus erat sicut arbor pluviae
this motionless listener was like a tree the rain
hic immobilis erat

this motionless man was the river itself
hic homo immotus erat ipse Deus
this motionless man was God himself
homo immobilis erat ipsum aeternum
the motionless man was the eternal itself
Siddhartha desiit cogitare de se et de vulnere suo
Siddhartha stopped thinking of himself and his wound
haec effectio Vasudeva mutatis moribus occupavit
this realisation of Vasudeva's changed character took possession of him
et quo plus introivit in illam, eo minus admirabile factum est;
and the more he entered into it, the less wondrous it became
quo magis omnia ordine naturalique intellexit
the more he realised that everything was in order and natural
intellexit Vasudeva iam diu sic fuisse
he realised that Vasudeva had already been like this for a long time
nuper non satis agnovit tamen
he had just not quite recognised it yet
Ipse paene eodem modo venerat
yes, he himself had almost reached the same state
Sensit, se iam videre senem Vasudeva sicut homines deos
He felt, that he was now seeing old Vasudeva as the people see the gods
sensitque hoc durare non posse
and he felt that this could not last
in corde suo valedicens proficiscitur Vasudeva .
in his heart, he started bidding his farewell to Vasudeva
Per haec omnia sine intermissione loquebatur
Throughout all this, he talked incessantly
Finito sermone, Vasudeva oculos suos ad eum convertit
When he had finished talking, Vasudeva turned his friendly eyes at him
oculi qui creverant leviter infirma
the eyes which had grown slightly weak

nihil dixit, sed tacitus amor et hilaritas luceat
he said nothing, but let his silent love and cheerfulness shine
intellectus et scientia eius fulgebant ab eo
his understanding and knowledge shone from him
Manus autem Siddharthae apprehendit et duxit eum ad sedem iuxta ripam
He took Siddhartha's hand and led him to the seat by the bank
sedit secum et subridens in flumine
he sat down with him and smiled at the river
"Ridere audisti", inquit
"You've heard it laugh," he said
"At non audistis omnia"
"But you haven't heard everything"
"Audiamus, audies plura".
"Let's listen, you'll hear more"
Leniter insonuit flumen, multis vocibus canens
Softly sounded the river, singing in many voices
Siddhartha inspexerat aquam
Siddhartha looked into the water
simulacra apparuerunt in aqua
images appeared to him in the moving water
pater, solus et lugens filii
his father appeared, lonely and mourning for his son
ipse apparuit in aqua viva
he himself appeared in the moving water
ipse etiam longinquo filio servitute devinctus
he was also being tied with the bondage of yearning to his distant son
filius apparuit, sola etiam
his son appeared, lonely as well
puer, ardenti cursu properans per vota iuvenum
the boy, greedily rushing along the burning course of his young wishes
unusquisque petebat metam
each one was heading for his goal
quisque obsessus est finis

each one was obsessed by the goal
quisque patiebatur ab studio
each one was suffering from the pursuit
Flumen cecinit voce doloris
The river sang with a voice of suffering
desideranter cantavit et ad suum metam profluebat
longingly it sang and flowed towards its goal
"Audisne?" Vasudeva quaesivit mutus aspectus
"Do you hear?" Vasudeva asked with a mute gaze
Siddhartha annuisset respondens
Siddhartha nodded in reply
"Audi melius!" Vasudeva susurrabant
"Listen better!" Vasudeva whispered
Siddhartha conatus est audire meliorem
Siddhartha made an effort to listen better
Imago patris apparuit
The image of his father appeared
sua imago immiscet patris sui
his own image merged with his father's
imago filii sui immiscet imaginem
the image of his son merged with his image
Kamala imago etiam apparuit et dispersa est
Kamala's image also appeared and was dispersed
et Govinda imago, et aliae imagines
and the image of Govinda, and other images
omniaque simulacro immiscet se
and all the imaged merged with each other
omne imaginatum in flumen
all the imaged turned into the river
cum flumen omnes peterent
being the river, they all headed for the goal
desiderare, desiderare, confluere
longing, desiring, suffering flowed together
et vox fluvii plena desiderii sonabat
and the river's voice sounded full of yearning
vox erat fluminis ardentis vae

the river's voice was full of burning woe
insatiabilis fluminis vox erat plena desiderio
the river's voice was full of unsatisfiable desire
Meta, flumen tenderet
For the goal, the river was heading
Siddhartha vidit fluvium festinantem ad metam
Siddhartha saw the river hurrying towards its goal
ad rivum illum et suos et omnes homines quos viderat
the river of him and his loved ones and of all people he had ever seen
Omnes hi fluctus et aquae currebant
all of these waves and waters were hurrying
sunt omnes cruciatus ad multa proposita
they were all suffering towards many goals
cataracta, lacus, rapids, mare
the waterfall, the lake, the rapids, the sea
ac fines perventum
and all goals were reached
et omnis meta secuta est a novo
and every goal was followed by a new one
et facta est aqua in vaporem et ascendit in caelum
and the water turned into vapour and rose to the sky
aqua in pluviam versa et demissa de caelo
the water turned into rain and poured down from the sky
aquam convertit in fontem
the water turned into a source
inde fons vertitur in rivum
then the source turned into a stream
amnis conversus in flumen
the stream turned into a river
flumenque urguente
and the river headed forwards again
Sed vox desiderans mutaverat
But the longing voice had changed
Resonabat adhuc, plenus doloris, inquisitionis
It still resounded, full of suffering, searching

sed aliae voces iunguntur flumine
but other voices joined the river
voces gaudii et doloris
there were voices of joy and of suffering
voces bonae et malae, ridentes et tristes
good and bad voices, laughing and sad ones
centum vocibus mille vocibus
a hundred voices, a thousand voices
Siddhartha audiebat omnes has voces
Siddhartha listened to all these voices
iam nihil nisi auditor erat
He was now nothing but a listener
omnino intentus audire
he was completely concentrated on listening
omnino vacua nunc
he was completely empty now
Sensit enim iam discere ad audiendum
he felt that he had now finished learning to listen
Saepius ante haec omnia audiverat
Often before, he had heard all this
has multas voces in flumine audiverat
he had heard these many voices in the river
hodie in flumine voces novae sonuerunt
today the voices in the river sounded new
Iam, multas voces seorsum iam dicere non poterat
Already, he could no longer tell the many voices apart
nulla differentia inter laetas voces et flentes erat
there was no difference between the happy voices and the weeping ones
voces infantium et hominum voces erant
the voices of children and the voices of men were one
Omnes voces simul
all these voices belonged together
luctus desiderio et risus sapientibus
the lamentation of yearning and the laughter of the knowledgeable one

et clamor irae et gemitus morientium
the scream of rage and the moaning of the dying ones
omne unum et omnia contexitur
everything was one and everything was intertwined
omnia connexa perplexa millies
everything was connected and entangled a thousand times
omnia simul omnes voces omnes metas
everything together, all voices, all goals
omnis amor, omnis dolor, omnis voluptas;
all yearning, all suffering, all pleasure
omnia bona et mala
all that was good and evil
totum hoc simul erat mundus
all of this together was the world
Omnes simul fluxus rerum
All of it together was the flow of events
omnibus erat musica vitae
all of it was the music of life
Cum Siddhartha attente audiebat hunc fluvium
when Siddhartha was listening attentively to this river
canticum mille vocum
the song of a thousand voices
cum nec dolorem nec risus
when he neither listened to the suffering nor the laughter
cum animam ad quamlibet vocem non ligavit
when he did not tie his soul to any particular voice
cum se in flumen immersit
when he submerged his self into the river
sed cum omnes audiret, totum unum
but when he heard them all he perceived the whole, the oneness
tum magnus millium vocum cantus uno verbo constabat
then the great song of the thousand voices consisted of a single word
id verbum om; perfectio
this word was Om; the perfection

"Audisne" iterum intuitus Vasudeva quaesivit
"Do you hear" Vasudeva's gaze asked again
Brightly, Vasudeva scriptor risus lucebat
Brightly, Vasudeva's smile was shining
volabat radians super omnes rugas veteris vultus
it was floating radiantly over all the wrinkles of his old face
Sic et Om fluebat in aere super omnes voces fluminis
the same way the Om was floating in the air over all the voices of the river
Risu splendide lucebat, cum amicum suum aspexit
Brightly his smile was shining, when he looked at his friend
clare eodem risu iam incipiens lucere in Siddhartha facies
and brightly the same smile was now starting to shine on Siddhartha's face
Vulnus eius floruit et dolor eius lucebat
His wound had blossomed and his suffering was shining
sui volaverunt in unum
his self had flown into the oneness
Hac hora, Siddhartha fatum suum pugnare desiit
In this hour, Siddhartha stopped fighting his fate
simul desiit dolorem
at the same time he stopped suffering
In facie ejus floruit hilaritas cognitionis
On his face flourished the cheerfulness of a knowledge
quae cognitio nulla voluntate amplius repugnabat
a knowledge which was no longer opposed by any will
cognitio quae cognoscit perfectionem
a knowledge which knows perfection
quae scientia cum rerum fluxu consentaneum est
a knowledge which is in agreement with the flow of events
scientia quae viget vitae
a knowledge which is with the current of life
plenus misericordiae pro dolor aliorum
full of sympathy for the pain of others
plenus misericordiae ad voluptatem aliorum

full of sympathy for the pleasure of others
fluere, ad unum
devoted to the flow, belonging to the oneness
Vasudeva resurrexit ab sede ad ripam
Vasudeva rose from the seat by the bank
inspexit Siddhartha oculos
he looked into Siddhartha's eyes
et hilaritatem cognitionis vidit in oculis eius fulgentem
and he saw the cheerfulness of the knowledge shining in his eyes
molliter umerum manu tetigit
he softly touched his shoulder with his hand
"Hanc horam exspectavi, fratres carissimi"
"I've been waiting for this hour, my dear"
"Nunc quod venit, sinite me abire".
"Now that it has come, let me leave"
"Ham horam diu expectavi".
"For a long time, I've been waiting for this hour"
"diu Vasudeva portitor fui"
"for a long time, I've been Vasudeva the ferryman"
"Nunc satis est. Vale"
"Now it's enough. Farewell"
"Vale flumen, vale Siddhartha!"
"farewell river, farewell Siddhartha!"
Siddhartha fecit arcum altum ei qui valedicens
Siddhartha made a deep bow before him who bid his farewell
"Novi" inquit
"I've known it," he said quietly
"Ibis in silvas?"
"You'll go into the forests?"
"Eo in silvas"
"I'm going into the forests"
"Ego in unum" locutus est Vasudeva cum splendido risu
"I'm going into the oneness" spoke Vasudeva with a bright smile
Cum splendido risu, discessit

With a bright smile, he left
Siddhartha observavit relinquens
Siddhartha watched him leaving
Magno cum gaudio, magna cum solemnitate, observavit eum licentia
With deep joy, with deep solemnity he watched him leave
vidit gressus suos pacem
he saw his steps were full of peace
vidit caput eius splendore plenum
he saw his head was full of lustre
vidit corpus eius lucidum
he saw his body was full of light

Govinda

Govinda diu fuerat cum monachis
Govinda had been with the monks for a long time
si non in peregrinationibus, in viridario commoratus est
when not on pilgrimages, he spent his time in the pleasure-garden
hortum quem meretrix Kamala sectatoribus Gotamae dederat
the garden which the courtesan Kamala had given the followers of Gotama
audierat garrulus de vete, qui vixit a via unius diei
he heard talk of an old ferryman, who lived a day's journey away
audivit multa eum sapientem esse
he heard many regarded him as a wise man
Cum Govinda reversus est, viam ad vada delegit
When Govinda went back, he chose the path to the ferry
cupiebat videre portitor
he was eager to see the ferryman
in omni vita per regulas vixerat
he had lived his entire life by the rules
a iunioribus monachis in veneratione habitus est
he was looked upon with veneration by the younger monks
aetatem ac modestiam
they respected his age and modesty
sed inquietudo eius ex animo non periit
but his restlessness had not perished from his heart
quaerebat quid non invenisset
he was searching for what he had not found
Venit ad flumen et rogavit senem ut vadas in eum
He came to the river and asked the old man to ferry him over
cum egrederetur scapham in altera parte, locutus est cum sene
when they got off the boat on the other side, he spoke with the old man

"Tu es valde bonus nobis monachis et peregrinis".
"You're very good to us monks and pilgrims"
"vos multos trans flumen transmisistis"
"you have ferried many of us across the river"
"Nonne tu quoque, portitor, rectam scrutator semitam?"
"Aren't you too, ferryman, a searcher for the right path?"
subridens oculis senex, Siddhartha locutus est
smiling from his old eyes, Siddhartha spoke
"O venerande, te perscrutorem vocas?"
"oh venerable one, do you call yourself a searcher?"
"Numquid adhuc scrutator es, licet iam bene sit annis?"
"are you still a searcher, although already well in years?"
"Quaeris dum toga monachi Gotamae gerens?"
"do you search while wearing the robe of Gotama's monks?"
Locutus est Govinda "verum sum"
"It's true, I'm old," spoke Govinda
"Sed inquisitione non cessavi"
"but I haven't stopped searching"
"Ego numquam desistas quaerere"
"I will never stop searching"
"Fatum meum hoc esse videtur"
"this seems to be my destiny"
"Tu quoque, ut mihi quidem videtur, quaesisti".
"You too, so it seems to me, have been searching"
"Vis aliquid dicere, o honeste?"
"Would you like to tell me something, oh honourable one?"
"Quid habeo quod dicam tibi, o venerabilis?"
"What might I have that I could tell you, oh venerable one?"
"Fortasse dicerem tibi quod nimium multa exquiris?"
"Perhaps I could tell you that you're searching far too much?"
"Ego tibi dicam quod tempus inveniendi non facis?"
"Could I tell you that you don't make time for finding?"
"Quomodo?" interrogavit Govinda
"How come?" asked Govinda
"Cum aliquis inquirit ut solum videant quid quaerant".

"When someone is searching they might only see what they search for"
"non posset aliquid aliud in mentem venire".
"he might not be able to let anything else enter his mind"
"Non videt quid non quaerit"
"he doesn't see what he is not searching for"
"quia semper nihil cogitat nisi de quo quaeritur".
"because he always thinks of nothing but the object of his search"
"propositum habet, quo obsessus est."
"he has a goal, which he is obsessed with"
"Quaerere significat propositum habens"
"Searching means having a goal"
"Invenire autem significat liberum esse, apertum et non habentem propositum";
"But finding means being free, open, and having no goal"
"Tu, venerande, forsitan perscrutor es".
"You, oh venerable one, are perhaps indeed a searcher"
"quia, cum ad propositum tendis, multa sunt quae non vides".
"because, when striving for your goal, there are many things you don't see"
"non videres ea quae sunt in conspectu oculorum tuorum directe"
"you might not see things which are directly in front of your eyes"
"Nihil satis intelligo", Govinda dixit, **"quid hoc vis?"**
"I don't quite understand yet," said Govinda, "what do you mean by this?"
"O venerabilis, ad hoc flumen ante diu fuisti"
"oh venerable one, you've been at this river before, a long time ago"
"et invenisti dormientem hominem ad flumen"
"and you have found a sleeping man by the river"
"Sedisti cum eo ad somnum suum custodiendum".
"you have sat down with him to guard his sleep"

"sed, o Govinda, dormientem non agnovisti".
"but, oh Govinda, you did not recognise the sleeping man"
Govinda obstupuit, quasi magico carmine obiectum fuisset
Govinda was astonished, as if he had been the object of a magic spell
monachus inspicitur portitor oculis
the monk looked into the ferryman's eyes
"Tune es Siddhartha?" interrogavit timida voce
"Are you Siddhartha?" he asked with a timid voice
"Noli te hoc tempore vel agnovisse!"
"I wouldn't have recognised you this time either!"
"Ex corde meo te, Siddhartha", salveo.
"from my heart, I'm greeting you, Siddhartha"
"Ex corde meo gaudeo te iterum videre!"
"from my heart, I'm happy to see you once again!"
"Multum mutasti, mi amice"
"You've changed a lot, my friend"
"et nunc portitor factus es?"
"and you've now become a ferryman?"
Amice, Siddhartha risit
In a friendly manner, Siddhartha laughed
"Immo portitor sum"
"yes, I am a ferryman"
"Multi homines, Govinda, multum mutare habent"
"Many people, Govinda, have to change a lot"
"habent stolas multas"
"they have to wear many robes"
"unus sum eorum qui multum muto";
"I am one of those who had to change a lot"
"Suscipe, Govinda, et in casa mea pernoctabimus".
"Be welcome, Govinda, and spend the night in my hut"
Govinda pernoctavimus in tugurio
Govinda stayed the night in the hut
dormivit in lecto, qui solebat esse in lecto Vasudeva
he slept on the bed which used to be Vasudeva's bed
multae quaestiones amico iuventutis

he posed many questions to the friend of his youth
Siddhartha debuit ei multa narrare de vita sua
Siddhartha had to tell him many things from his life

et facta est altera mane
then the next morning came
tempus diei initium venerat
the time had come to start the day's journey
sine haesitatione Govinda unum plura quaesivit
without hesitation, Govinda asked one more question
"Antequam iter pergo, Siddhartha, permitte mihi unam quaestionem quaerere".
"Before I continue on my path, Siddhartha, permit me to ask one more question"
"Habesne doctrinam quae te ducit?"
"Do you have a teaching that guides you?"
"Tu fidem habes, vel notitiam tui sequeris";
"Do you have a faith or a knowledge you follow"
"Estne scientia quae te juvat recte vivere et facere?"
"is there a knowledge which helps you to live and do right?"
"Bene scis, mi karissime, semper me magistrorum diffidere";
"You know well, my dear, I have always been distrustful of teachers"
"Iuvenem iam coepi dubitare magistri"
"as a young man I already started to doubt teachers"
"cum in silva viximus cum paenitentibus, diffisi doctrinam eorum".
"when we lived with the penitents in the forest, I distrusted their teachings"
"et dorsum meum ad illos".
"and I turned my back to them"
" diffidens magistris fui"
"I have remained distrustful of teachers"
"Tamen ego multos magistros habui ex tunc";
"Nevertheless, I have had many teachers since then"
"Formosa meretrix diu magister meus fuit"

"A beautiful courtesan has been my teacher for a long time"
"Mercator dives fuit magister meus"
"a rich merchant was my teacher"
" et quosdam aleatores cum aleis me docuit ";
"and some gamblers with dice taught me"
"Olim, etiam sectator Buddha magister meus fuit".
"Once, even a follower of Buddha has been my teacher"
"Pedatum iter faciebat, peregrinatio"
"he was travelling on foot, pilgering"
"et sedit mecum cum in silva dormieram"
"and he sat with me when I had fallen asleep in the forest"
"Ego quoque ab eo didici, quod habeo gratiam".
"I've also learned from him, for which I'm very grateful"
"Sed maxime ab hoc flumine didici".
"But most of all, I have learned from this river"
"et ego a Decessore Nostro, Portitor Vasudeva".
"and I have learned most from my predecessor, the ferryman Vasudeva"
"Is erat valde simplex, Vasudeva, non erat excogitator".
"He was a very simple person, Vasudeva, he was no thinker"
"sed sciebat necessarium sicut Gotama".
"but he knew what is necessary just as well as Gotama"
" vir perfectus fuit, vir sanctus ".
"he was a perfect man, a saint"
"Siddhartha adhuc amat homines irridere, mihi videtur"
"Siddhartha still loves to mock people, it seems to me"
"Credo in te et scio quod magistrum non secutus es"
"I believe in you and I know that you haven't followed a teacher"
"At non invenisti aliquid a te?"
"But haven't you found something by yourself?"
"Quamvis doctrinas non inveneris, cogitationes tamen quasdam invenisti".
"though you've found no teachings, you still found certain thoughts"
"Perspectiones quaedam, quae tua sunt".

"certain insights, which are your own"
"Insecta quae tibi vivere"
"insights which help you to live"
"Nonne invenisti aliquid simile hoc?"
"Haven't you found something like this?"
"Si dicas mihi, cor meum delectabis".
"If you would like to tell me, you would delight my heart"
"Recte dicis; cogitationes habui et multas perceptiones habui".
"you are right, I have had thoughts and gained many insights"
" Aliquando per horam sensi scientiam in me "
"Sometimes I have felt knowledge in me for an hour"
" alias per totum diem sensi scientiam in me " ;
"at other times I have felt knowledge in me for an entire day"
"Eadem scientia quis sentit, cum quis vitam in corde sentit";
"the same knowledge one feels when one feels life in one's heart"
" Multae cogitationes"
"There have been many thoughts"
"sed mihi difficile esset has cogitationes ad te perferre".
"but it would be hard for me to convey these thoughts to you"
"mi Govinda, haec una est cogitationum mearum quas inveni".
"my dear Govinda, this is one of my thoughts which I have found"
"Sapientia non potest transmittere"
"wisdom cannot be passed on"
"Sapientia, quam transire conatur sapiens, semper stultitiam sonat".
"Wisdom which a wise man tries to pass on always sounds like foolishness"
"Tu es kidding?" interrogavit Govinda
"Are you kidding?" asked Govinda
"Non kidding, dico tibi quod inveni"
"I'm not kidding, I'm telling you what I have found"
"Scientia ferri potest, sapientia non potest".

"Knowledge can be conveyed, but wisdom can't"
"Inveniri potest sapientia, potest vivere".
"wisdom can be found, it can be lived"
"Potest ferri sapientia"
"it is possible to be carried by wisdom"
"Miracula cum sapientia perfici possunt".
"miracles can be performed with wisdom"
"sapientia autem non potest exprimi verbis aut doceri".
"but wisdom cannot be expressed in words or taught"
"Hoc fuit quod aliquando suspicatus sum etiam adulescens";
"This was what I sometimes suspected, even as a young man"
"Hoc est quod me a magistris deiecit".
"this is what has driven me away from the teachers"
" Inveni quam stultitiam putes "
"I have found a thought which you'll regard as foolishness"
"Sed haec cogitatio mea optima fuit"
"but this thought has been my best"
"Omni vero contrarium est perinde ac verum."
"The opposite of every truth is just as true!"
"omnis veritas exprimi non potest nisi cum una pars est".
"any truth can only be expressed when it is one-sided"
"Una tantum erant res in verbis ponere possunt"
"only one sided things can be put into words"
"Omne quod cogitari potest est quadratum".
"Everything which can be thought is one-sided"
"Omnis una pars est, ut dimidium solum est"
"it's all one-sided, so it's just one half"
"Omne caret omni perfectione, rotunditate et unitate".
"it all lacks completeness, roundness, and oneness"
"Locutus est excelsus Gotama in doctrina mundi".
"the exalted Gotama spoke in his teachings of the world"
"sed mundum in Sansara et Nirvana dividere debuit".
"but he had to divide the world into Sansara and Nirvana"
"divisit mundum in deceptionem et veritatem";
"he had divided the world into deception and truth"
" mundum in passione et in salute divisit ".

"he had divided the world into suffering and salvation"
"Mundus aliter explicari non potest".
"the world cannot be explained any other way"
"non est alius modus explicandi, iis qui docere volunt".
"there is no other way to explain it, for those who want to teach"
"Sed mundus ipse numquam est postesque"
"But the world itself is never one-sided"
"Mundus circa nos et intra nos existit".
"the world exists around us and inside of us"
"Persona vel actus numquam est omnino Sansara vel omnino Nirvana";
"A person or an act is never entirely Sansara or entirely Nirvana"
"homo numquam est omnino sanctus aut omnino vitiosus".
"a person is never entirely holy or entirely sinful"
"Videtur sicut mundus dividi potest in hec opposita";
"It seems like the world can be divided into these opposites"
"sed id quod subiacet errori"
"but that's because we are subject to deception"
"sicut deceptio est aliquid reale"
"it's as if the deception was something real"
"Tempus non est verum, Govinda"
"Time is not real, Govinda"
" Hoc saepe et saepe iterum expertus sum "
"I have experienced this often and often again"
"quando tempus non est verum, medium mundi et aeternitatis est deceptio"
"when time is not real, the gap between the world and the eternity is also a deception"
"medium inter dolorem et beatitudinem non est verum"
"the gap between suffering and blissfulness is not real"
"Nulla distantia inter malum et bonum"
"there is no gap between evil and good"
"Hi omnes hiatus deceptiones";
"all of these gaps are deceptions"

"Sed hi hiatus nobis nihilominus apparent".
"but these gaps appear to us nonetheless"
"Quomodo?" timide interrogavit Govinda
"How come?" asked Govinda timidly
"Audi, mi," respondit Siddhartha
"Listen well, my dear," answered Siddhartha
" Peccator, quod ego sum et qui es, peccator est " ;
"The sinner, which I am and which you are, is a sinner"
"sed in futuro peccator Brahma iterum erit".
"but in times to come the sinner will be Brahma again"
"Perveniet Nirvana et Buddha erit"
"he will reach the Nirvana and be Buddha"
"Tempora ventura deceptio"
"the times to come are a deception"
" Ventura tempora parabola tantum sunt."
"the times to come are only a parable!"
"Non est peccator in itinere suo fieri Buddha"
"The sinner is not on his way to become a Buddha"
"Non est in processu developing"
"he is not in the process of developing"
"Cogitandi facultas nostra non scit quomodo haec proponitur".
"our capacity for thinking does not know how else to picture these things"
"Nullum, in peccatore iam Buddha futurum est"
"No, within the sinner there already is the future Buddha"
"In posterum iam omnia"
"his future is already all there"
"In Buddha peccatorem adorare debes"
"you have to worship the Buddha in the sinner"
"Tu adorare Buddha occulta in omnibus"
"you have to worship the Buddha hidden in everyone"
"Buddha occulta quae exsistat possibilis".
"the hidden Buddha which is coming into being the possible"
"Mundus, amice Govinda, imperfectus non est".
"The world, my friend Govinda, is not imperfect"

"**Mundus non tardat viam ad perfectionem**"
"the world is on no slow path towards perfection"
"**Immo mundus omni momento perfectus est**"
"no, the world is perfect in every moment"
« **iam omne peccatum veniae divinae in se portat** ».
"all sin already carries the divine forgiveness in itself"
"**Omnes infantes iam senex in se**"
"all small children already have the old person in themselves"
"**Omnes infantes iam habent mortem in eis**".
"all infants already have death in them"
"**Omnes homines morientes vitam aeternam habent**".
"all dying people have the eternal life"
"**Non possumus videre quam longe alius in via sua iam profecerit**".
"we can't see how far another one has already progressed on his path"
"**in latro et aleator, Buddha exspectat**"
"in the robber and dice-gambler, the Buddha is waiting"
"**in Brahman latro exspectat**".
"in the Brahman, the robber is waiting"
"**in alta meditatione est possibilitas tempus exsistendi**"
"in deep meditation, there is the possibility to put time out of existence"
"**Est facultas videndi omnem vitam simul**"
"there is the possibility to see all life simultaneously"
"**Potest videre omnem vitam, quae fuit, est, et erit**".
"it is possible to see all life which was, is, and will be"
"**et ibi omnia bona et perfecta et Brahman**".
"and there everything is good, perfect, and Brahman"
"**Video igitur quidquid bonum est**".
"Therefore, I see whatever exists as good"
"**mors mihi vita placet**".
"death is to me like life"
"**peccatum mihi sicut sanctitas**";
"to me sin is like holiness"
"**Sapientia potest esse similis stultitia**".

"wisdom can be like foolishness"
" omnia sic habet ut est "
"everything has to be as it is"
"Omne solum requirit consensum et voluntatem meam"
"everything only requires my consent and willingness"
"Omne quod sententia mea requirit bonum est mihi bonum esse consensum meum"
"all that my view requires is my loving agreement to be good for me"
"Mihi visum est nihil facere nisi opus ad utilitatem meam"
"my view has to do nothing but work for my benefit"
" et tunc sensus meus mihi nocere non potest " ;
"and then my perception is unable to ever harm me"
"Expertus sum quod mihi peccanti valde indigui";
"I have experienced that I needed sin very much"
hoc expertus sum in corpore meo et in anima mea.
"I have experienced this in my body and in my soul"
"Opus desiderium, desiderium possessionum et vanitas".
"I needed lust, the desire for possessions, and vanity"
"et mihi turpissima desperatione opus est".
"and I needed the most shameful despair"
"ut discat quomodo omnem resistentiam cederet".
"in order to learn how to give up all resistance"
"ut discas quomodo mundum ames"
"in order to learn how to love the world"
"ut desinas alicui mundo comparare quae optavi".
"in order to stop comparing things to some world I wished for"
"Fingebam perfectionem aliquam quam constitueram";
"I imagined some kind of perfection I had made up"
"sed de mundo ut dictum est discedere didici"
"but I have learned to leave the world as it is"
"Te mundum ut dictum est amare didici";
"I have learned to love the world as it is"
"Et didici quod pars sit frui"
"and I learned to enjoy being a part of it"

"Haec, o Govinda, sunt nonnullae cogitationes quae in mentem meam venerunt".
"These, oh Govinda, are some of the thoughts which have come into my mind"

Siddhartha inclinavit se et sustulit lapidem de terra
Siddhartha bent down and picked up a stone from the ground
appendit lapidem in manu eius
he weighed the stone in his hand
"Hic hic" inquit ludentem saxo "saxum est";
"This here," he said playing with the rock, "is a stone"
"lapis hic, quodani tempore, in humum fortasse conversus";
"this stone will, after a certain time, perhaps turn into soil"
"de solo convertetur in plantam vel animalem vel hominem".
"it will turn from soil into a plant or animal or human being"
" Olim lapis iustus lapis est " .
"In the past, I would have said this stone is just a stone"
" Potui dictum nequam est " ;
"I might have said it is worthless"
"Dixi tibi hic lapis ad mundum Maianae pertinet".
"I would have told you this stone belongs to the world of the Maya"
"sed nolui vidisse momentum habere".
"but I wouldn't have seen that it has importance"
"possit fieri spiritus in cyclo mutationum".
"it might be able to become a spirit in the cycle of transformations"
ideo etiam illud concedo momenti.
"therefore I also grant it importance"
"Sic ego forsitan antea senserim".
"Thus, I would perhaps have thought in the past"
"At hodie de lapide aliter sentio"
"But today I think differently about the stone"
"lapis hic lapis est, estque etiam animal, deus, et Buddha".
"this stone is a stone, and it is also animal, god, and Buddha"

"**Non illud veneror et amabo quod in hunc vel illum converti possit**".
"I do not venerate and love it because it could turn into this or that"
"**Amo, quia ea res est**".
"I love it because it is those things"
"**Hic lapis iam omnia**"
"this stone is already everything"
nunc mihi videtur et hodie ut lapis.
"it appears to me now and today as a stone"
"**Id est, quod amo**"
"that is why I love this"
"**Quare in singulis venis et cavitatibus ejus pretium et propositum video**".
"that is why I see worth and purpose in each of its veins and cavities"
"**Video valorem in croceo, cinereo, et duritia**";
"I see value in its yellow, gray, and hardness"
"**Ego gratum sonum facit cum pulso**".
"I appreciated the sound it makes when I knock at it"
"**Diligo siccitatem vel humiditatem superficiei**";
"I love the dryness or wetness of its surface"
"**Sunt lapides qui sentiant sicut oleum vel saponem**"
"There are stones which feel like oil or soap"
"**et alii lapides sentiunt sicut folia aut arenam**"
"and other stones feel like leaves or sand"
" **et omnis lapis specialis est et om in suo modo orat** " .
"and every stone is special and prays the Om in its own way"
"**Quisque lapis est Brahman**"
"each stone is Brahman"
simul autem et tantundem est lapis.
"but simultaneously, and just as much, it is a stone"
"**Lapis, sive oleum sive pubentes**"
"it is a stone regardless of whether it's oily or juicy"
"**et hoc, quare mihi placet, et hunc lapidem specto**".
"and this why I like and regard this stone"

"Mirum est et cultu dignum".
"it is wonderful and worthy of worship"
"Sed de hoc amplius non loquar".
"But let me speak no more of this"
"Verba non sunt bona tradendi sensum secretum"
"words are not good for transmitting the secret meaning"
"Omnia semper in paulum diversa fiunt, simul ac in verba ponuntur".
"everything always becomes a bit different, as soon as it is put into words"
"Omnia deprauata verbis paulum"
"everything gets distorted a little by words"
"et tunc explicatio fit inepta paulum"
"and then the explanation becomes a bit silly"
"est, et hoc etiam valde bonum est, et mihi multum placet".
"yes, and this is also very good, and I like it a lot"
"Ego quoque huic valde assentior";
"I also very much agree with this"
"thesaurus hominis et sapientia semper stultitiam sonat alteri"
"one man's treasure and wisdom always sounds like foolishness to another person"
Govinda tacite auscultavit quid Siddhartha diceret
Govinda listened silently to what Siddhartha was saying
mora est et Govinda cunctanter interrogavit quaestionem
there was a pause and Govinda hesitantly asked a question
quare hoc mihi indicasti de lapide?
"Why have you told me this about the stone?"
" Id feci sine certa intentione ";
"I did it without any specific intention"
fortasse quod volui, amem hunc saxum et flumen.
"perhaps what I meant was, that I love this stone and the river"
"et amo haec omnia spectamus"
"and I love all these things we are looking at"
"et ex his omnibus possumus cognoscere"

"and we can learn from all these things"
"Non possum lapidem amare, Govinda"
"I can love a stone, Govinda"
"Et possum etiam amare lignum vel fragmen corticis"
"and I can also love a tree or a piece of bark"
"Sunt res, et res amari possunt".
"These are things, and things can be loved"
"Sed non possum amare verba"
"but I cannot love words"
"non sunt ergo mihi bona doctrina".
"therefore, teachings are no good for me"
"doctrina non habent duritiem, mollitiem, colorum, acutam, olfactum, gustum";
"teachings have no hardness, softness, colours, edges, smell, or taste"
"Docmenta nihil habent nisi verba"
"teachings have nothing but words"
fortassis verba quae te prohibent pacem.
"perhaps it is words which keep you from finding peace"
quia salus et virtus sunt verba.
"because salvation and virtue are mere words"
"Sansara et Nirvana etiam solum verba, Govinda" sunt.
"Sansara and Nirvana are also just mere words, Govinda"
"non est res quae esset Nirvana"
"there is no thing which would be Nirvana"
" Nirvana ergo est verbum "
"therefore Nirvana is just the word"
Govinda obiecit "Nirvana verbum non solum, mi amice".
Govinda objected, "Nirvana is not just a word, my friend"
"Nirvana verbum est, sed etiam est cogitatio";
"Nirvana is a word, but also it is a thought"
Siddhartha continuavit, "ut esset cogitatio"
Siddhartha continued, "it might be a thought"
"Fateor, non multum differo inter cogitationes et verba".
"I must confess, I don't differentiate much between thoughts and words"

"quod honestum sit, ego quoque nullam cogitationem habeam".
"to be honest, I also have no high opinion of thoughts"
"Meliorem sententiam habeo de rebus quam cogitationibus"
"I have a better opinion of things than thoughts"
"Hic in hac phasellus, enim quis, auctor mi"
"Here on this ferry-boat, for instance, a man has been my predecessor"
" Fuit etiam unus de magistris meis " ;
"he was also one of my teachers"
"vir sanctus, qui per multos annos simpliciter credidit in flumine";
"a holy man, who has for many years simply believed in the river"
"et nihil aliud credidit"
"and he believed in nothing else"
" Animadvertit quod flumen ei locutus est " ;
"He had noticed that the river spoke to him"
"Didicit a flumine"
"he learned from the river"
"Fluvius erudivit et docuit eum."
"the river educated and taught him"
"Fluvius illi deus esse videbatur"
"the river seemed to be a god to him"
" per multos annos nesciebat omnia divina esse sicut flumen "
"for many years he did not know that everything was as divine as the river"
"ventus, omnis nubes, omnis avis, omnis scarabaeorum";
"the wind, every cloud, every bird, every beetle"
"Docere tantum quantum flumen possunt"
"they can teach just as much as the river"
"Sanctus autem vir ille in silvas ingressus, omnia noverat".
"But when this holy man went into the forests, he knew everything"
"plus sciebat quam me et me sine magistris aut libris"

"he knew more than you and me, without teachers or books"
" plus sciebat quam nos solum quia in flumine credidit " .
"he knew more than us only because he had believed in the river"

Govinda adhuc dubitat et quaestiones
Govinda still had doubts and questions
"At estne id quod dicis actu aliquid reale?"
"But is that what you call things actually something real?"
"Numquid haec existunt?"
"do these things have existence?"
"Nonne maiva est deceptio"
"Isn't it just a deception of the Maya"
"Nonne haec omnia imago et illusio?"
"aren't all these things an image and illusion?"
"Laxum tuum, lignum tuum, flumen tuum";
"Your stone, your tree, your river"
"An vere res sunt?"
"are they actually a reality?"
"Hoc quoque" dixit Siddhartha, **"non valde curo".**
"This too," spoke Siddhartha, "I do not care very much about"
"Quae sint fallaciae vel non"
"Let the things be illusions or not"
"post omnia, volo etiam esse fallacia".
"after all, I would then also be an illusion"
"et si haec fallaciae sunt, tunc similes sunt mihi";
"and if these things are illusions then they are like me"
"Hoc est quod eos tam dilectos ac venerandos pro me facit".
"This is what makes them so dear and worthy of veneration for me"
"haec sunt sicut me et hoc est quomodo eas amem".
"these things are like me and that is how I can love them"
"Haec doctrina deridebis".
"this is a teaching you will laugh about"
"Amor, o Govinda, mihi videtur esse omnium primum"

"love, oh Govinda, seems to me to be the most important thing of all"
"Ut penitus cognoscat mundus sit quod magni cogitantes faciunt"
"to thoroughly understand the world may be what great thinkers do"
explicant mundum et contemnunt.
"they explain the world and despise it"
"At ego tantum quaero quod mundum amare possim".
"But I'm only interested in being able to love the world"
"Non quaero contemnendo mundum"
"I am not interested in despising the world"
"Nolo odisse mundum"
"I don't want to hate the world"
"et nolo me mundum odisse"
"and I don't want the world to hate me"
"Vellem mundum intueri potero meque amore".
"I want to be able to look upon the world and myself with love"
"Omnium entium cupio intueri cum admiratione"
"I want to look upon all beings with admiration"
"Magnum habere cupio omnia reverentia"
"I want to have a great respect for everything"
"Hoc intelligo" locutus est Govinda
"This I understand," spoke Govinda
"Sed hoc ipsum ut deceptio ab excelso reperta est".
"But this very thing was discovered by the exalted one to be a deception"
"Imperat benevolentiam, clementiam, misericordiam, tolerantiam";
"He commands benevolence, clemency, sympathy, tolerance"
"sed non imperat amori"
"but he does not command love"
"prohibuit nos cor nostrum in amore ligare ad terrena"
"he forbade us to tie our heart in love to earthly things"
"Scio, Govinda", Siddhartha dixit, et risus eius aureus fulsit

"I know it, Govinda," said Siddhartha, and his smile shone golden
"Et ecce, cum hoc recte tenemus in conplexu sententiarum".
"And behold, with this we are right in the thicket of opinions"
"nunc in controversia verborum sumus"
"now we are in the dispute about words"
"Nam negare non possum, mea verba contradictio sunt".
"For I cannot deny, my words of love are a contradiction"
"videntur verbis Gotamae contradicere"
"they seem to be in contradiction with Gotama's words"
"Qua de causa diffido verbis tantum"
"For this very reason, I distrust words so much"
"quia contradictionem hanc scio esse deceptio";
"because I know this contradiction is a deception"
"Scio me consentire cum Gotama";
"I know that I am in agreement with Gotama"
"Quomodo ille amorem non cognoscit cum omnia elementa humanae vitae reperit"
"How could he not know love when he has discovered all elements of human existence"
"Perpetuam eorum et vanitatem deprehendit".
"he has discovered their transitoriness and their meaninglessness"
"et tamen populum valde amabat"
"and yet he loved people very much"
"longam, laboriosam vitam tantum adiuvare ac docere!"
"he used a long, laborious life only to help and teach them!"
"Etiam praeceptore tuo magno, rebus verbis antepono"
"Even with your great teacher, I prefer things over the words"
"Magis in actis et vita quam in orationibus ponam".
"I place more importance on his acts and life than on his speeches"
"Gestus manuum magis quam sententias aestimamus".
"I value the gestures of his hand more than his opinions"
" nihil mihi erat in oratione et cogitatione " ;
"for me there was nothing in his speech and thoughts"

" Magnitudinem eius tantum in factis et in vita video ".
"I see his greatness only in his actions and in his life"

Duo senes diu nihil dixerunt
For a long time, the two old men said nothing
Tunc Govinda locutus est, vale pro inclinato
Then Govinda spoke, while bowing for a farewell
"Gratias tibi ago, Siddhartha, quod aliquas cogitationes tuas mihi narras"
"I thank you, Siddhartha, for telling me some of your thoughts"
« **Hae cogitationes partim sunt mihi alienae** ».
"These thoughts are partially strange to me"
"Non omnes istae cogitationes statim mihi comprehensae sunt".
"not all of these thoughts have been instantly understandable to me"
"Quod cum ita sit, ago tibi";
"This being as it may, I thank you"
"et volo tibi habere tranquillitatem dierum"
"and I wish you to have calm days"
Sed aliud occulte sibi cogitabat
But secretly he thought something else to himself
"Haec Siddhartha prodigiosum hominem est"
"This Siddhartha is a bizarre person"
"Exprimit prodigiosum cogitationes"
"he expresses bizarre thoughts"
"Stultam doctrinam sonant"
"his teachings sound foolish"
" **Purae doctrinae altae valde diversae sonant** " ;
"the exalted one's pure teachings sound very different"
"Ea doctrina clarior, purior, comprehensibilis".
"those teachings are clearer, purer, more comprehensible"
"Nihil mirum, nihil stultum, nihil ineptum in illis doctrinis".
"there is nothing strange, foolish, or silly in those teachings"

"Sed manus Siddharthae visae sunt a cogitatione eius diversae".
"But Siddhartha's hands seemed different from his thoughts"
pedes, oculi, frons, anhelitus;
"his feet, his eyes, his forehead, his breath"
" Risus, salutatio, deambulatio "
"his smile, his greeting, his walk"
"Non alium virum similem conveni quia Gotama unus cum Nirvana factus est".
"I haven't met another man like him since Gotama became one with the Nirvana"
"ex eo quod non sensi praesentia sancti viri".
"since then I haven't felt the presence of a holy man"
"Solum Siddhartham inveni, quae talis est".
"I have only found Siddhartha, who is like this"
"ut sit aliena doctrina, et stulta verba sonant".
"his teachings may be strange and his words may sound foolish"
"sed pudicitia ex visu et manu elucet".
"but purity shines out of his gaze and hand"
" Pellis et comae puritas ;"
"his skin and his hair radiates purity"
de omni parte eius refulget puritas.
"purity shines out of every part of him"
ex eo lucet tranquillitas, hilaritas, mansuetudo, sanctitas.
"a calmness, cheerfulness, mildness and holiness shines from him"
quod vidi in nullo alio.
"something which I have seen in no other person"
"Non vidi post ultimam mortem excelsi doctoris nostri".
"I have not seen it since the final death of our exalted teacher"
Dum hoc cogitavit Govinda, certatum est in corde suo
While Govinda thought like this, there was a conflict in his heart
et iterum adoravit Siddhartha
he once again bowed to Siddhartha

sentiebat protractum amore
he felt he was drawn forward by love
ei qui placide sedebat
he bowed deeply to him who was calmly sitting
"Siddhartha" dixit, "senes facti sumus".
"Siddhartha," he spoke, "we have become old men"
"Verisimile est unum nostrum alterum iterum in hac incarnatione videre".
"It is unlikely for one of us to see the other again in this incarnation"
"Video, dilectissime, quod pacem invenisti";
"I see, beloved, that you have found peace"
"Fateor me non invenisse"
"I confess that I haven't found it"
"Dic mihi, o honestum, verbum unum".
"Tell me, oh honourable one, one more word"
" da mihi aliquid in via mea quam capere possum " .
"give me something on my way which I can grasp"
"da mihi aliquid quod intelligam!"
"give me something which I can understand!"
"Da mihi quid possum capere mecum in viam meam"
"give me something I can take with me on my path"
"via mea saepe dura et obscura est, Siddhartha".
"my path is often hard and dark, Siddhartha"
Siddhartha nihil dixit et intuens eum
Siddhartha said nothing and looked at him
eum semper immutata quiete aspexit risus
he looked at him with his ever unchanged, quiet smile
Govinda intuita faciem eius cum timore
Govinda stared at his face with fear
in oculis eius est labor et dolor
there was yearning and suffering in his eyes
in eius vultu visibilis aeterna quaestio fuit
the eternal search was visible in his look
aeternam posses invenire
you could see his eternal inability to find

Siddhartha vidit et risit
Siddhartha saw it and smiled
"Inclina ad me!" Govinda in aurem insusurrans
"Bend down to me!" he whispered quietly in Govinda's ear
"Hoc fac, et propius accede!"
"Like this, and come even closer!"
"Oscula fronti meae, Govinda!"
"Kiss my forehead, Govinda!"
Obstupuit Govinda, sed nimio amore et exspectatione attractus
Govinda was astonished, but drawn on by great love and expectation
obediens dictis et inclinans se ad eum
he obeyed his words and bent down closely to him
et tetigit labra sua
and he touched his forehead with his lips
cum hoc faceret, accidit ei miraculosum
when he did this, something miraculous happened to him
cogitationes eius adhuc habitabant in Siddhartha mirabilibus verbis
his thoughts were still dwelling on Siddhartha's wondrous words
adhuc invitus laborabat cogitare tempus
he was still reluctantly struggling to think away time
et Nirvana et Sansara quasi unum conari adhuc temptabat
he was still trying to imagine Nirvana and Sansara as one
erat tamen quidam contemptus verborum amici
there was still a certain contempt for the words of his friend
verba illa adhuc pugnabant in eo
those words were still fighting in him
verba illa adhuc contra amorem immensum ac venerationem pugnabant
those words were still fighting against an immense love and veneration
atque in his omnibus cogitationibus aliquid aliud ei accidit

and during all these thoughts, something else happened to him
Non amplius vidit faciem amici sui Siddhartha
He no longer saw the face of his friend Siddhartha
loco Siddhartha facies alias facies vidit
instead of Siddhartha's face, he saw other faces
vidit longa serie facies
he saw a long sequence of faces
vidit fluens flumen facierum
he saw a flowing river of faces
centum milia faciei, quae omnes venerunt et disparuerunt
hundreds and thousands of faces, which all came and disappeared
et tamen omnes simul esse videbantur
and yet they all seemed to be there simultaneously
perpetuo se mutaverunt et renovaverunt
they constantly changed and renewed themselves
ipsi erant, et adhuc omnes facies Siddhartha
they were themselves and they were still all Siddhartha's face
vidit faciem piscis cum dolore os in infinitum
he saw the face of a fish with an infinitely painfully opened mouth
facie morientis pisces, oculis decidentibus
the face of a dying fish, with fading eyes
vidit faciem pueri recentis nati rubicundi et rugae
he saw the face of a new-born child, red and full of wrinkles
deformatus est clamor
it was distorted from crying
vidit faciem homicidae
he saw the face of a murderer
vidit eum in alterius corpus cultrum immittere
he saw him plunging a knife into the body of another person
Vidit eodem momento scelestum hunc servitutem
he saw, in the same moment, this criminal in bondage
turbam flexo vidit
he saw him kneeling before a crowd

viditque abscissum a spiculatore caput
and he saw his head being chopped off by the executioner
corpora virorum ac mulierum vidit
he saw the bodies of men and women
nudi sunt loca et cramps furentis amoris
they were naked in positions and cramps of frenzied love
cadavera vidit extenta, immota, frigida, inane;
he saw corpses stretched out, motionless, cold, void
vidit capita animalium
he saw the heads of animals
aprorum capita, crocodilorum et elephantorum
heads of boars, of crocodiles, and of elephants
capita taurorum et volucrum vidit
he saw the heads of bulls and of birds
di vidit; Krishna et Agni
he saw gods; Krishna and Agni
has omnes figuras et facies videbat in mille relationibus inter se
he saw all of these figures and faces in a thousand relationships with one another
unaquaque figura est auxilium alterum
each figure was helping the other
unaquaque figura erat amandi necessitudinem suam
each figure was loving their relationship
singulae figurae necessitudinem suam oderant, eam destruebant
each figure was hating their relationship, destroying it
et singulae figurae ad eorum relationem renascentes
and each figure was giving re-birth to their relationship
unaquaque figura erat voluntas mori
each figure was a will to die
confessiones excruciatas transeuntium
they were passionately painful confessions of transitoriness
et tamen nullus eorum mortuus est, sed unus transfiguratus est
and yet none of them died, each one only transformed

semper renascuntur et plus ac magis novas facies
they were always reborn and received more and more new faces
nullum tempus inter faciem unam et alteram
no time passed between the one face and the other
Omnes hi figurae et facies requievit
all of these figures and faces rested
influebant et generantur
they flowed and generated themselves
ferebatur et inducitur inter se
they floated along and merged with each other
et omnes continue tenues
and they were all constantly covered by something thin
nullum proprium
they had no individuality of their own
sed tamen existebant
but yet they were existing
quasi tenuis vitreum aut glaciem
they were like a thin glass or ice
sicut diaphanum cutem
they were like a transparent skin
quasi testa aut forma aut persona aquae
they were like a shell or mould or mask of water
et haec persona subridens
and this mask was smiling
et haec persona erat Siddhartha blanditur
and this mask was Siddhartha's smiling face
persona quam Govinda tangebat labiis suis
the mask which Govinda was touching with his lips
Et hoc vidit Govinda
And, Govinda saw it like this
in risu de persona
the smile of the mask
risus unum supra fluens formas
the smile of oneness above the flowing forms
risus simultatis supra mille nativitates et mortes

the smile of simultaneousness above the thousand births and deaths
Siddhartha scriptor risus erat ipsum
the smile of Siddhartha's was precisely the same
Risus Siddhartha idem fuit quod Gotama quies risus, Buddha
Siddhartha's smile was the same as the quiet smile of Gotama, the Buddha
erat delicata et impenetrabilis risu
it was delicate and impenetrable smile
fortasse benevolus et oum et sapiens
perhaps it was benevolent and mocking, and wise
millesimum risum Gotamae Buddha
the thousand-fold smile of Gotama, the Buddha
ut ipse centies in magna veneratione viderat
as he had seen it himself with great respect a hundred times
Hoc simile, Govinda cognovit, perfecti rident
Like this, Govinda knew, the perfected ones are smiling
nesciebat amplius an tempus esset
he did not know anymore whether time existed
nesciebat utrum visio secunda an centum annorum permansisset
he did not know whether the vision had lasted a second or a hundred years
nesciebat utrum Siddhartha an Gotama exstiterit
he did not know whether a Siddhartha or a Gotama existed
nesciebat si a me vel esses
he did not know if a me or a you existed
sentiebat in sua quasi divina sagitta vulneratum
he felt in his as if he had been wounded by a divine arrow
sagitta intima sui
the arrow pierced his innermost self
iniuriam divinae sagittae gustavit
the injury of the divine arrow tasted sweet
Govinda in intima sui ipsius cantata ac dissoluta est
Govinda was enchanted and dissolved in his innermost self

et stetit usque ad tempus modicum
he stood still for a little while
placidam Siddharthae faciem inclinavit, quam mox osculatus est
he bent over Siddhartha's quiet face, which he had just kissed
faciem, in qua mox viderat scenam omnium manifestationum
the face in which he had just seen the scene of all manifestations
faciem omnium mutationum et omnium existentiae
the face of all transformations and all existence
faciem spectabat immutatus
the face he was looking at was unchanged
sub eius superficie mille caularum altitudo iterum occlusa est
under its surface, the depth of the thousand folds had closed up again
subridens tacite, tacite et leniter
he smiled silently, quietly, and softly
fortasse risit benevole ac deridens
perhaps he smiled very benevolently and mockingly
hoc ipsum erat quomodo sublimis risit
precisely this was how the exalted one smiled
Penitus Govinda adoravit Siddhartha
Deeply, Govinda bowed to Siddhartha
lachrymis nihil sciebat decurrere vultum suum
tears he knew nothing of ran down his old face
lachrymae ardentes sicut ignis intimae amoris
his tears burned like a fire of the most intimate love
sensit humillimam venerationem in corde suo
he felt the humblest veneration in his heart
Inclinavit, tangens terram
Deeply, he bowed, touching the ground
Et adoravit eum sedentem
he bowed before him who was sitting motionlessly

eius risu admonuit de omnibus, quos semper dilexit in vita sua
his smile reminded him of everything he had ever loved in his life

subridens eum admonebat omnia in vita sua, quae pretiosam et sanctam invenit
his smile reminded him of everything in his life that he found valuable and holy

www.ingramcontent.com/pod-product-compliance
Lightning Source LLC
Chambersburg PA
CBHW012003090526
44590CB00026B/3851